20 SEASONS: BROADWAY MUSICALS OF THE 21ST CENTURY

20 Seasons: Broadway Musicals of the 21st Century catalogues, categorizes, and analyzes the 269 musicals that opened on Broadway from the 2000–2001 season through the 2019–2020 season.

This book is the first to comprehensively examine the musicals that premiered on Broadway during this important historical period, which was bookended by the 9/11 terrorist attacks on one end and the Coronavirus pandemic on the other. It begins by exploring the historical context for the first 20 years of the 21st century and how this impacted American culture and theatre. Rather than chronologically, the musicals are then organized into categories based on their source material and whether they were original musicals or revivals, painting a detailed picture of the Broadway musical in first 20 years of the 21st century. Jukebox musicals, screen-to-stage musicals, revivals, and other original musicals are all covered, and each chapter ends with reading guides and discussion prompts. The book not only discusses what was produced, but by whom, uncovering the stark lack of representation for women and artists of color on Broadway musical creative and design teams. Additionally, the last chapter discusses the COVID-19 pandemic, the Broadway shutdown, and what happened to the Broadway musical during the shutdown, including the response to the Black Lives Matter movement in the summer of 2020.

20 Seasons: Broadway Musicals of the 21st Century will appeal to fans and scholars of musical theatre, as well as students of Musical Theatre, Musical Theatre History, American Studies, and Pop Culture Studies.

Dr. Amy S. Osatinski is a faculty member in the School of Theatre at Oklahoma City University, where she teaches courses in Theatre History and Dramaturgy and serves as a director, intimacy director, and dramaturg for productions in the School of Theatre's production season. She is the author of *Disney Theatrical Productions: Producing Broadway Musicals the Disney Way* (Routledge, 2019).

20 SEASONS: BROADWAY MUSICALS OF THE 21ST CENTURY

Amy S. Osatinski

NEW YORK AND LONDON

Designed cover image: canbedone / Shutterstock.com

First published 2024
by Routledge
605 Third Avenue, New York, NY 10158

and by Routledge
4 Park Square, Milton Park, Abingdon, Oxon OX14 4RN

Routledge is an imprint of the Taylor & Francis Group, an informa business

© 2024 Amy S. Osatinski

The right of Amy S. Osatinski to be identified as author of this work has been asserted in accordance with sections 77 and 78 of the Copyright, Designs and Patents Act 1988.

All rights reserved. No part of this book may be reprinted or reproduced or utilised in any form or by any electronic, mechanical, or other means, now known or hereafter invented, including photocopying and recording, or in any information storage or retrieval system, without permission in writing from the publishers.

Trademark notice: Product or corporate names may be trademarks or registered trademarks, and are used only for identification and explanation without intent to infringe.

Library of Congress Cataloging-in-Publication Data
A catalog record for this title has been requested

ISBN: 978-0-367-68822-6 (hbk)
ISBN: 978-0-367-68821-9 (pbk)
ISBN: 978-1-003-13917-1 (ebk)

DOI: 10.4324/9781003139171

Typeset in Bembo
by Taylor & Francis Books

For Rob

CONTENTS

List of illustrations	*viii*
Foreword: To Make Art or to Make Commerce:	
Broadway in the 2000s	*x*
Acknowledgements	*xvii*
Introduction: 20 Seasons by the Numbers	1
1 20 Years/20 Seasons	14
2 An Introduction to Original Musicals	48
3 Jukebox Musicals and Revues	54
4 Screen-to-Stage Musicals	85
5 Other Original Musicals	114
6 Revivals and Remounts	145
7 Beyond 20 Seasons	173
Appendix A	*186*
Appendix B	*193*
Bibliography	*200*
Index	*215*

ILLUSTRATIONS

Figures

0.1 Number of musicals that opened on Broadway by season	5
0.2 Percentage of musicals in the 20 seasons that were originals, revivals, and remounts	6
0.3 Number of originals, revivals, and remounts by season	7
2.1 Percentage of musicals in each of the five categories for original musicals	50
2.2 Number of musicals in each of the five categories for original musicals by season	51
5.1 Percentage of musical in the "other original" category by source material	119

Tables

0.1 Distribution of roles by race 2006–2016	11
3.1 Jukebox musicals in 20 seasons	54

3.2 Revues in 20 seasons	57
4.1 Screen-to-stage musicals in 20 seasons	85
5.1 Other original musicals in 20 seasons	114
6.1 Revivals in 20 seasons	145
6.2 Remounts in 20 seasons	147
A.1 Shows by opening date	186
B.1 Shows by number of performances	193

FOREWORD: TO MAKE ART OR TO MAKE COMMERCE: BROADWAY IN THE 2000S

On June 3, 2001, Mel Brooks stepped up on stage at Radio City Music Hall, where he name-dropped a certain dictator. "I want to thank Hitler, for being such a funny guy on stage," Brooks said, upon receiving the Tony Award for Best Musical. Brooks had co-written the musical *The Producers*, which contained a farcical musical-within-a-musical sequence called "Springtime for Hitler," featuring tap-dancing Nazis and a campy Hitler played by Gary Beach.

That night at the Tony Awards, *The Producers* made musical theater history by winning a record 12 Tony Awards, a number that has still not been beaten. *The Producers* was a bona fide hit when it premiered on Broadway at the St. James Theatre, where it set box office records: selling more than $3 million worth of tickets the day after opening night. Audiences flocked to the theater to witness the dual star power of Nathan Lane and Matthew Broderick.

Not bad for a show based on a film that was a flop. Said Brooks on that Tonys stage, surrounded by the real producers of *The Producers*, "'Behind me you see a phalanx—an avalanche—of Jews who have come with their talent, their money, but most of all their spirit and their love for the theater."

The Producers didn't just make Broadway history through its numbers. It was a musical of the new millennium and its success foretold

Foreword: To Make Art or to Make Commerce: Broadway in the 2000s **xi**

several trends that would dominate commercial musicals in the next two decades. It was based on a film. It had well-known celebrities at its center (so much so that *The Producers'* box office dipped significantly when Broderick and Lane left the show). And it was expensive, both in how much it cost to make and the eye-popping box office receipts.

In the 2000s, the cost of putting on a musical on Broadway sky-rocketed—going into several millions because of numerous factors (such as increasing costs of theater rentals and labor). Broadway became more expensive to produce, which also led to it being more expensive to attend. The average ticket price has risen from an inflation adjusted $74 in 1984 to $124 in 2019.[1]

This has put Broadway further and further outside the reaches of the middle class, who can now find more affordable entertainment through film and television. As the old adage goes, you cannot make a living on Broadway but you can make a killing. For the last two decades, producers have needed to be more calculating if they wanted to make a killing on Broadway, or if they just wanted to break even. They are in a constant push-and-pull between commercial profits and artistic expression. Is Broadway in the business to make great art or to make money? Or is it an idealistic mix of both?

In *The Producers*, Max Bialystock and Leo Bloom chase money, trying to use Broadway as a get-rich-quick-by-putting-on-a-show scheme. They didn't care about creating art, that's why it's so ironic when they stumble onto greatness. In real life, countless Broadway producers have tried to balance those two motives of art and commerce. In doing so, they have shaped the American musical in the new millennium.

The Rise of IP

It is rare for a musical to be entirely original. Musical theater creators are usually inspired by something in the world, whether it's a biography of Alexander Hamilton in *Hamilton*, a classic German play in *Spring Awakening*, or Greek mythology in *Hadestown*. But the 2000s saw a dramatic rise of a new kind of musical: the IP musical (or what I also like to call the nostalgia musical).[2]

This can be seen in the growth of two sub-genres of such musicals: the jukebox musicals, which use popular songs, and the musical based

xii Foreword: To Make Art or to Make Commerce: Broadway in the 2000s

on a hit film. While in the 1980s and 1990s there were only 12 jukebox musicals, in the 2000s and 2010s the popular song genre exploded, with 56 musicals. A similar explosion occurred with the screen-to-stage genre.

In the 2000s, there have been 269 musicals presented on Broadway: 56 have been jukebox musicals and a whopping 80 have been musicals adapted from film. Those two genres of musicals have widely outnumbered original musicals, of which there have been 78. In fact, in the 2017–2018 season on Broadway, there were no new original musicals at all. Every new musical that premiered was either a jukebox musical, or a musical adapted from a film.

Those two genres of musicals have an inherent advantage that other musicals do not have: they usually benefit from prior knowledge from the audience. Unlike a musical that is based on an obscure book or play, musicals based on already-written music or a hit film benefit from audience familiarity—the audience already knows what to expect. When it's a musical containing the music of a popular artist—such as Carole King, ABBA, the Temptations, Tina Turner—audiences come in already knowing the songs. When it's a musical based on a hit film—such as *Pretty Woman*—audiences come in already knowing where the story will go, the only surprise is what the songs will sound like. When these musicals succeed, they do so because they tap into one specific feeling: nostalgia. They give audiences what they already know, just in a new medium. And they make audiences feel safe in spending over $100 on a ticket, because even if they don't love everything about a show, at least they'll like *something*.

When the alternative is an all-new musical, where producers pray that word-of-mouth and reviews will be positive, and have to actively find an audience that will want to risk their hard-earned money on a show they are wholly unfamiliar with, those nostalgia musicals are relatively safe.

The growth of those genres of nostalgia musicals is arguably inspired by Disney, who planted its flag on Broadway in the 1990s with *The Lion King* and *Beauty and the Beast*, both based on the Disney animated films and containing the songs from those films. The successes of those two musicals showed Broadway producers a genre of musical that could consistently work. With the growth of Disney Theatricals, the

Foreword: To Make Art or to Make Commerce: Broadway in the 2000s **xiii**

theater producing arm of the Disney Company, the Mouse has been a prime source of musicals that audiences already sort-of know. That's not to denigrate all musicals based on film or to say they're all equal in their ploy for nostalgia. Musicals such as *The Band's Visit* and *Waitress* were based on indie films, and were box office hits on Broadway. But they were rare. A large majority of movies that have served as the basis for musicals were either blockbusters, classic films, or animated films. Only 34% were cult films or indie films with no prior mass name recognition.

In the 2000s, on the Great White Way, IP Became King

Some of those musicals did become long-running hits for a time, such as *Mamma Mia* and *Beautiful: The Carole King Musical*. But IP has not been fool-proof. Perhaps the most notorious IP flop on Broadway was *Spider-Man: Turn Off the Dark*. The musical was Broadway's attempt to capitalize off of the 2000s growth of superheroes in Hollywood, and was based on the Spider-Man comic books. At that point, Spider-Man and X-Men had made their big screen debut and were box office hits. No expenses were spared in realizing Spider-Man's story for the stage. The Foxwoods Theatre was retrofitted to allow Spider-Man to fly above the audience's head. Bono and the Edge were brought in to compose the songs, even though they had never composed a musical before. At a $70 million production budget, it's still currently the most expensive musical ever made, and the biggest flop in Broadway history (its investors lost a reported $60 million). *Spider-Man* closed on Broadway after only two years—because no spectacle and no amount of Spider-Men flying through the air could make up for a lackluster book or unmemorable songs.

But that doesn't mean that original musicals, works that are wholly unfamiliar to the audience, have died on Broadway. The 2000s also saw the premiere of several original musicals that have become long-running hits on Broadway, including *Wicked, The Book of Mormon*, and *Hamilton* (where at one point, tickets being sold for $1,200 apiece).

In fact, it is notable that in the current list of best-selling musicals on Broadway, a majority of them are not IP musicals. Yes there's *The Lion*

xiv Foreword: To Make Art or to Make Commerce: Broadway in the 2000s

King and *Aladdin*, but there's also *The Book of Mormon, Hadestown*, and *Wicked*. They are works that slowly built an audience until they became recognizable names. Because at a certain point, nostalgia cannot replace the key building blocks of a musical: artistry and a killer 11 o'clock number.

The Rise of Diversity

Despite Broadway's in the 2000s being more risk-averse, there has been growth in one key area: diversity. A key example of how Broadway has become more diverse, even if it has become more restrictive in artistic originality, can be found in Rodgers and Hammerstein's classic musical *Oklahoma!* The musical has been revived twice since 2000: once in 2002 and then again in 2019. The 2002 revival featured a mostly white cast led by Patrick Wilson, with period-appropriate clothing such as petticoats and leather vests. Directed by British director Trevor Nunn, the revival looked and sounded like what you would expect from *Oklahoma!*.

By contrast, the 2019 Broadway revival of *Oklahoma!* was nicknamed by many theater fans as "Sexy Oklahoma!" Directed by Daniel Fish, the recent revival was set in the present day, with the cast in tight jeans and tank tops. The score was stripped down and given a country/bluegrass feel. The cast was diverse, including Black actor Rebecca Naomi Jones as Laurie, the female lead, and Ali Stroker as Ado Annie—who imbued her show stopping song "I Cain't Say No" with an infectious mix of lust and zeel. Stroker became the first actor in a wheelchair to win a Tony Award. And that new version of *Oklahoma!* made musical theater fans so angry that it inspired walkouts and one headline that read: "'Oklahoma!' Wreaks Havoc on a Musical Theater Classic."

Sure, *Oklahoma!* is a well-known property that could sell tickets based on the power of its name, and with a well-cast celebrity. And many Broadway revivals have taken that route, such as *The King and I* with Ken Watanabe, *A Little Night Music* with Catherine Zeta-Jones, or *Cabaret* with Michelle Williams.

But many Broadway revivals and original musicals have also taken the opposite approach, depending not on audience familiarity or

Foreword: To Make Art or to Make Commerce: Broadway in the 2000s **xv**

pushing nostalgia buttons. Instead, they have focused on making theater for the now, and focused on speaking to the audience in the moment with a daring, new work or a treatment of an older musical that challenged expectations—aside from *Oklahoma!, Spring Awakening* and *West Side Story* both received revivals that provided a divisive new take on the material.

This focus on contemporary storytelling has also led to more diversity on Broadway. The past two decades have seen many firsts on Broadway: the first musical about Latinx people written by a Latino composer (*In the Heights*, and Lin-Manuel Miranda was the first Latino composer to win a Tony Award), the first Black writer to win a Tony Award for best book (Stew for *Passing Strange*), the first musicals composed by and written by Asian creators (*Bombay Dreams* and then later *Allegiance*), the first female composing team to win a Tony Award (Lisa Kron and Jeanine Tesori for *Fun Home*). Then at the 2016 Tony Awards, also known as the night *Hamilton* swept the Tonys, four Black actors won in four major musical performance categories for the first time.

These firsts reflect a Broadway that, very slowly, has welcomed artists from a more diverse array of backgrounds. In the 2018–2019 season, 34% of actors cast on Broadway[3] were BIPOC actors, a sizable jump from the 2006–2007 season when actors of color only made up 14% of all roles.[4] Though sadly, those numbers are still inadequate.

Change has still been frustratingly slow. Out of the 269 musicals that have premiered in the last 20 years, only 59 shows have been created (or co-created) by women and only 27 have been composed or written by BIPOC writers. Yet it's been a slow and consistent upwards trend, a reassurance in arguably one of the most challenging times to produce theater.

As Broadway enters its third decade of the 2000s, post-90s-Disney-takeover, post-80s-mega-musical, it remains to be seen whether producers will continue to prioritize familiar IPs or if there will still be room for challenging new musicals. While original musicals like *Six, Hamilton,* and *Hadestown* continues to lead the Broadway box office, the COVID-19 pandemic has made it more difficult for challenging new works to survive: after only running on Broadway for seven months, *A Strange Loop* announced its closure on Broadway despite xvi Foreword: To Make Art or to Make Commerce: Broadway in the 2000s

winning the Tony Award for Best Musical and the Pulitzer Prize for Drama. Meanwhile, this Broadway season so far only contains three new original musicals, while there are two musicals based on hit films and two jukebox musicals. As Patti LuPone complained to Variety, "Broadway has also changed considerably," saying that the audience has been "dumbed down" and saying that Broadway is "turning into Disneyland, a circus, and Las Vegas."

In those ways, Broadway as it exists is a reflection of the realities of living in contemporary America, where capitalism controls the choices we all make. Within that, we all search for some beauty and meaning, and a song we can keep singing.

- Diep Tran is the editor-in-chief of *Playbill*. She was previously the features editor of Broadway.com and the senior editor of *American Theatre* magazine. Her writing has been featured in the *New York Times, New York Magazine, Washington Post*, and many other publications.

Notes

1 Mark Dent, "The Economics of Broadway Shows: How the Pandemic Has Made Broadway's Risky Business Even Riskier," The Hustle, last modified November 20, 2021, accessed December 6, 2022, https://thehustle.co/the-economics-of-broadway-shows/.

2 IP stands for *intellectual property* and in this context "IP musical" refers to musicals that are based on pre-existing intellectual property that is already popular and widely known.

3 *The Visibility Report: Racial Representation on NYC Stages* (n.p.: AAPAC, 2021), 52.

4 "2006/07–2010/11 Report," Asian American Performers Action Coalition, accessed December 6, 2022, http://www.aapacnyc.org/200607-201011.html.

ACKNOWLEDGEMENTS

I would like to start by thanking my husband Rob for his continued support and willingness to follow me wherever a career in academia leads us. Thank you to my family for your love and support. Thanks also to my students, both current and former, whose enthusiasm and curiosity inspires me every day. Thanks to my colleagues who continue to inspire me to be a better artist and scholar. This book would also not have been possible without the community of scholars in Musical Theatre Studies who continue to push the boundaries of our field. My gratitude to one of those scholars in particular, Barrie Gelles, whose support and encouragement throughout the writing process kept me writing.

A sincere thank you to the incomparable Diep Tran for writing the foreword to this volume. Thanks also to my editor, Stacey Walker, and editorial assistant, Lucia Accorsi, who are an incredible team and have supported me through the process of publishing two books. Thank you to the University of Northern Iowa and Oklahoma City University for providing funding at various stages of the process to facilitate the research and writing of this book.

Finally, thank you to all the artists whose dedication and fortitude led to the creation of the 269 musicals discussed in this book.

INTRODUCTION

20 Seasons by the Numbers

Musical theatre is one of only a few performance forms that is truly "American."[1] Throughout its short history, the American musical as a cultural object has served as a mirror for the culture of the United States at large. In his 2005 book, *The American Musical and the Formation of National Identity*, musical theatre scholar Raymond Knapp argues that "American musicals represent a large slice of our national life and heritage."[2] If the musical is a snapshot of American life, then examining the musicals of a particular period can open a window into the zeitgeist of that time. Since the late 20th century, musical theatre scholars have turned a critical eye to the connection between musical theatre and the culture of the United States during many formative periods in the history of the United States. This volume is submitted as a "next chapter" in the lineage of the musical as it will turn a critical eye toward the musicals of the first twenty years of the 21st century with a specific focus on Broadway (commercial) musical theatre.

In these 20 seasons, Broadway musicals reflected the culture of the United States not only in their form and content but also in the ways that they were brought to the Broadway stage and who was on the teams that developed them. In the second edition of his book, *The*

DOI: 10.4324/9781003139171-1

2 Introduction

Great White Way: Race and the Broadway Musical, musical theatre scholar Warren Hoffman observes that musicals "contribute significantly to the construction of whiteness" in the United States "by thinking about whose stories get told and produced and how we consume culture, we can begin to chip away at the system of white supremacy…"[3] Thinking about not only whose stories are being told and produced, but who is telling and producing those stories can extend the process of "chipping away." Though the history of musical theatre includes a great number of marginalized people, in particular Black, Jewish, and queer people,[4] and there has been some diversification in the stories that are told (though more work in this area is certainly needed) in Broadway musicals, the identities of the people who get to tell those stories continue to be narrow. Additionally, In the Introduction to her edited collection, *Reframing the Musical: Race, Culture, and Identity,* editor Sarah Whitfield observes that the way the history and historiography of musical theatre has been framed "some people, places and events have been privileged as more important, more worth remembering and paying attention to than others …"[5] She continues by pointing out that the field of musical theatre studies has contributed to the erasure of marginalized people by making some groups central to the historical narrative and by leaving others out entirely.[6] Framing the historical and popular narrative of the musical through a white, male lens has contributed to the lack of representation for marginalized artists in all roles at all levels of commercial musical theatre. While in the 21st century there was representation at the top of Broadway musicals productions for some marginalized groups like queer people and Jewish people, the "table" is still filled with white men. The table of power on Broadway looks a lot like the table of power in many other US institutions, from universities to the government. One only needs to look at the numbers to see how glaringly white and male the Broadway "table" actually is.

Examining these 20 Seasons

This book will explore the 269 musicals that opened on Broadway from the 2001–2002 season to the shortened 2019–2020 season by cataloging, categorizing, and analyzing them. Rather than moving

Introduction 3

through these musicals chronologically, these shows will be examined together and divided by type or category in order to wholistically assess the entire period rather than comparing productions year to year.

First, this introduction will break down the musicals "by the numbers," looking at what was produced and by who. The first chapter will then examine the historical and cultural context of the 20 seasons and broadly explore some of the major trends and controversies of the period, shedding light on both the culture of the time and the impact that culture had on the Broadway musical. Chapters 3–5 will illuminate the musicals that fall into the "original" category, examining each subcategory in its own chapter. Chapter 3 will examine jukebox musicals and revues, Chapter 4 will unpack screen-to-stage musicals, and Chapter 5 will tackle "other original" musicals. Chapter 6 will dive into revivals, uncovering the various types of revivals that were common in the period. Chapter 7 will bring the exploration to a close by looking at 2020 and the Broadway COVID-19 shutdown, and discuss the possibilities for the Broadway musical as it moves into its next historical era.

20 Seasons by the Numbers

Between October 26, 2000, and March 11, 2020, 269 musicals opened on Broadway. These 269 productions represent a variety of types and styles of musicals, including original musicals that are new to Broadway and revivals of older productions. For this study, only productions designated as musicals by the Broadway league that opened in a Broadway theatre between October 2000 and March 2020 (hereafter referred to as the 20 seasons) will be included. Shows designated "specials" will not be included. The categorization of a production as "original" or "revival" will also be determined by how the production is designated by the Broadway League. This means that a musical that has not before played in a Broadway theatre, even if it is not a "new" musical and has had major productions outside of Broadway, will be designated as an original. For example, *Rodgers and Hammerstein's Cinderella* was written in 1957 for television and subsequently staged all over the world, but was never mounted on Broadway prior to the 2013 production, making it an original musical during the 20 seasons.

4 Introduction

The "original" designation will also be used regardless of the source material for the musical.

The Shows

During the 20 seasons, there were an average of 13.5 musicals that opened on Broadway every year. The 2016–17 season saw the most openings with 19 productions and the 2019–2020 season the least with only six. However, had all the shows in previews and scheduled to open in the latter half of the 2019–2020 season opened, there would have been 13, making 2001–2002 the season with the fewest openings at nine. It is not surprising that the 2001–2002 and 2019–2020 seasons saw the fewest number of shows as both seasons were impacted by national events.

The 9/11 terrorist attacks happened early in the 2001–2002 season and had a large impact on tourism in New York. In an interview with *The New York Times*, Christopher Heywood, a senior vice president of NYC & Company shares that after 9/11 "the number of international visitors declined from about 6.8 million in 2000 to about 5.7 million in 2001, with most of that loss coming after Sept. 11."[7] Heywood also notes that it took five years to return to pre-9/11 levels for tourism in New York City despite an uptick in 2002 from what he refers to as domestic "patriotic tourism."[8] In addition to the drop in tourism, the psychological aftermath of 9/11 impacted what was and was not opened in the following months. For example, the revival of the Stephen Sondheim and John Weidman musical *Assassins* was originally scheduled to open in November 2001 but was postponed indefinitely.[9] Though the show would eventually open in 2004, its postponement was not surprising given its topic: presidential assassinations.

At the other end of the 20 seasons, the 2020 COVID-19 pandemic prematurely cut off the 2019–2020 season at the height of spring Broadway musical openings. On March 12 there were four shows that were in previews, including *Six: The Musical*, which was scheduled to open on March 12. There were also three additional shows that were scheduled to open in April 2020. If all these shows had opened, the 2019–2020 season would have seen 13 musicals open, placing it squarely in the middle of the pack for the number of musicals to open in a season.

Broadway Openings by Season

Figure 0.1 shows the number of musicals that opened on Broadway for each of the 20 seasons. Approximately 186 (or 70%) of the musicals that opened on Broadway were original musicals, while 83 (or 30%) were revivals or remounts (Figure 0.2). This can be further broken down by season (Figure 0.3).

Breaking down the original musical category further reveals that there are six categories in which the original musicals reside: *screen-to-stage, jukebox, other original source, revue, dansical, opera/etta*. Screen-to-stage musicals are musicals that are stage adaptations of an existing film. These musicals may be adaptations of musical films that utilize the music from the film (in which case they are also jukebox musicals) or they may be musical adaptations of non-musical films. Musicals in the jukebox category are those that utilize a score of existing music, that is, the majority of the music in the production was not composed for the production. In order to be classified as a jukebox musical, these productions also must be plot-driven book musicals. Musicals that utilize existing music but do not have a plot are categorized as revues. Other original source musicals draw their source material from a variety of

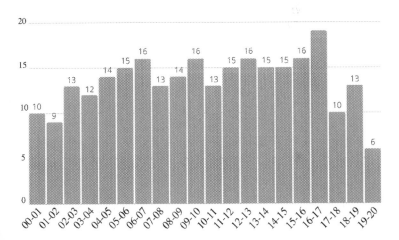

FIGURE 0.1 Number of musicals that opened on Broadway by season.

6 Introduction

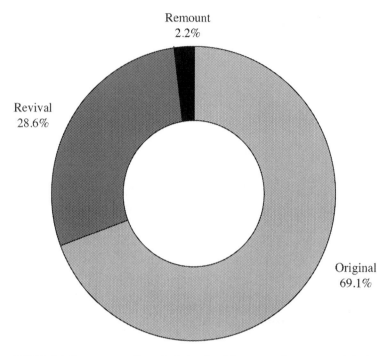

FIGURE 0.2 Percentage of musicals in the 20 seasons that were originals, revivals, and remounts.

places including but not limited to books, plays, and historical events. Finally, dansicals are a specific type of dance-driven musical that appeared at the beginning of the 20 seasons. These categories will be explored in detail in section 2 of this book, but the numbers are as follows: There were 78 musicals that fall into the other original source category, 72 screen-to-stage musicals, 55 jukebox musicals, six revues, three dansicals, and two opera/ettas.

It should be noted that there are shows that fit into multiple categories. These shows have been counted in both categories, which accounts for the discrepancy between the total number of original musicals and the sum of all the categories. These categories will be explored in detail in Chapters 3–5.

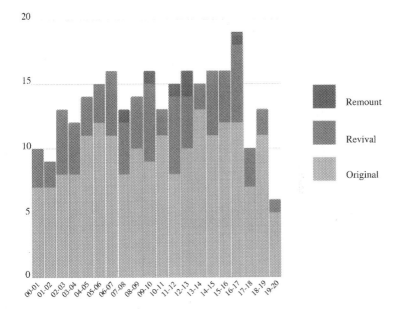

FIGURE 0.3 Number of originals, revivals, and remounts by season.

The Artists

In addition to breaking down and categorizing the types of musicals that were mounted in the 20 seasons, it is also possible to catalog who filled the major creative roles in each production. For this study, the gender and race of the artists in the following categories were compiled: Director, choreographer, book writer, composer, lyricist, scenic designer, costume designer, sound designer, lighting designer, and video/projection designer.

Before presenting the numbers for these artists, it is important to acknowledge that there are several artists whose race could not be verified. Though this was only the case for a few artists, it is still imperative to acknowledge that those data points are missing. Artists whose race could not be verified have not been counted in the Black, Indigenous, and People of Color (BIPOC) artist tally.

8 Introduction

Directors and Choreographers

Of the 269 musicals that opened on Broadway, 133 (or 49% of them) had no women or people of color in the role of director or choreographer; 158 productions (59%) had an all-male team and 217 (81%) had an all-white team. In the role of director, only 39 productions (14%) had a female director and only 15 different women directed a musical on Broadway during the 20 seasons. Only 14 productions (5%) had a BIPOC director and only nine different BIPOC artists directed a musical on Broadway. Of those nine artists, one was a woman, therefore, only one woman of color directed a musical on Broadway in these 20 seasons. This means that only 0.37% of productions in the 20 seasons employed a woman of color as director.

There were 10 productions during the 20 seasons that had no choreographer credited, so the numbers for choreography are calculated for 259 musicals. Of the 259 musicals that opened on Broadway and credited a choreographer, 66 productions (or 26%) had a female choreographer, while 36 productions (14%) had a BIPOC choreographer. There were 36 women and 17 BIPOC[10] artists who were credited as choreographers for a Broadway musical in the 20 seasons.

Writing Team: Book Writers, Composers, Lyricists

In the 20 seasons, 22% of productions, or 59 productions, had at least one woman on the writing team. Ten percent (or 27 productions) had at least one person of color on the writing team, and 3% or eight productions had at least one woman of color on the writing team. In total there were 23 women, 14 BIPOC, and 3 women of color credited as composers for a Broadway musical in this period.[11] There were 34 women, 18 BIPOC, and five women of color credited as book writers. And there were 26 women, 14 BIPOC, and three women of color credited as lyricists. As the original writer in all three categories is credited for revivals, some of these artists were not alive at the time of production, reducing the number of actively participating women and BIPOC artists even further.

Designers

In the 20 seasons, 35% of productions, or 95 productions had an all-white design team. While at first glance this seems to be a better number than the numbers for writers, directors, or choreographers, it isn't. That can be seen when breaking down the design roles and looking at how many female or BIPOC artists had the opportunity to design one of the 269 musicals that opened on Broadway.

Costume Design

In costume design, 39% of productions or 105 productions were designed by a woman and 47 different women designed a Broadway musical in this period. 13% or 34 productions had a BIPOC designer and eight different artists of color had the opportunity to design a production.

Scenic Design

In scenic design, 14% of productions or 38 productions were designed by a woman and there were 15 different women credited as scenic designers for a musical. Six percent of productions (or 17 productions) had a BIPOC scenic designer. Additionally, there were only two women of color credited as scenic designers in this period.

Lighting Design

In lighting design, 15% of productions or 41 productions had a female lighting designer. However, there were only four women who were given the opportunity to design lighting for a Broadway musical in this period. Of the 41 productions designed by a woman, 59% or 24 productions were designed by Natasha Katz. Fourteen of the 41 productions (34%) were designed by Peggy Eisenhauer with a white, male co-designer, leaving three other productions to two other white women. No musical produced on Broadway in the 20 seasons had a BIPOC lighting designer.

10 Introduction

Projection/Video Design

Projection/video design is an interesting category because it was a new area of design in the 21st century. For the first part of the 20 seasons, it was almost all white women designing projections, then as projection/video design became more prevalent and prominent toward the middle of the period, the identity of the designers shifted and at the end of the 20 seasons, it was primarily white men with a few white women designing projections and video.[12] Additionally, only 94 of the 269 productions had a credited projection or video designer, so the percentages are calculated out of 94. In the 20 seasons, 18 productions, or 19% of the productions that credited a projection/video designer employed a female designer. Eight different white women were credited in the projection/video category in the 20 seasons. There are no people of color credited as projection or video designers in the 20 seasons.[13]

Sound Design

Only two women have ever been credited for sound design for a Broadway musical. In 2010 Ashley Hanson was the first woman to ever sound designing a musical on Broadway. Those two productions account for 0.74% of the productions in the 20 seasons. During the 20 seasons, there was one male sound designer, Kai Hereda, who is half white and half Japanese, who designed 11 musicals. Therefore 4% of musicals in this period had a BIPOC sound designer.[14]

Across all areas of design, there were 76 different women and 23 different people of color who had the opportunity to design a Broadway musical. Assuming that all productions have a scenic, costume, lighting, and sound designer, and then adding in the 94 productions that credited a video/projection designer, there were 1439 opportunities for designers in this period. Of those 1439 opportunities, 204, or 14% of them were given to women. Of those 1439 opportunities, 62 or 4% were given to people of color.

If this is expanded to include opportunities for directors (269), choreographers (259), and writers (807),[15] there were 2774 opportunities to work on a Broadway musical in the 20 seasons. 362 or 13% of these opportunities went to women and 158 or 6% went to a person of color. Across all areas, Broadway has a representation problem.

Representation on Stage

During the 20 seasons, there were far more conversations about the representation of women and people of color on stage than there were about the creative teams. However, Broadway also fell short in the roles that were available to women and BIPOC performers and in the casting of women and BIPOC performers in roles where gender or race is not fixed.

In 2018 the Asian American Performers Action Coalition (AAPAC) published a report that examined representation on New York stages for ten years (2006–2016). AAPAC is an organization whose mission is to "expand the perception of Asian American performers in order to increase their access to and representation on New York City's stages."[16] As a part of this work, since its founding in 2011, the organization has been tracking representation on New York stages. The data gathered each year is compiled into a report and in 2018 the organization looked at ten years of that data in order to analyze trends and progress. In looking at Broadway (both plays and musicals) from year to year the percentage of roles that went to BIPOC[17] actors are as follows:

TABLE 0.1 Distribution of roles by race 2006–2016.[18]

Year	White	BIPOC
2006–2007	89%	11%
2007–2008	77%	23%
2008–2009	85%	15%
2009–2010	81%	19%
2010–2011	75%	25%
2011–2012	75%	25%
2012–2013	79%	21%
2013–2014	75%	25%
2014–2015	78%	22%
2015–2016	64%	36%

12 Introduction

These numbers show that though the representation of BIPOC performers on stage was better than their counterparts off stage, Broadway was still overwhelmingly white. It should be noted that these numbers do include both plays and musicals. The 2015–2016 season was broken out into plays and musicals in the report with musicals showing better representation. For 2015–2016 musicals 64% of roles were filled by white performers and 36% were filled by BIPOC performers[19] whereas for plays 85% went to white performers and 15% to BIPOC performers.[20] AAPAC has continued to track these numbers and each year their data and analysis become deeper and richer. At the time of this writing, the 2018–2019 season is the most recent report available and that report shows that little progress was made between the 2015–2016 and 2018–2019 seasons despite a great deal of conversation about representation in and outside of the theatre industry. For the 2018–2019 season, 65.9% of roles went to white actors, which is consistent with the 66.4% from the 2017–2018 season, showing no further progress.[21] When musicals are examined on their own, there was some progress, with 58.9% of roles going to white actors and 41.1% to BIPOC actors. However, AAPAC also reported that for Broadway musicals, 80% of the lead roles were filled by white actors showing that even as more bodies of color are appearing on Broadway musical stages, they are most often filling secondary or ensemble roles.[22] Clearly, though progress has been made on stage, there is still a long way to go for equitable representation.

Notes

1 The term "American" here is being used to represent the United States of America and is in quotation marks to acknowledge the fact that there are multiple Americas but that here, the term refers to culture that is of the United States.
2 Raymond Knapp, *The American Musical and the Formation of National Identity*, 2nd ed. (Princeton, NJ: Princeton Univ. Press, 2005), 10.
3 Warren Hoffman, *The Great White Way: Race and the Broadway Musical*, 2nd ed. (New Brunswick, NJ: Rutgers University Press, 2020), xi.
4 Knapp, *The American*, 5–8.
5 Sarah Whitfield, "Framing and Reframing: Existing Ways of Looking," introduction to *Reframing the Musical: Race, Culture and Identity* (London: Methuen Drama, 2021), xii.

Introduction   **13**

6 Whitfield, "Framing and Reframing," introduction, xii.
7 Jonathan Wolfe and Nick Corasaniti, "New York Today: Terrorism and Tourism," *New York Times*, November 3, 2017, www.nytimes.com/2017/11/03/nyregion/new-york-today-terrorism-and-tourism.html.
8 Wolfe and Corasaniti, "New York."
9 Jesse McKinley, "Read, Aim, Sing: 'Assassins' Hits Broadway," *New York Times*, April 22, 2004, sec. E, 1, www.nytimes.com/2004/04/22/theater/ready-aim-sing-assassins-hits-broadway.html.
10 Please see above note about verification of race.
11 There are several Jukebox musicals with many writers credited for writing music or lyrics who are not counted here.
12 There is also a production company that employs a variety of people who did the video for a few productions, but those individuals are not credited, the production company is, so they are not included in this tally.
13 During this period there are several productions that credit a company as the video/projection designer. In these cases, the individuals who worked on the production are unknown.
14 There are several male sound designers whose race could not be verified and who are, therefore, not included in this tally.
15 It must be acknowledged that these calculations are hypothetical and for illustrative purposes as there were multiple people credited in some of these categories.
16 "About," The Asian American Performers Action Coalition, accessed September 16, 2022, www.aapacnyc.org/.
17 It must be noted that AAPAC also includes disabled actors of any race with BIPOC actors.
18 *Ethnic Representation on New York Stages: Special 10-Year Edition* (n.p.: AAPAC, 2018), 8.
19 *Ethnic Representation*, 9.
20 *Ethnic Representation*, 10.
21 *The Visibility Report: Racial Representation on NYC Stages* (n.p.: AAPAC, 2021), 53.
22 *The Visibility*, 54–55.

1

20 YEARS/20 SEASONS

20 Seasons of History

From 2000–2020 there were many historical and cultural events that shaped the Broadway musical. The first 20 years of the 21st century are truly a historic period due to two significant events that shifted life and culture in the United States. On September 11, 2001, just one year into the 20 seasons, the terrorist group Al-Qaeda hijacked four passenger airplanes. Two of those planes were flown into the twin towers of the World Trade Center in Lower Manhattan. The third crashed into the Pentagon and a group of heroic passengers brought down the fourth in a field in Pennsylvania. Though the attacks that occurred on the morning of September 11 were a national tragedy, New York bore the devastation locally. Over 2500 people died in the World Trade Center in lower Manhattan. Prior to September 11, the threat of a terrorist attack was abstract to many Americans in the 21st century, it was something that happened half a world away and would never happen at home in the United States. 9/11 proved that nowhere was safe and had lasting impacts on U.S. life and liberties. 9/11 also had an immediate impact on Broadway. Broadway performances were suspended for two days, September 11 and September 12. Though the

DOI: 10.4324/9781003139171-2

theatres reopened, and performances resumed on September 13, productions played to mostly empty houses for weeks. To entice audiences back to Broadway, on September 28, hundreds of Broadway performers gathered in Times Square to perform the John Kander and Fred Ebb song "New York, New York" for a commercial entitled "I Love New York" that would run on major networks and in movie theatres across the country.[1] Ticket sales on Broadway were abysmal in the month of September 2001 and would slowly begin to recover throughout the 2001–2002 season.

It was not just Broadway that experienced a drop off in revenue after 9/11, the attacks had a large impact on tourism in New York in general. As mentioned in the introduction, there was a significant decline in both international and domestic tourism in New York and it would take several years for the tourists to return. The attacks also impacted what was deemed appropriate subject matter for Broadway, further stifling musical openings. Because of 9/11, the 2001–2002 season had the fewest number of musicals open on Broadway (other than the pandemic shortened 2019–2020 season). It would take years for Broadway grosses to recover fully, but they did recover and the latter part of the 20 seasons saw record-breaking attendance and revenue.

The 9/11 shutdown of all theatres on Broadway was unprecedented. Prior to 9/11 Broadway had shut down several times due to labor disputes, but never because of an incident like 9/11. During the 20 seasons theatres went dark several times for several days at a time because of natural disasters and blackouts. Still, these isolated events did not have a lasting impact on ticket sales or attendance the way 9/11 did. In addition, in the history of Broadway, there were several times that labor disputes led to prolonged closures. In 1919 Actors' Equity went on strike for a month, leading to all productions shutting down. In 1975 Broadway closed for 25 days due to a strike of The American Federation of Musicians, the musician's union. During the 20 seasons, there were several labor disputes with the longest happening in In 2007 when Broadway shut down for three weeks because of a stagehand strike, which until March 2020 was the longest closure of Broadway productions in the 21st century. Though a month or three weeks is a lot of time and a lot of lost revenue, each of these closures was finite and not caused by outside factors. The Broadway shutdown in 2020 was different.

16 20 Years/20 Seasons

On March 12, 2020, the lights on Broadway went out. Amid the global COVID-19 pandemic and a growing number of cases in New York City, including in the companies of several Broadway productions, the city shut down all theatres. The shutdown came in the middle of a busy and exciting season. There were several musicals in previews and several slated to open in the coming weeks ahead of the Tony Awards nomination deadline. One production, *Six: The Musical* had to close just hours before its opening night. There was much speculation in the days and months that followed about when Broadway theatres would reopen and as the shutdown dragged on, it became clear that this time it was different. Even as theatres in other parts of the country and the city began to reopen and found creative ways for the show to go on, Broadway remained dark. Broadway productions were some of the last productions to reopen post-COVID, which is not surprising given the politics and economics of Broadway.

Politically, Broadway has to contend with multiple unions that all have different priorities for their members. Navigating the rules for one or two unions was a herculean task for the many smaller professional theatres that produced work during the COVID-19 pandemic, navigating the rules for more than one or two, which would have been necessary on Broadway, was nearly impossible. It also didn't make financial sense for large-scale commercial productions to reopen. Broadway shows cost a lot of money to run each week and often must run at near capacity just to break even. The restrictions on audience numbers and the reduction in tourism and therefore in ticket demand meant that productions would likely run at a loss for months, something that no production could survive. So, Broadway stayed dark. It would take 471 days for a paying audience to sit in a Broadway theatre once again. On June 26, 2021, an unprecedented 15 months after Broadway closed, Bruce Springsteen walked out onto the stage at the St. James Theatre in front of a crowd of 1721 vaccinated (but mostly unmasked) theatregoers and brought the closure to its end.[2] Though the production, *Springsteen on Broadway*, was a musical special and therefore is not included in the productions covered in this book, the concert is important as it was the first production to open post-COVID-19.

It would take a few more months before plays and musicals would open. The first was Antoinette Chinonye Nwandu's modern absurdist play *Pass Over*, which played its first preview on August 4, 2021.[3] A month later, on September 2, 2021, two musicals would finally open, signaling an end to the pandemic closures, but not an end to the pandemic. *Hadestown*, which was running at the time of the shutdown, reopened, and *Waitress*, which had closed a few months before the pandemic hit, returned for a limited run. Many other productions also opened or re-opened in the following weeks and months, however, many of the productions experienced intermittent closures that lasted from one to several days and even up to weeks as they were forced to close due to COVID cases in their companies. Very few productions during this period were able to avoid COVID closures.

The attacks of September 11, 2001, and the 2020 global COVID-19 pandemic bookended the 20 seasons, making the years between a discrete historical period. However, it was not only these major events that shaped these two decades. This period also saw rapid changes in technology that had enormous impacts on culture. For example, Facebook was founded in 2004, ushering in the rise of social media. Social media would have a huge impact on the ways that Broadway musicals were marketed and discovered by audiences. YouTube made internet video free for everyone in 2005 and would quickly become a place where fans could find Broadway musical content (both legal and illegal) any time and from anywhere. YouTube quickly became the place where fans could find Broadway content and productions and creators began to use the platform in creative ways to drive ticket sales and fan engagement. In the early years of YouTube, productions like *In the Heights* (2005), *Xanadu* (2007), and *Rock of Ages* (2009) took advantage of the platform to engage with fans online.[4]

In 2007, the iPhone hit the market and within a few years, huge numbers of people across the world always had a computer in their purse or pocket leading to massive shifts in the ways that companies do business and people live their lives. The swiftly changing technology and the ways that technology rapidly shifted culture were unprecedented. For example, the industrial revolution, which was one of the most impactful cultural shifts of any time and ushered in the modern era happened over an almost 100-year period. Even if one points to the rise of the Internet, which became available publicly in 1991, as the beginning of this seismic cultural shift, that is still only 30 years for a societal paradigm shift. The new cultural paradigm of the 21st century

18 20 Years/20 Seasons

profoundly impacted the Broadway musical. It influenced its form and content, its casting trends and practices, as well as its economics and marketing. Social media and technology not only changed the way that Broadway musicals were designed and run but appeared as props and plot points in many productions. Society changed rapidly from 2000 to 2020 and the Broadway musical changed alongside it.

20 Seasons of U.S. Politics

The 20 seasons also spanned three US presidencies: George W. Bush, Barack Obama, and Donald Trump.[5] These three administrations and the culture that existed under them were vastly different. George W. Bush's presidency was defined by 9/11 and the war on terror. The period immediately after 9/11 saw a rise in patriotism as Americans came together to mourn a national tragedy. That patriotism and desire to punish those responsible for events led to policy shifts that might otherwise never have come to pass. Bush's two terms saw the enactment of The Patriot Act, which instituted sweeping changes to the investigative powers of law enforcement in the name of stopping terrorism. Bush's presidency began the "War on Terror," a 20-year-long unwinnable war in Iraq and Afghanistan that would span this entire period. It was also later determined that the justification for the invasion of Iraq, the "weapons of mass destruction" they were said to have possessed, was a lie. In response to his presidency, George W. Bush's name was invoked in several musicals in this period. *Avenue Q* (2005) included a line in the song "For Now," which stated, "George Bush is only for now," which often elicited cheers from the audience. Bush was also mentioned in the 2009 Green Day jukebox musical *American Idiot*. That musical was set during the Bush presidency, though it premiered under the next administration, and explored the unhappy fate of a young man sent to Iraq to fight in the war on terror.

In 2008, Bush's two terms were up, and Barack Obama was elected. Obama ran on the ideas of hope and change, and his presidency was the first time the United States elected a Black president. The Obama era saw many progressive policies come to the forefront including the federal legalization of gay marriage. For many on the left, the eight years that Obama spent in the White House brought about the change that they had hoped for. Even though the dominant discourse during the Obama administration was one of hope and change, and discourse about how progressive the US was for its choice and for the policies that Obama enacted was common, the reality was that not much had changed. In the mainstream, white culture, America was "beyond racism" but under the surface, the same systemic inequities that have existed since the birth of the United States persisted. That racism was not only baked into the systems and structures of the country despite its Black leader but also dug even deeper fissures between left and right, liberal, and conservative, as a backlash against the new paradigm in the country stoked fires of white nationalism.

The years of the Obama presidency also played out on stage, most notably in the 2015 smash hit *Hamilton*. The musical was praised for the progressiveness of its casting as it tells the story of founding father Alexander Hamilton by casting a diverse array of BIPOC performers. However, like the Obama presidency, the act of presenting bodies of color in office or on stage does not solve the systemic racism in the United States or the theatre industry. In his article, "Why *Hamilton* Is Not the Revolution You Think It Is," theatre scholar James McMaster observes, "in *Hamilton*, the fact that the white men who founded the United States—colonizers all, slaveholders some—are played by men of color actually obfuscates histories of racialized violence in the United States."[6]

In addition to its erasure of the true history of people of color in the United States, musical theatre Scholar Donatella Galella observes:

> [*Hamilton*] upholds ... "nationalist neoliberal multicultural inclusion." In other words [creator Lin-Manuel] Miranda and the musical occupy a centrist position that mobilizes performers of color and the myth of meritocracy in order to extol and envision the United States as a multiracial utopia where everyone has a fair chance to compete for access to "The Room Where It Happens."[7]

Much of the discourse surrounding *Hamilton* asserted that because the United States had a Black president, it was possible for anyone, regardless of race, to work hard and succeed, and racism and the obstacles that the nation's systemic inequities presented to people of color were a thing of the past. However, that was far from the truth.

20 20 Years/20 Seasons

The election of Donald Trump in 2016 showed just how far from the truth *Hamilton*'s assertions about the state of racism in the United States really were. The Trump campaign and presidency brought many white Americans who felt disenfranchised and left behind by the politics of the Obama presidency and frankly, by the idea that their whiteness no longer made them superior, out of hiding. The swift rise in overt displays of white nationalism, racism, and antisemitism during the campaign and first years of the Trump presidency proved that the nation had not left racism behind, it had just buried it. And in combination with the rise of misinformation on social media and the Internet, hate speech and racism only grew more prolific and more overt. The gap between the political right and left also widened in this period as the right moved further right and the left moved further left making any common ground increasingly harder to come by.

This divide was also on display on Broadway, notably at the November 18, 2016, performance of *Hamilton*. Vice President-elect Mike Pence attended the show and during the curtain call, the actor who played Aaron Burr, Brandon Victor Dixon, addressed Pence directly by reading a letter from the cast. He thanked him for attending and asked him to "hear them out." Then Dixon shared the cast's concerns about the new administration he stated:

> We, sir—we—are the diverse America who are alarmed and anxious that your new administration will not protect us, our planet, our children, our parents, or defend us and uphold our inalienable rights ... We truly hope that this show has inspired you to uphold our American values and to work on behalf of all of us.[8]

In the wake of the 2016 election many marginalized people including women, people of color, Jews, and Muslims were afraid and with good reason. That fear manifested itself on stages across the United States, including on Broadway.

20 Seasons of Cultural Movements

In addition to presidential politics, Broadway was also impacted by wider cultural movements during this period. Two examples are the

Occupy Wallstreet Movement and the Black Lives Matter Movement. The Occupy Wallstreet movement began in September 2011 when several hundred protestors marched on Wallstreet to protest income disparity. The gap between the rich and the poor had been steadily widening exacerbated by the Great Recession that began in 2008, and the Occupy Movement was protesting the fact that 1% of people held the vast majority of the nation's wealth. As the protestors marched, Disney Theatrical Productions, the theatrical producing arm of the Walt Disney Corporation was about to open the much-anticipated stage version of *Newsies*, a beloved early 1990s cult classic film that told the story of the 1899 newsboys' strike. The musical was scheduled for a pilot production at the Papermill Playhouse in New Jersey and then planned to be released for licensing, but the popularity of the title coupled with its keen connection to current events (the newsboys were a perfect stand-in for the Occupy movement) led the production to Broadway.[9] Broadway musicals are a part of the culture and when a musical, like *Newsies* in 2011, is able to capture the feeling of a specific moment on stage, it can lead to success.

However, Broadway has not always been in step with the current moment. That was clear in 2020 when the Black Lives Matter movement entered mainstream consciousness after the murder of George Floyd by Minneapolis police officers. The nation erupted and Broadway finally took notice. Perhaps because Floyd's murder was just the next in a long line of unjust deaths of Black men and women at the hands of law enforcement, but more likely because the nation was under lockdown because of the global COVID-19 pandemic with few distractions, the long overdue conversation about the injustice and inequality experienced by Black Americans was finally heard by white ears. In 2020 several theatrical movements emerged including "We See You White American Theatre." The "About" page of the website for "We See You White American Theatre" shares the origin of the organization:

In reaction to civil unrest in our country, we—Black, Indigenous and People of Color (BIPOC) theatremakers—formed a collective of multi-generational, multi-disciplinary, early career, emerging and established artists, theater managers, executives, students, administrators, dramaturges and producers, to address the scope and pervasiveness of anti-Blackness and racism in the American theater. Our response was to draft a strong testimonial letter, "DEAR WHITE AMERICAN THEATER", collectively crafted by theatremakers from across the country, exposing the indignities and racism that BIPOC, and in particular Black theatremakers, face on a day-to-day basis in the theater industry.[10]

The 300+ BIPOC theatremakers who made up the membership of the organization published both a list of principles for creating an Anti-racist theatre industry and a list of demands for the American Theatre. The organization and other anti-racist theatre practitioners started a long-overdue conversation that had a visible impact on theatres around the United States in the years after the 20 seasons. Unfortunately, the Broadway musical was slow to change and as will be discussed in the conclusion to this book, Broadway musicals post-COVID weren't that different from Broadway musicals pre-COVID. "We See You White American Theatre" was one of many organizations doing the work of pushing the theatre industry toward anti-racist practices. As the numbers presented in the introduction show, Broadway musicals have a long way to go to even begin to address the issues of representation both on stage and off. Though important conversations about equity and access were finally acknowledged by those in power (who are overwhelmingly white and male) at the end of the 20 seasons, only time will tell if these conversations will continue and if action will be taken, or if long-standing inequities will continue to be the norm on Broadway.

20 Seasons of Trends and Controversies

In looking at these 20 seasons as a period in the history of the Broadway musical, several trends rise to the surface as prominent features. Additionally, there were several major controversies that ignited a dialogue about Broadway musicals and what stories are told, and who gets to tell those stories. Though by no means comprehensive, the following section will illuminate some of the prominent trends that can be observed and some of the most visible controversies that arose during the period.

Trend #1: Recycling Material

Though reviving musicals and basing musicals on known properties was not a new development for the Broadway musical during the 20 seasons, the sheer number of musicals that recycled material, particularly from films (in the form of screen-to-stage musicals) and that used existing music (in the form of jukebox musicals) was unprecedented. During the 20 seasons, 47% of the musicals that opened on Broadway were either jukebox or screen-to-stage musicals. That is a staggering figure and certainly points to a trend. As will be discussed at length later in this book, the incredibly high cost of mounting a musical on Broadway makes any production risky and one way to lessen the risk is to choose source material with which audiences, particularly tourists, already have some familiarity. A big-budget musical based on a beloved film already has an audience built in and when fighting to be one of the few shows for which the tourists will purchase tickets, producers bet on that familiarity to capture those coveted dollars.

The proliferation of musicals based on existing films or that included existing music led to many within the field of Musical Theatre Studies and Broadway critics to complain that there was nothing new on Broadway. For example, in his article for *Vanity Fair*, "Pop Goes the Great White Way," James Wolcott observes that many "Broadway purists" want to "turn off the popcorn machine."[11] Musical Theatre Scholar Mark N. Grant titles the last chapter of his 2004 book *The Rise and Fall of Broadway Musicals* "The Age of McMusicals." This title invokes the idea of an assembly line and asserts that musicals in the 21st century are devoid of any artistic merit. Grant's position is further made clear when at the end of the chapter he declares, "Adaptations have played out their string. They are now killing the musical and foreclosing its artistic development."[12] The desire to "turn off the popcorn machine" because adaptations are "killing the musical" just isn't supported by the large number of successful jukebox and screen-to-stage musicals in this period. It must be acknowledged that not all musicals that are financially successful are artistically successful and vice versa, but if musicals playing on Broadway are finding any kind of success, can it really be argued that the musical is dead? Additionally, in each era of the musical, those that subscribed to whatever the musical

24 20 Years/20 Seasons

was in its last era pronounce the musical "dead." And yet, the form continues to grow and change from each era to the next, and will continue to grow and change for many eras to come.

Another form of recycling that was prevalent in the 20 seasons was the revival. As will be discussed in detail in Chapter 6, revivals are new productions of musicals that have already had a production on Broadway. If the number of revivals and remounts is added to the number of jukebox and screen-to-stage musicals, the percentage of recycled musicals in this period jumps to 78%. Additionally, one could argue that many of the musicals in the "other original" category are also recycled as only one subcategory of "other original musicals" are not based on some sort of source material. If these musicals are added, the percentage of musicals that played on Broadway that were "recycled" hits 88% as there are only 33 musicals that opened during the 20 seasons that were newly invented. Clearly, recycling was a major trend during this period.

Trend #2: Technologically Advanced Scenography and Staging

As was the case for culture and society at large, the 20 seasons saw huge leaps in the technology used to bring musicals to life on Broadway stages. Though technological advances occurred across all areas of the theatre, the most visible of those advances were in digital scenography. None were more prevalent and present during the 20 seasons than the LED screen. LED stands for light-emitting diode, which is "a semiconductor device that emits light when an electric current is passed through it."[13] As different wavelengths of energy are passed through the diode, it emits different colors of light. The technology that is used in an LED was first discovered in the early 20th century and the first patent for an LED (an infrared LED) was filed in the early 1960s. Throughout the 1960s and 1970s, more LEDs were developed and eventually, LEDs that lit up in multiple colors were invented. The technology was not widely used in the 20th century due to its high cost but in the 1990s and into the first decade of the 21st century, the cost was reduced, and LED technology became standard for many applications including televisions and large-scale screens for sporting events.[14] Throughout the 21st century, LED technology has improved and become more precise in its ability to replicate color and images.

During the 20 seasons, the use of large-format LED screens became standard practice, particularly in new musicals. Take for example 2018's *Mean Girls*. Based on the 2004 film of the same name, *Mean Girls* follows the story of Cady Heron, an American teenage girl who grew up in Kenya and returns to the US only to find that the wilds of high school are just as vicious as the savannas of Africa. The musical follows her adventures with "The Plastics" a group of popular "mean" girls who turn Cady's world upside down and bring out the worst in her and everyone around them.

The musical, like the film, is kinetic and moves through scenes and locations quickly. To support the cinematic nature of the libretto, the designers turned to digital technology. In his June 2018 article for *Lighting & Sound America*, scenic designer Scott Pask shares, "The key to the design proved to be a large-scale video system ... video [helps] facilitate the show's fast pace by allowing for rapid transitions; it's also suitable for a show about a generation that has grown up permanently attached to their digital devices."[15] The video team decided that utilizing LED screens rather than projectors was the right choice for several reasons. Adam Young shares that using the screens allowed for brighter images and the use of "colors and tones" that would not be possible with projections and the screens are able to compete with the stage lighting in ways that projections cannot.[16]

To create the digital world of the musical, the production utilized "two huge curved LED screens with various sliding panels and six LED screen legs that go into the wings."[17] In all, the screens were "6,000 pixels across and about 2,000 pixels high."[18] This enormous system is used throughout the musical in two ways, first to represent the locations within the show with high-resolution images of the various places that the teens inhabit. It's also used to get inside the characters' heads and "represent the character's psychology."[19] This dual use of video is reflective of the source material for the musical as digital imagery allows the production to have a cinematic feel and to jump quickly from moment to moment like a film, which is particularly appropriate for a screen-to-stage musical. In the case of *Mean Girls*, it also allowed the team to share pages from the iconic "Burn Book" which plays a

26 20 Years/20 Seasons

major role in the plot and that the audience really needs to be able to see to get the jokes.

Utilizing a video system like the one in *Mean Girls* is not without its challenges. For one, it is very expensive. High-quality LED panels like the ones in *Mean Girls* cost hundreds of thousands of dollars for small systems and the custom system created for the musical likely accounted for a great deal of the musical's $17 million budget. Next, the panels are incredibly bright and can be dangerous for the performers and crew. In fact, backstage at *Mean Girls*, some crew members apparently opted to wear sunglasses to protect their eyes because the scenery was so bright.

The screens also pose a challenge for timing. Unlike analog scenery, any small hiccup in the timing of the video on the displays can have an enormous impact on the production meaning that the video must be carefully programmed and deployed with virtually no room for error. This was evident in 2011's *Ghost: The Musical*, which also utilized giant LED screens. During the dance numbers in the show, the screens displayed silhouetted versions of the dancers on stage doing the show's choreography in tandem with the live performers. On multiple occasions during the production, the LED dancers and the live dancers were slightly out of sync and that discrepancy was glaringly obvious and greatly detracted from the experience of the show.

Despite the failure of its LED dancers, *Ghost: The Musical* was able to harness technology to create never before seen on Broadway illusions to support its storytelling. The musical is based on the 1990 film of the same name which tells the story of Sam and Molly. When Sam is killed, his girlfriend Molly uses a medium to communicate with his ghost, and Sam's ghost is a main character in the film. Part of the rising action of the film follows Sam as he learns how to be a ghost. He walks through walls and manipulates objects in the real world. To transfer the film to the stage, the musical had to recreate these iconic moments. To do that, the team hired an illusionist, Paul Kieve, who created original illusions for the production. These illusions included Sam learning to move objects. At one point in the show, Sam passes his hand through the image of a soda cup in one moment and then sends that same cup flying across the stage in the next. In another scene, Sam walks through the closed door of Molly's apartment. Though the production never shared how these illusions were created, it was clear that they were aided by digital projection technology.[20] Producing a stage version of *Ghost* would likely not have been possible a decade or two before.

Mean Girls and *Ghost* are just two of the many musicals during the 20 seasons that made use of digital video technology to varying degrees of success. As was mentioned in the introduction, by the middle of the period, projection and video designers were standard members of a creative team and throughout the second half of the period, many of the video elements in large-scale Broadway musicals utilized LED panels rather than projectors.

In addition to video and projection technologies, the 20 seasons also saw advances in other areas that were aided by technology. For example, flying technology took great leaps forward due to the innovations brought by two productions. First, Disney's *Tarzan: The Musical* (2006). Transferring *Tarzan* from screen-to-stage necessitated the development of new technology for flying as Tarzan and the apes in the show had to be able to swing through the space as if they were swinging through the trees in the jungle, often with multiple actors in the air at once. The production hired the company Flying By Foy who was responsible for making Peter Pan fly on stage in 1954 and who had since developed a computerized system for flying. Though Flying By Foy had a computerized system, traditional methods of flying the actors didn't fit with the aesthetics and needs of the production, so new methods and technologies needed to be developed. According to Associate Director Jeff Lee, this eventually led to the design of a "Mother Grid ... a framework of trussing that hangs over the entire footprint of the stage and channels ropes from electronic, computerized winches, up to drop points that are in the overhead system of the stage."[21] This system worked in tandem with rope-wielding stagehands backstage to create the dynamic flying in the production. The storytelling in *Tarzan* necessitated advancements in flying technology which were developed and then deployed in the production. Though the musical was not necessarily successful, the flying was.

Another production that led to advances in theatrical flight was 2011's *Spider-Man: Turn Off the Dark,* which employed Hollywood stunt coordinator Scott Rogers to design the aerial stunts for the show. In his 2013 book, *Song of Spider-Man: The Inside Story of the Most Controversial Musical in Broadway History*, Glen Berger reports that Rogers

28 20 Years/20 Seasons

"appropriated an innovation from pro football coverage." Prior to 2011, TV networks had "added a camera suspended by four cables above the playing field, which enabled an operator to send the suspended camera roving around the field via remote control."[22] Berger also shares that unlike the system used in *Tarzan*, Rogers determined that the system would have to be fully automated to achieve the cinematic flying effects the production was after. No stagehands would be involved, all flight would happen at the push of a button.[23] This advancement led to never before seen in the theatre feats of flight and it landed several performers in the hospital.

Broadway musicals in the 20 seasons were the site of many innovations in scenography that were driven by advances in technology. At times these advances enhanced the material and sometimes these advances stole focus from the material. Screen-to-stage musicals were especially technologically driven with many innovations occurring out of necessity to bring cinematic properties to life on stage. Regardless of whether the final product was successful, these innovations that were developed for Broadway musicals impacted theatre at all levels as many stage technologies continued to advance and become more affordable during this period.

Trend #3: Social Media and the Broadway Musical

As was mentioned in the section on the cultural context of this period, the rise of social media had an outsized impact on the culture of the United States in the first twenty years of the 21st century. Social media also impacted the Broadway musical. As contemporary musicals set in contemporary times began to play on Broadway, social media, of course, became a plot point and a design element. There is no better example of this than 2016's *Dear Evan Hansen*. The popular production utilizes social media in its plot and design to portray the world of contemporary teenagers. The show tells the story of Evan Hansen, a high school senior who suffers from anxiety, as he gets caught up in a lie about being best friends with a classmate who committed suicide. Rather than explain the truth, Evan uses his newfound social position to elicit sympathy from his classmates and to date his dead classmate's sister. Though the story is truly appalling, its frank discussions of mental illness and the contemporary teen experience spoke to young audience members and their parents. The production ran for almost six years and spawned a popular national tour and a film adaptation. But putting its problematic narrative aside, the way that the production utilized social media was very connected to the culture in which it was created. Not only is social media a plot point in the show, but it is also utilized in the scenography. The digital world of the teenagers in the production was projected as scenery behind much of the action, lending authenticity to the teen experience depicted and providing a window into the character's thoughts and motivations.

Social media was not only on stage on Broadway during the 20 seasons, but it also played a role in the marketing of Broadway musicals and even in determining which musicals landed on Broadway, take for example Disney's *Newsies*. The musical is based on the 1992 Disney box office disaster of the same name. Though the film was unsuccessful at the box office, it grew a cult following after repeated play on the Disney Channel. As social media rose to prominence, these fans, lovingly known as "fansies," created online communities and utilized social media as a major part of their fandom. It was because of these communities that Disney knew there was a market for a stage adaptation. Though multiple factors contributed to the decision to bring *Newsies* to Broadway, which will be discussed in more detail in Chapter 4, the fansies were the catalyst for Disney even considering an adaptation.[24]

The influence of social media did not end at the stage door. Disney Theatrical Productions also utilized the power of social media in the marketing efforts for the production. Just prior to *Newsies*, Disney Theatricals hired a digital media coordinator (who would later become the digital media manager), Greg V. Josken. In this author's 2019 book, *Disney Theatrical Productions: Producing Broadway Musicals the Disney Way*, Josken explains the impact of digital media on the marketing of the production:

> [Disney] used video content in a new way for us. We relied very heavily on a Newsies cast member Andrew Keenan-Bolger, who played Crutchie, to actually create video content for us on a regular basis ... [this] did a few things: one, it just caught the authenticity of the cast members and the energy of the show in a

30 20 Years/20 Seasons

> very, very unique way, that really showcased the cast and the relationship that existed among them... so it didn't feel like a talking head interview, it truly felt like you were backstage with the cast and you got to know their personalities and the antics that happened backstage, in a way that was very true to the show.[25]

This approach combined with the creation of what the media team called "bumpers," digital mini posters that can easily be shared on multiple platforms, helped the production to harness the power of the "fansies" and their existing networks to promote the show. The practice was so successful that bumpers became standard for Disney productions and each production began to designate a social media captain, a company member who was in charge of capturing authentic backstage content to help promote their show.

Another production that only landed on Broadway because of social media is 2018's *Be More Chill*. The musical by Joe Iconis and Joe Tracz is based on Ned Vizzini's young adult novel of the same name. *Be More Chill* had its first production at the Two Rivers Theatre in New Jersey in 2015 where it received lukewarm reviews and so no future production was planned. However, the team made the decision to record an original cast album. That album was shared on Spotify and was heard by young musical theatre fans across the country because of the algorithms that Spotify uses to suggest music to its users based on what they are already listening to. *Be More Chill* was suggested as people listened to better-known musicals that were similar in tone and lyric content. That lead to thousands of new fans for the musical. Those fans were sharing their love of the musical on social media and clamoring for another production, which led to an Off-Broadway run. That production was buoyed by the fans of the album and their online presence, which in turn led *Be More Chill* to a Broadway opening. The musical would never have landed on Broadway without the viral popularity of the cast album and the outpouring of support it received on social media.

In addition to landing musicals on Broadway, social media also kept musicals playing on Broadway or at least tried to keep musicals playing on Broadway. The 2019 production of *Beetlejuice the Musical* is a prime example. *Beetlejuice*, based on a 1988 cult classic film of the same name, opened at the Winter Garden Theatre, one of Broadway's largest venues, in April 2019. Despite the production's name recognition and mind-blowing scenography, due to less-than-stellar reviews and weak ticket sales, the production struggled through the summer. However, come November 2019, it would be breaking records.

In December 2019, the production announced that it would close in June 2020 to launch a national tour. The production was not closing, however, because of a lack of ticket sales, in fact, the show was selling very well. *Beetlejuice* was selling so well that it set a record for ticket sales at the Winter Garden Theatre by grossing almost $1.6 million the week of Thanksgiving 2019.[26] But still, the production would have to close because the Shubert Organization, which owns the Winter Garden Theatre, invoked a "stop clause" that allows them to kick out a production that falls below an agreed-upon gross for two weeks in a row. Though in December 2019, *Beetlejuice* was exceeding the minimum number of sales, the production had fallen below the mark in May 2019 and the Shubert Organization promised the theatre to producer Scott Rudin for his revival of *The Music Man* starring Sutton Foster and Hugh Jackman.[27]

Though the dealings of Broadway producers and theatre owners are interesting, the reason why ticket sales for *Beetlejuice* rebounded is even more interesting. In October 2019, Brendan Wetmore of *Paper* Magazine reported on the enormous presence the musical suddenly had on social media and that even non-theatregoing fans were engaging with *Beetlejuice* across multiple platforms. He informs, "A quick scroll through the #BeetlejuiceBroadway hashtag on Twitter shows that not only is there discussion around the musical itself, but a true multi-platform, multi-medium fandom has formed: fan art, show-inspired foods, and cover songs litter the internet."[28] While Broadway going viral was not new, what was new was the presence that the musical suddenly had on TikTok. Wetmore explains:

> One differentiating form of expression in the *Beetlejuice* fandom, however, happens to be an unlikely ally: everyone's favorite lip-syncing app, TikTok. TikTokers everywhere have taken clips of songs from the Broadway musical—including, but not limited to, "Say My Name," "Girl Scout," and "Day-O (The Banana Boat

Song)"—and started *Beetlejuice*-inspired trends of cosplays, duets, and general clownery.[29]

In his book, *TikTok Broadway: Musical Theatre Fandom in the Digital Age*, Musical Theatre and TikTok scholar Trevor Buffone explains, that the way theatre critics discussed "Beetlejuice is reminiscent of how critics discuss TikTok aesthetics and cultures. TikTok's critics (both positive and negative) use similar language. TikTok is loud, cheeky, excessive, frantic, always in hyperdrive, and filled with off-the-wall humor. But all-in-all, it's a pretty fun time."[30] Buffone also points out that *Beetlejuice* had actual teenagers in its cast, something that doesn't often happen on Broadway, and one of those teens, "Presley Ryan, the Lydia understudy, was a 'veteran' TikToker ready to introduce Broadway to the TikTok revolution."[31] Ryan created TikToks backstage with other members of the cast in makeup and costume. As she engaged with viral TikTok trends, *Beetlejuice* engaged with viral TikTok trends and "the virality of their TikToks soon became a form of free advertising for the Beetlejuice marketing team."[32]

The musical's authentic presence on the platform led to engagement with teens who might never have otherwise discovered the production. It also engaged in social media in a way that few other Broadway musicals had. Though eventually the marketing team got involved, the fact that the original videos were created by a teen actor backstage lent a sense of authenticity to the campaign. It didn't feel like marketing, it just felt like fun! Buffone shares, "Beetlejuice distinguished itself from its peers because its cast was creating Beetlejuice-inspired TikToks alongside fans, often in conversation with fans."[33] That conversation led to a new audience, an audience that was rabid for *Beetlejuice* content and for whom the ability to see the show live (and visit the stage door afterward) was the pinnacle of their fandom. These fans not only attended the production, but they also even engaged in cosplay when they attended. When this author attended the production in June 2022, there were many young audience members in varying degrees of show-inspired costumes including a young person in a black and white striped suit and Beetlejuice-inspired makeup.

Beetlejuice ended up playing its last performance at the Winter Garden on March 11, 2020, due to the COVID-19 pandemic, which shut down all Broadway theatres on March 12. However, rather than embarking on a national tour once Broadway was back up and running, *Beetlejuice* reopened on Broadway at the Marquis Theatre in April 2022 and announced a National Tour to begin in December 2022.[34] Social media and specifically TikTok was able to bring a floundering screen-to-stage adaptation back from the brink of financial ruin and spawn a brand new fandom in the process.

Social media is changing the way Broadway musicals are marketed and is having tangible impacts on ticket sales and even on what properties end up on Broadway. It offers avenues to reach new audiences, both because it can catch younger demographics and because social media users who are not already Broadway fans or followers interact with Broadway content and sometimes become fans or ticket buyers in the process. It is likely that the influence of social media on the Broadway musical in the 21st century, both on stage and off, will only continue to grow.

Trend #4: Superfans and "Stagedooring"

Though there have always been fans of particular musicals who see the show multiple times, the rise of digital platforms for fan engagement has taken musical theatre fandom to another level. In his chapter "Play It Again (and Again, and Again): The Superfan and Musical Theatre," Musicologist James Deaville observes that "the proliferation of online platforms has enabl[ed] the sharing of information and personal experiences, interaction with other fans, and the creation of fan fiction and audiovisual media …"[35] "Superfan" is a term that cuts across many industries from sports, to retail, to the arts, and refers to fans who obsess over the object of their admiration. For Broadway musicals, the ability of these fans to interact with each other and to interact with content from and even sometimes the performers in the musical with which they are obsessed has led to a rise in fanaticism about musicals. These fans attend the musical object of their adoration as often as possible in as many places as possible, leading to an incredible outlay of money to indulge their obsessions. One manifestation of this fandom during the 20 seasons happened at the stage door.

Deaville explains that "stagedooring" is "a longstanding tradition for fans of Broadway …whereby spectators wait at the stage door after the

34 20 Years/20 Seasons

performance of a show to express their appreciation for the actors' efforts, get cast members' autographs or photos as memorabilia, and engage with an actor regarding their performance that night."[36] This practice has become so common that many Broadway news outlets including *Playbill.com* and *Broadwayworld.com* have published articles that outline tips and etiquette for visiting the stage door and that provide information about where to go at each theatre to visit the stage door. Stagedooring is not without controversy as there has been a backlash against actors who decide not to visit the stage door by the fans who wait for them. For example, in 2017 in response to fan complaints that he did not visit the stage door at the musical *Dear Evan Hansen*, star Ben Platt, Tweeted a response:

> Performing Dear Evan Hansen every night is wonderful but also hugely tough- as much as I would like to be out there every night, very often I cannot come to the stage door after the performance. My priority must always be self-care so I can recreate the same quality show each night. That's my job, and what each and every audience member is paying for and deserves. Before you tweet hateful things about how I don't value our incredible fans when I can't come to the door, please pause to consider that my responsibility to them is first and foremost to give my all each night. I preserve myself because I value each of them deeply.[37]

Platt is responding to the growing expectation in the latter half of the 20 seasons that Broadway performers, particularly stars, visit the stage door to engage with their fans after every performance. There have been many documented cases where fans have taken to social media to express outrage that a performer has not come to the stage door. This started a discourse at the end of the 20 seasons about fan entitlement and the fact that the purchase of a ticket to see a show does not guarantee access to a performer or that performer's autograph. The outbreak of COVID-19 and the subsequent actor safety protocols, which shut down the stage doors for a time, also added to the discourse around the practice as the possibility of viral transmission made visiting the stage door risky for the performers.

Controversy #1: The Scottsboro Boys (2010)

The Scottsboro Boys opened on Broadway in October 2010 and raised questions about how stories are told on Broadway and who gets to tell them.[38] The musical tells the true story of nine teenage Black boys, dubbed the Scottsboro Boys, who were wrongfully accused and later convicted of raping two white women on a train in Alabama in the 1930s. The case spent decades in the courts, including appearing before the Supreme Court twice and had a lasting impact on culture in the United States. The trial was widely covered and widely discussed in the culture at large in the mid-20th century and the case is often cited as an important event in the lead-up to the civil rights movement. Despite the impact of the case in its time and shortly after, by the 21st century, the Scottsboro Boys had been all but forgotten.

In the early years of the 20 seasons, director Susan Stroman and writer David Thompson wanted to collaborate with legendary composers John Kander and Fred Ebb (*Cabaret, Chicago*) on a historical musical. Thompson did some research and came back to the team with the Scottsboro Boys having been shocked by the injustice of the case and the anger and racism in the court transcripts he had found.[39] The team would spend the next decade developing the material for Broadway.

As it became clear that the project was likely headed for a commercial run, questions began to surface about the production and its team. Stroman, Thompson, Kander, and Ebb are all white. Though an all-white team telling a Black story was not new to Broadway (in fact, it is historically quite common), there was an additional layer added to this particular production. The framing device for the narrative was a minstrel show. Blackface minstrelsy is an American (US) performance form that rose to prominence in the early 19th century and continued to be popular well into the 20th century. The tradition began with white performers "blacking up" by putting burnt cork makeup on their faces and performing exaggerated stereotypes that mocked Black people. The tradition is incredibly racist and permeated entertainment in the 19th and early 20th centuries contributing to the culture of anti-Black racism, hate, and systemic injustice in the United States.[40]

Unsurprisingly, there was concern about utilizing the form of a minstrel show for a 21st century Broadway musical and in particular

36 20 Years/20 Seasons

that the creative team making that decision was white. In her 2020 article for *Playbill.com*, "The Oral History of *The Scottsboro Boys*," Felicia Fitzpatrick notes, "While the intention of *The Scottsboro Boys* was to deconstruct a minstrel show—to emphasize the inherent racism and flaws of the form—many took issue with the story being framed through the lens of a white writing team."[41] These concerns led to protests. On November 6, the *Freedom Party*, a political group concerned about the historical marginalization of Black and Latinx peoples, gathered in front of the theatre to protest the musical and its use of the minstrel form.[42] The Freedom Party released a statement about the protest in which they shared their concerns: "This racist play has reduced the tragedy of the Scottsboro Boys case to a Step n Fetchit comedic, minstrel exhibition."[43] The protests, which began shortly after the production opened, would continue throughout its short 49-performance run. When the production closed in December 2010, the producers cited ticket sales as the cause and denied any connection between the closure and the protests.[44] However, the activists who organized the protest disagreed and cited the protests as a primary reason for the show's shutdown.[45]

In contrast to the views of those protesting outside the theatre, many critics and scholars who saw the production thought it successfully told the story of the Scottsboro Boys in a way that provoked conversation. In the second edition of his book *The Great White Way: Race and the Broadway Musical*, musical theatre scholar Warren Hoffman observes that the framing of the musical, though not without controversy, allows the production to connect the historical racism that the Scottsboro Boys endured to the contemporary racism that Black Americans still endure. He shares, "In the show's particularly chilling finale, in which the young men tell of the horrible fates that befell them at the end of their lives, the actors playing the Scottsboro Boys appear in actual blackface, fully hitting home the show's minstrel conceit: to be black in America is, to great extent, to be forced to perform in a never-ending minstrel show for whites."[46] Though Hoffman seems to have hit on the heart of what the musical was trying to say, he arrived there by way of a very specific subject position. Hoffman is a highly trained scholar and a theatre professional who studies musicals as a part of his vocation. The average theatregoer who saw the musical did not have the same frame of reference. It should also be noted that Hoffman along with most of the critics who reviewed the production, is not Black, so his perspective is informed by his own positionality in relation to the source material.

Another nuance in the discussion is the fact that many of the protestors never saw the production and were protesting the framing of the story without actually seeing how the material and that framework were handled. In fact, several protestors commented that they would not see it because it was too difficult for them to engage with. One protestor, 84-year-old Flora Polk (who attended a rally in support of freeing the Scottsboro Boys in Harlem in 1933), commented, "I resent the 'Scottsboro Boys' show. I don't want to see it. I don't want to sit through it."[47] Producers cited the fact that many of the protestors had not seen the show as a reason to ignore them. But some of them did see the production. Dr. Kwando M. Kinshasa[48] of the African American Studies Department in the John Jay College of Criminal Justice at the City University of New York and expert on the Scottsboro Boys and their case was one such person. He wrote an op-ed for the Amsterdam News wherein he describes his objection to the material. After discussing how the production is akin to lynching "in the format of a cultural exhibition" he shares:

> Tragically, the attempt to address a major event in African-American history through the stage format of a minstrel show is both absurd and an affront to the cultural and political integrity of this ethnic group and the ongoing experiences of people of the African Diaspora ... Nor does it explore the reality that the Scottsboro defendants were, in truth, a tragic metaphor for hundreds of thousands of African-American youths trying to maintain a level of survival within a nation, America, whose laws were actively functioning to eliminate any semblance that their social, cultural and political wellbeing was a recognized fact.[49]

He continues by noting that the production "reeks with an intent to profit from the anguishing experiences of victims, whose experiences of institutionalized racial barbarity are well documented."[50]

Furthermore:

38 20 Years/20 Seasons

> To then utilize a musical format, the minstrel show concept that in itself emerges from a racist pre-Civil War 1850s format that utilized whites actors in black face to portray enslaved or marginalized American Blacks as buffoons, is not only to commit a cultural felony of the highest and most debasing kind, but is to suggest a political stance that desires strife and controversy for profit.[51]

Regardless of whether the production's use of a minstrel show as a framing device was appropriate, one thing is certain: The production had an all-white creative team telling a Black story that centers on race and in this case, utilizes a racist performance form as a framework to comment on that story. There was no Black representation at the table when decisions were being made or when the show was being conceived. This is a trend that was repeated many times during the 20 seasons and a concern that was only beginning to be taken seriously at the end of the period.

With that said, many of the performers in the production did comment that the experience of creating the musical was a positive one in which they were granted agency as members of the team and in which the white director acknowledged her lack of context. Coleman Domingo, who played Mr. Bones in the original production, commented, "They were very specific about making sure they had artists in the room who were going to interrogate the process, interrogate the work, and interrogate the text." He continues, "I think this was true advocacy. This is exactly what our advocates can do if they are so interested in telling a tale like this. No one had picked up the pen to write about these nine African American boys in the musical form."[52] The production was illuminating a troubling piece of history and brought it back into the contemporary conversation. The production was also providing jobs for many Black performers at a time when representation on stage on Broadway was abysmal. But even as the production provided work for many Black performers, those performers were required to be the spokespeople for their own identities during the development process, which in itself, is problematic.

There is no easy answer about whether the production should have happened, but the circumstances of the show's creation shine a light on

20 Years/20 Seasons **39**

the need for greater representation behind the scenes in Broadway musicals. A first step to rectifying the inequities that exist on Broadway is to ensure that those whose stories are being told are included in positions of power on creative teams.

Controversy #2: **West Side Story** *(2019)*

On February 20, 2020, a new revival of *West Side Story* opened at the Broadway theatre. While there had been much conversation about the production due to its new choreography from Anna Teresa de Keersmaeker[53] and new vision from director Ivo Van Hove in the year leading up to the opening, the biggest story on opening night wasn't the show itself, it was what happened on the sidewalk outside the theatre. Over 100 protestors lined the entrance to the theatre carrying signs and shouting their demands that Amar Ramasar, the actor playing Bernardo, be removed from the production.[54]

Two years earlier, New York City Ballet dancer Alexandra Waterbury discovered that her boyfriend and fellow NYCB dancer, Chase Finley, had been taking nude photographs and videos of her and sharing them in group chats with his friends, including other dancers in the company. The chat also contained derogatory comments including comparing the women to farm animals. One of those dancers was Amar Ramasar. In that same chat, Ramasar also shared photographs of his girlfriend, Alexa Maxwell, in the chat. Waterbury filed a lawsuit and the resulting investigation led to Finley resigning from the NYCB and Ramasar and another male dancer being fired. The dancer's union eventually challenged their dismissal and Ramasar and the other dancer were reinstated and assigned mandatory counseling.[55]

Ramasar was subsequently cast in the revival of *West Side Story* despite the production's knowledge of his prior conduct, which led to the protests. On February 13, 2020, while the show was in previews, the producers released the following statement:

> The management of *West Side Story* stands, as it always has stood, with Amar Ramasar. While we support the right of assembly enjoyed by the protestors, the alleged incident took place in a different workplace—the New York City Ballet—which has no

affiliation of any kind with *West Side Story*, and the dispute in question has been both fully adjudicated and definitively concluded according to the specific rules of that workplace, as mandated by the union that represents the parties involved in that incident. Mr. Ramasar is a principal dancer in good standing at the New York City Ballet ... He is also a member in good standing of both AGMA (representing the company of NYCB) and Actors' Equity Association (representing the company of *West Side Story*) ... There is zero consideration being given to his potentially being terminated from this workplace, as there has been no transgression of any kind, ever, in this workplace. The *West Side Story* Company does not as a practice terminate employees without cause. There is no cause here ... He is a valued colleague who was hired to play a principal role in this production, which he is doing brilliantly, and which he will continue to do for the entire unabated length of his agreement.[56]

The producers were correct that there was "no cause" to fire him from the production based on prior bad acts as Ramasar had not been caught doing anything inappropriate while employed on the production. However, when casting was announced in July 2019, the producers would have been aware of his prior behavior and cast him anyway. The protestors asserted that he should never have been cast given knowledge of what he did to women at the New York City Ballet. This controversy brought the conversations of the #MeToo-era to Broadway and raised questions about what the punishment for men who prey on women should be. For the later part of the twenty-teens, Hollywood was engaging in this same conversation which led to some men who had preyed upon women, perpetrating sometimes inappropriate and sometimes illegal acts, to be held accountable. Many of these men were sidelined from their careers for their conduct and others ended up prosecuted in court. In popular discourse, this was often referred to as "canceling" and led to conversations about "cancel culture." However, the inclusion of Ramasar in the cast of *West Side Story* even after his abuse of his female coworkers at NYCB was evidence of the fact that Broadway was not having the same conversations as Hollywood.

In April 2021, just as Broadway productions were beginning to plan their reopenings after the COVID-19 shutdown, the producer of the production (and many others on Broadway), Scott Rudin, resigned from the Broadway League amidst accusations of abusive behavior going back decades. Rudin was the person responsible for Ramasar's casting and for his remaining in the production despite the outcry. This fact demonstrates the ways in which the hierarchies in commercial theatre can protect abusers and lead to unsafe workplaces. When there is no accountability at the top, how can there be accountability in the company on stage? Should Amar Ramasar have been fired from *West Side Story*? Legally, probably not. But should he have been cast in the first place given his prior bad behavior? Definitely not.

Controversy #3: Jagged Little Pill *(2019)*

When *Jagged Little Pill*, the Jukebox musical based on Alanis Morissette's 1995 hit album of the same name, opened on Broadway in December 2019, it had made a few changes to its libretto from its out-of-town tryout in Boston. Adjusting a production between the tryout and Broadway is common practice, in fact, the purpose of an out-of-town tryout is to adjust and hone the show before opening in New York. However, in the case of *Jagged Little Pill*, some of those adjustments led to controversy and a conversation about gender and representation.[57]

The pre-Broadway iteration of the libretto included many lines in which it was implied that the character Jo was nonbinary, but these lines were removed or changed before the production opened on Broadway.[58] Though the character was never explicitly referred to as nonbinary, many of the reviews of the Boston production mentioned the character's gender identity, referring to the fact that Jo's gender was fluid and/or that Jo was exploring gender identity. Clearly, the character read as nonbinary even if the text of the script was not explicit.

There is very little representation in theatre for trans and nonbinary people and that representation becomes almost non-existent on Broadway. The existence of a nonbinary character who is exploring their gender identity in a Broadway musical is not common, therefore, the erasure of Jo's nonbinary identity prior to the production opening on Broadway was a big deal. The controversy was furthered by the

42 20 Years/20 Seasons

response of Lauren Patten, the actor playing Jo on Broadway. In an interview with Madison Malone Kircher of *Vulture*, Patten, who uses she/her pronouns, stated that "Jo was never written as anything but cis."[59] Once the show opened on Broadway, Patten received a great deal of attention, including multiple award nominations and wins, for her performance. Her denial of the nonbinary identity of the character was refuted in *The Brooklyn Rail* by Christian Lewis, who pointed out that during an earlier production at the A.R.T in Massachusetts, Patten retweeted a thread in which someone called out critics for using she/her pronouns for Jo and thanked the post's author for recognizing what she was trying to do with the character. This post was one of many that Patten would later delete as the controversy heated up on Broadway.[60] From the beginning of the development process, Patten's performance of "You Oughta Know" was lauded as a showstopper and hailed as one of the best performances in the production, so it was unlikely that Jo would be recast. Therefore, Lewis conjects, "Sometime between Cambridge and Broadway, Cody and Paulus made the decision to make Jo cis, possibly because of negative feedback about the way they wrote the character but also perhaps due to concern about potential backlash over Patten, a cis woman, playing a nonbinary role."[61] Lewis also points out that a scene between Jo and their mother about clothing and gender presentation was left in the script, further evidencing Jo's nonbinary identity.

At first, the producers repeated Patten's assertions that Jo was not intended to be a nonbinary character and publicly stated that the character was not written or conceived as nonbinary. However, in September 2021, ahead of the production's reopening, the producers released a statement:

> In Jo, we set out to portray a character on a gender expansive journey without a known outcome … Throughout the creative process, as the character evolved and changed, between Boston & Broadway, we made mistakes in how we handled this evolution. In a process designed to clarify and streamline, many of the lines that signaled Jo as gender non-conforming, and with them, something vital and integral, got removed from Jo's character journey … Compounding our mistake, we then stated publicly and categorically that Jo was never

written or conceived as non-binary. That discounted and dismissed what people saw and felt in this character's journey. We should not have done that … We should have protected and celebrated the fact that the non-binary audience members saw in Jo a bold, defiant, complex, and vibrant representation of their community. For all of this we are deeply sorry.[62]

Additionally, Patten apologized in a video conversation with her friend Shakina Nayfack, a trans performer, that was posted on Patten's Instagram. In the video, she stated that she was "profoundly sorry for the harm" and that she hoped "for Jo to be a character that can be claimed and owned by folks of many queer identities."[63] Patten also acknowledged that the development of the character was not straightforward and that she, a cis actor, had not taken the role of a character that was clearly already written to be trans or nonbinary.[64]

This controversy points to larger conversations about nonbinary and trans representation that began at the end of the 20 seasons and continued during and after the 2020 shutdown. Musicals like *Tootsie* and *Mrs. Doubtfire* that relied on outdated jokes about men in dresses stoked the conversations. The first character in a Broadway musical written specifically as trans, Pythio, appeared in the 2018 short-lived jukebox musical *Head Over Heels*. There was movement in the last few years of the 20 seasons toward better trans and nonbinary representation, but that movement was slow, and the conversations were just beginning. The *Jagged Little Pill* controversy also led to calls for better trans and nonbinary representation on creative teams when trans and nonbinary stories are being told, and only time will tell if that call is answered.

Reading Questions

1. What connections do you see between what was on Broadway in the 20 seasons and what was happening in history and culture at the time?
2. What were the major Broadway musical trends during the 20 seasons?
3. What do those trends tell us about the Broadway musical in the 21st century?

44 20 Years/20 Seasons

4. What do the controversies discussed tell us about the conversations that were happening in the culture at large in the first 20 years of the 21st century?

Notes

1 Casey Mink, "How a TV Ad Enticed Broadway Crowds Right after 9/11," *New York Times* (New York, NY), September 12, 2021, sec. AR, 4, accessed July 30, 2022, www.nytimes.com/2021/09/09/theater/9-11-broadway-new-york-commercial.html#:~:text=Following%20the%20Sept.,near%2Dempty%20houses%20for%20weeks.

2 Nick Corasaniti, "Bruce Springsteen Reopens Broadway, Ushering in Theater's Return," *New York Times* (New York, NY), June 27, 2001, sec. C, 1, accessed July 30, 2022, www.nytimes.com/2021/06/27/theater/bruce-springsteen-broadway.html?smid=url-share.

3 Reuters, "First Broadway Play Opens in NY since Lengthy Pandemic Shutdown," Reuters, last modified August 5, 202`, accessed July 30, 2022, www.reuters.com/world/us/first-broadway-play-opens-ny-since-lengthy-pandemic-shutdown-2021-08-05/.

4 Trevor Buffone, *TikTok Broadway: Musical Theatre Fandom in the Digital Age* (New York, NY: Oxford UP, 2023).

5 The beginning of the 20 seasons occurred in the last few months of Bill Clinton's presidency, but as the Clinton presidency was at its end when this period began, it is not being included here.

6 James McMaster, "Why 'Hamilton' Is Not the Revolution You Think It Is," *Howlround Theatre Commons*, last modified February 23, 2016, accessed July 31, 2022, https://howlround.com/why-hamilton-not-revolution-you-think-it.

7 Donatella Galella, "Being in 'The Room Where It Happens': *Hamilton*, Obama, and Nationalist Neoliberal Multicultural Inclusion," *Theatre Survey* 59, no. 3 (July 27, 2018): 364, https://doi.org/10.1017/S0040557418000303.

8 Qtd in Christopher Mele and Patrick Healy, "'Hamilton' Had Some Unscripted Lines for Pence. Trump Wasn't Happy," *New York Times* (New York, NY), November 19, 2016, sec. A, 10, accessed July 31, 2022, www.nytimes.com/2016/11/19/us/mike-pence-hamilton.html.

9 Amy Sara Osatinski, *Disney Theatrical Productions: Producing Broadway Musicals the Disney Way* (New York, NY: Routledge, 2019), 141.

10 "About," We See You White American Theatre, accessed July 31, 2022, www.weseeyouwat.com/about.

11 James Wolcott, "Pop Goes the Great White Way," *Vanity Fair*, July 1, 2011, accessed September 2, 2022, www.vanityfair.com/culture/2011/07/musicals-201107.

12 Mark Grant, *The Rise and Fall of the Broadway Musical* (Lebanon, NH: University Press of New England, 2005), 314.

20 Years/20 Seasons **45**

13 "What is an LED?," LEDs Magazine, last modified September 1, 2004, accessed September 2, 2022, www.ledsmagazine.com/leds-ssl-design/ma terials/article/16701292/what-is-an-led.

14 "LEDs and OLEDs," History of Lighting, accessed September 2, 2022, https://edisontechcenter.org/LED.html.

15 Qtd. in David Barbour, "High School Confidential: Mean Girls Takes Broadway in a Production That Pushes the Technology Envelope," *Lighting&Sound America*, June 2018, 66.

16 Qtd. in Barbour, "High School," 66.

17 Barbour, "High School," 67.

18 Barbour, "High School," 67.

19 Barbour, "High School," 68.

20 Amy Sara Osatinski, "Ghosts in the Machine: Digital Technology and Screen to Stage Musicals," in *IBroadway: Musical Theatre in the Digital Age*, ed. Jessica Hillman-McCord (Basingstoke: Palgrave Macmillan, 2018), 78–79.

21 Qtd. in Amy Sara Osatinski, *Disney Theatrical Productions: Producing Broadway Musicals the Disney Way* (New York: Routledge, 2019), 106.

22 Glen Berger, *Song of Spider-Man: The inside Story of the Most Controversial Musical in Broadway History* (New York: Simon & Schuster, 2014), 67.

23 Berger, *Song of Spider-Man*, 68.

24 For the entire story, please see "Watch What Happens: *Newsies: The Musical*," ch. 6 in Osatinski, *Disney Theatrical Productions*.

25 Osatinski, *Disney Theatrical Productions*, 149.

26 Sarah Bahr, "'Beetlejuice' Will Return to Broadway in April," *The New York Times*, September 13, 2021, accessed August 1, 2022, www.nytimes. com/2021/09/13/theater/beetlejuice-broadway-return.html.

27 Michael Paulson, "Despite Turnaround, 'Beetlejuice' Being Forced out of Theater," *The New York Times*, December 11, 2019, sec. C, 1, accessed August 1, 2022, www.nytimes.com/2019/12/09/theater/beetlejuice-broa dway-evicted.html.

28 Brendan Wetmore, "'Beetlejuice' on Broadway is Breaking TikTok," *Paper*, October 3, 2019, accessed August 1, 2022, www.papermag.com/beetleju ice-broadway-tiktok-trend-1-2640689936.html?rebelltitem=1#rebelltitem1.

29 Wetmore, "'Beetlejuice' on Broadway."

30 Trevor Buffone, *TikTok Broadway: Musical Theatre Fandom in the Digital Age* (New York: Oxford UP, 2023).

31 Buffone, *TikTok Broadway*.

32 Buffone, *TikTok Broadway*.

33 Buffone, *TikTok Broadway*.

34 The production would end up running for nine months closing in January 2023.

35 James Deaville, "Play It Again (and Again, and Again): The Superfan and Musical Theatre," in *The Routledge Companion to the Contemporary Musical*, ed. Jessica Sternfeld and Elizabeth L. Wollman (New York, NY: Routledge, 2020), 355.

36 Deaville, "Play It Again," 360.

46 20 Years/20 Seasons

37 Qtd in Robert Diamond, "Dear Evan Hansen's Ben Platt Tweets Back at Stage Door Complainers," *BroadwayWorld.com*, last modified July 3, 2017, accessed September 2, 2022, www.broadwayworld.com/article/DEAR-EVAN-HANSENs-Ben-Platt-Tweets-Back-at-Stage-Door-Complainers-20170703.

38 This is the first controversy being explored in this volume, but it is by no means the first controversy tied to the Broadway musical in the 20 seasons. There were many controversies and this book lays out only a few.

39 Felicia Fitzpatrick, "The Oral History of the Scottsboro Boys," *Playbill.com*, last modified October 30, 2020, accessed September 23, 2022, https://playbill.com/article/the-oral-history-of-the-scottsboro-boys.

40 For more information about blackface minstrel performance see Ayanna Thompson's book *Blackface*, Bloomsbury, 2021.

41 Fitzpatrick, "The Oral History."

42 Patricia Cohen, "'Scottsboro Boys' Is Focus of Protest," *Arts Beat*, accessed September 23, 2022, https://archive.nytimes.com/artsbeat.blogs.nytimes.com/2010/11/07/scottsboro-boys-is-focus-of-protest/.

43 Qtd. in Kenneth Jones, "Protestors Take Aim at Scottsboro Boys Musical," *Playbill.com*, last modified November 8, 2010, accessed September 23, 2022, https://playbill.com/article/protestors-take-aim-at-scottsboro-boys-musical-com-173373.

44 Patrick Healey, "'Scottsboro Boys' to Close on Dec. 12," *ArtsBeat*, last modified November 30, 2010, accessed September 23, 2022, https://archive.nytimes.com/artsbeat.blogs.nytimes.com/2010/11/30/scottsboro-boys-to-close-on-december-12/.

45 Nayaba Arinde, "Protests Shut Down Offensive Scottsboro Boys Play," *Amsterdam News* (New York, NY), April 22, 2013, accessed September 23, 2022, https://amsterdamnews.com/news/2013/04/22/protests-shut-down-offensive-scottsboro-boys-play/.

46 Warren Hoffman, *The Great White Way: Race and the Broadway Musical*, 2nd ed. (New Brunswick, NJ: Rutgers University Press, 2020), 231.

47 Nayaba Arinde, "'Scottsboro Boys' Fallout Continues," *Amsterdam News* (New York), April 12, 2011, accessed September 23, 2022, https://amsterdamnews.com/news/2011/04/12/scottsboro-boys-fallout-continues/.

48 Kinhasa also wrote a book about the Scottsboro Boys: *The Scottsboro Boys In Their Own Words: Selected Letters 1931–1950* (Mcfarland, 2014).

49 Kwando M. Kinshasa, editorial, *On Committing a Cultural Felony: "The Scottsboro Boys" Minstrel Show* (New York, NY), April 12, 2011, https://amsterdamnews.com/news/2011/04/12/on-committing-a-cultural-felony-the-scottsboro/.

50 Kinshasa, editorial.

51 Kinshasa, editorial.

52 Qtd. in Fitzpatrick, "The Oral History."

53 Just prior to the first previews, Broadway Choreographer Sergio Trujillo was brought in to "consult" and ended up restoring much of Robbins original choreography.

20 Years/20 Seasons **47**

54 Rebecca Rubin and Brent Lang, "'West Side Story' Broadway Opening Night Sparks Protests," *Variety*, February 21, 2020, accessed September 30, 2022, https://variety.com/2020/legit/news/west-side-story-broadway-opening-night-protests-1203509630/.

55 Lila Shapiro, "'We Stand with Alexandra Waterbury': Inside a Protest of West Side Story on Broadway," *Vulture.com*, last modified February 1, 2020, www.vulture.com/2020/02/west-side-story-broadway-protest-alexandra-waterbury-amar-ramasar.html.

56 Qtd. in The Playbill Staff, "Broadway's New West Side Story Releases Statement Regarding Casting Controversy," *Playbill.com*, last modified February 13, 2020, accessed September 30, 2022, https://playbill.com/article/broadways-new-west-side-story-releases-statement-regarding-casting-controversy.

57 This volume is only covering the controversy surrounding the representation of non-binary characters in the production, however, the show was also subject to an Actors' Equity investigation because of allegations by cast member Nora Schell that the production team forced them to put off necessary surgery and that they were intimidated into performing even though they were unwell.

58 Ashley Lee, "'Jagged Little Pill' Fumbled a Character's Gender Identity. The Tour Vows to do Better," *LA Times*, September 16, 2022, accessed September 30, 2022, www.latimes.com/entertainment-arts/story/2022-09-16/jagged-little-pill-jo-gender-identity-revisions?fbclid=IwAR1E7TmktBZAopUxReg NWzy0eXLUpDt0cI3AqCFkDZ1oQrQW5eORKyJVBvo.

59 "Cis" is short for "cis-gender," which refers to a person whose gender identity corresponds to the gender they were assigned at birth; qtd. in Madison Malone Kircher, "Jagged Little Pill's Lauren Patten Will Not Admit That She Steals the Show," *Vulture.com*, last modified June 13, 2020, accessed September 30, 2022, www.vulture.com/2020/06/jagged-little-pills-lauren-patten-steals-the-show.html.

60 Christian Lewis, "One Step Forward, Two Steps Back: Broadway's Jagged Little Journey Toward Nonbinary Inclusion," *The Brooklyn Rail*, April 2021, accessed September 30, 2022, https://brooklynrail.org/2021/04/theater/One-Step-Forward-Two-Steps-Back-Broadways-Jagged-Little-Journey-Toward-Nonbinary-Inclusion.

61 Lewis, "One Step."

62 Qtd in Greg Evans, "Actor Lauren Patten Speaks Out On Broadway's 'Jagged Little Pill' Controversy & Reveals Her Future With The Show As Producers Apologize For Erasing A Nonbinary Character – Update," *Deadline*, last modified September 18, 2021, accessed September 30, 2022, https://deadline.com/2021/09/jagged-little-pill-broadway-producers-nonbinary-erasure-lauren-patten-1234839144/.

63 Qtd in Evans, "Actor Lauren," *Deadline*.

64 Evans, "Actor Lauren," *Deadline*.

2

AN INTRODUCTION TO ORIGINAL MUSICALS

In the 20 seasons, there were 186 musicals that opened on Broadway that can be called "original." As was mentioned in the introduction, this book uses the designations from the Broadway League. Therefore, any musical that has not previously had a production in a Broadway theatre is considered an original musical. This means that there are several productions from the 20 seasons that are categorized as original musicals that have had previous productions. For example, *Rodgers and Hammerstein's Cinderella* was written in 1957 for television and subsequently staged all over the world but was never mounted on Broadway prior to the 2013 production, making it an original musical during the 20 seasons. Revivals are not included here, even if they conform to one of the categories listed below. Remounts of productions that opened in the 20 seasons (and closed and opened again) are also not included here. Musicals in this category are designated original regardless of their source material, however, this section will categorize these musicals based on both their source material and their form.

There are six categories in which these original musicals reside: screen-to-stage, jukebox, other original source, revue, dansical, and opera/etta. The two opera/ettas in this period, *La Boheme* and *The Threepenny Opera*, will not be discussed further other than to note their presence on Broadway in this period. Therefore, from here on out, five categories, rather

DOI: 10.4324/9781003139171-3

An Introduction to Original Musicals **49**

than six, will be discussed. Screen-to-stage musicals are musicals that are stage adaptations of an existing film. These musicals might be adaptations of musical films that utilize the music from the film (in which case they are also Jukebox musicals) or they may be musical adaptations of non-musical films. Musicals in the jukebox category include a score of existing music, that is, the majority of the music in the production was not composed for the production but at another time. To be classified as a jukebox musical, these productions also must be plot-driven book musicals. Musicals that utilize existing music but do not have a plot are categorized as revues. The next category is the other original source category. These musicals draw their source material from a variety of places including but not limited to books, plays, and myths. These sources will be discussed in more detail in Chapter 5.

The next category is the dansical. The dansical is an interesting trend that appeared at the beginning of this period and drew attention as a possible "next big thing" for the Broadway musical but fizzled out after only a few productions. In her article "Because She Said So…: How Twyla Tharp and *Movin' Out* Legitimized the 'Dansical' as a Choreographic Domain/Diversion on Broadway," musical theatre scholar Pamyla Stihl offers the following two-part definition for the genre:

(1) The dansical is a dance-dominant production created by a choreographic auteur and intended as a musical theatre work for Broadway; (2) The dansical moves choreography/dance to the forefront where it dominates (and sometimes diminishes) the score and libretto, while the production's star is the choreographer who asserts authorial control and content through her signature movement. In other words, the dansical is a "musical" creation by a "self-expressive" choreographer.[1]

At the beginning of the 20 seasons, it appeared that the dansical was going to be a dominant trend on Broadway. However, the form died out quickly and only three dansicals, all conceived and choreographed by Twyla Tharp, premiered in the 20 seasons: *Movin' Out* (2002), *The Times They Are a-Changin'* (2006), and *Come Fly Away* (2010). Because these three productions each used the music of a well-known artist (Billy Joel, Bob Dylan, and Frank Sinatra), they also fall into the Jukebox category.

50 An Introduction to Original Musicals

The only one of these productions that had any staying power on Broadway was 2002's *Movin' Out*, which ran for over 1300 performances and was just as much about the excellent performance of Billy Joel by a string of talented singer/piano players as it was about the dance.

For the twenty seasons the breakdown for the number of musicals in the five categories is shown in Figure 2.1. It should be noted that there are shows that fit into multiple categories. These shows have been counted in both categories, which accounts for the discrepancy between the total number of original musicals and the sum of all the categories. The corresponding numbers for the categories are as follows: 72 screen-to-stage musicals, 55 jukebox musicals, 77 other original source musicals, six revues, and three daniscals. The breakdown can also be looked at by season (Figure 2.2).

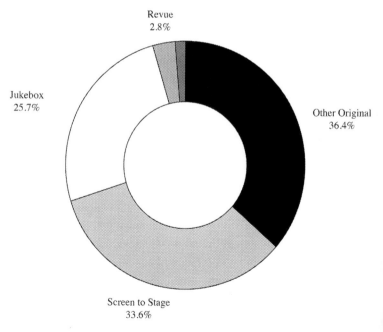

FIGURE 2.1 Percentage of musicals in each of the five categories for original musicals.

An Introduction to Original Musicals 51

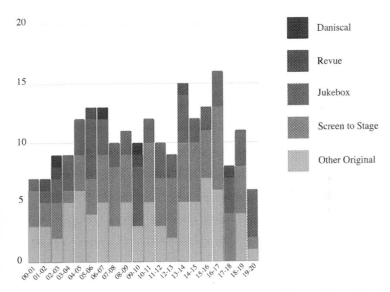

FIGURE 2.2 Number of musicals in each of the five categories for original musicals by season.

There are no seasons in which there are no jukebox musicals, only one where there is no screen-to-stage musical, though in that season there were several revivals of screen-to-stage musicals, and only one season where there is not a musical that falls into the other original category. In comparing the number of musicals in each category to earlier periods, there is a noticeable uptick in both jukebox musicals and screen-to-stage musicals:

> From January 1, 2010, to December 31, 2015, a total of 84 original musicals (not revivals) played on Broadway. Of those 84 musicals, 31 of them were based on films. In contrast, in the middle of the Golden Age of musical theatre, there were far fewer movie adaptations. From January 1, 1950, to December 31, 1955, there were 79 original musicals [that] played on Broadway. Of those 79 musicals, only five of them were based on films.[2]

52 An Introduction to Original Musicals

While screen-to-stage musicals (and Jukebox musicals) are not new, there is a sizable difference in the percentage of new musicals that fall into one of the two categories. In the 20 seasons, approximately 68% of original musicals that opened on Broadway were either a screen-to-stage or a jukebox musical. In total, approximately 47% of all musicals (original and revival) that opened on Broadway in this period were either a screen-to-stage or a jukebox musical. However, both screen-to-stage musicals and jukebox musicals are original to Broadway and despite the outcries from many in the Broadway establishment, the original musical thrived during this period with 186 of them opening on the Great White Way.

Original musicals also greatly outnumber revivals in the 20 seasons. Approximately 69% of the productions that opened on Broadway in this period were original to Broadway. Additionally, the most successful musicals of this period were original. There are 13 musicals that played over 2000 performances in the 20 seasons and all those musicals were original musicals. In fact, of the 20 longest-running musicals to open in this period, only one, 2001's *42nd Street*, is a revival. Drilling down further, there are 29 musicals that played over 1000 performances and only two are revivals, the aforementioned production of *42nd Street*, and the 2014 production of *Les Misérables*.

Chapters 3–5 will take a deep dive into four of the five categories of original musicals mentioned above. The fifth, dansicals, has been covered in enough detail here so as not to require further examination as, despite early-21st-century predictions, the dansical did not have a significant presence in the 20 seasons. Chapter 3. will cover jukebox musicals and revues, illuminating the characteristics of a genre that became ubiquitous in the 20 seasons. Though several jukebox musicals had landed on Broadway before 2000, the form exploded and was codified within this period. Chapter 4 will examine the screen-to-stage musical, which has been pointed to as a new phenomenon in the 20 seasons, but in fact, dates to the early 20th century. However, as was mentioned earlier in this chapter and will be discussed in further detail, the number of screen-to-stage musicals took a very noticeable jump in the 20 seasons. Chapter 4 will unpack some of the possible reasons for the uptick. Chapter 5 will illuminate the musicals that fall into the other original source material category. This group of musicals encompasses a broad spectrum of productions and includes some of the most and least successful musicals of the 20 seasons.

Notes

1 Pamyla Stiehl, "Because She Said So: How Twyla Tharp and *Movin' Out* Legitimized the 'Dansical' as a Choreographic Domain/Diversion on Broadway," *Journal of American Drama and Theatre* 22, no. 2 (Spring 2010): 85.
2 Amy S. Osatinski, "Ghosts in the Machine: Digital Technology and Screen-to-Stage Musicals," in *iBroadway: Musical Theatre in the Digital Age*, ed. Jessica Hillman-McCord (Cham, Switzerland: Palgrave Macmillan, 2017), 76–77.

3

JUKEBOX MUSICALS AND REVUES

TABLE 3.1 Jukebox musicals in 20 seasons

Show Title	Season	Run	Category(ies)	Jukebox Type
A Class Act	2000–2001	105	Jukebox	Single artist: autobiographical
Mamma Mia	2001–2002	5758	Jukebox	Single artist: new story
Movin' Out	2002–2003	1303	Jukebox/dansical	Single artist: new story
Never Gonna Dance	2003–2004	84	Jukebox/screen-to-stage	Movie musical adaptation
Taboo	2003–2004	100	Jukebox	Single artist: autobiographical
The Boy From Oz	2003–2004	364	Jukebox	Single artist: autobiographical
All Shook Up	2004–2005	213	Jukebox	Single artist: new story
Chitty Chitty Bang Bang	2004–2005	285	Jukebox/screen-to-stage	Movie musical adaptation
Good Vibrations	2004–2005	94	Jukebox	Single artist: new story
Hot Feet	2005–2006	97	Jukebox	Single artist: new story

DOI: 10.4324/9781003139171-4

Jukebox Musicals and Revues 55

Show Title	Season	Run	Category(ies)	Jukebox Type
Jersey Boys	2005–2006	4642	Jukebox	Single artist: autobiographical
Lennon	2005–2006	49	Jukebox	Single artist: autobiographical
Ring of Fire	2005–2006	57	Jukebox	Single artist: autobiographical
Tarzan	2005–2006	486	Jukebox/screen-to-stage	Movie musical adaptation
Lovemusik	2006–2007	60	Jukebox	Single artist: autobiographical
Mary Poppins	2006–2007	2619	Jukebox/screen-to-stage	Movie musical adaptation
The Times They Are a-Changin'	2006–2007	28	Jukebox/dansical	Single artist: new story
The Little Mermaid	2007–2008	685	Jukebox/screen-to-stage	Movie musical adaptation
Xanadu	2007–2008	512	Jukebox/screen-to-stage	Movie musical adaptation
Irving Berlin's White Christmas	2008–2009	53	Jukebox/screen-to-stage	Movie musical adaptation
Rock of Ages	2008–2009	2328	Jukebox	Multiple artists: new story
American Idiot	2009–2010	422	Jukebox	Single artist: new story
Come Fly Away	2009–2010	188	Jukebox/dansical	Single artist: new story
Everyday Rapture	2009–2010	85	Jukebox	Multiple artists: new story
Fela!	2009–2010	463	Jukebox	Single artist: autobiographical
Million Dollar Quartet	2009–2010	489	Jukebox	Multiple artists: biographical
Baby It's You	2010–2011	148	Jukebox	Multiple artists: biographical
Priscilla Queen of the Desert	2010–2011	526	Jukebox/screen-to-stage	Multiple artists: new story
Newsies	2011–2012	1004	Jukebox/screen-to-stage	Movie musical adaptation
Nice Work If You Can Get It	2011–2012	478	Jukebox	Single artist: new story

56 Jukebox Musicals and Revues

Show Title	Season	Run	Category(ies)	Jukebox Type
Once	2011–2012	1168	Jukebox/screen-to-stage	Movie musical adaptation
Motown: The Musical	2012–2013	738	Jukebox	Multiple artists: biographical
Rodgers + Hammerstein's Cinderella	2012–2013	769	Jukebox/screen-to-stage	Movie musical adaptation
A Night with Janis Joplin	2013–2014	140	Jukebox	Single artist: autobiographical
Aladdin	2013–2014	2732★	Jukebox/Screen-to-stage	Movie musical adaptation
Beautiful: The Carole King Musical	2013–2014	2416	Jukebox	Single artist: autobiographical
Soul Doctor	2013–2014	66	Jukebox	Single artist: autobiographical
An American in Paris	2014–2015	623	Jukebox/Screen-to-stage	Single artist: new story
Holler If Ya Hear Me	2014–2015	38	Jukebox	Single artist: new story
Disaster!	2015–2016	72	Jukebox	Multiple artists: new story
On Your Feet	2015–2016	746	Jukebox	Single artist: autobiographical
Anastasia	2016–2017	808	Jukebox/Screen-to-stage	Movie musical adaptation
Charlie and the Chocolate Factory	2016–2017	305	Jukebox/Screen-to-stage	Movie musical adaptation
Holiday Inn: The New Irving Berlin Musical	2016–2017	117	Jukebox/Screen-to-stage	Movie musical adaptation
Escape to Margaritaville	2017–2018	124	Jukebox	Single artist: new story
Frozen	2017–2018	825	Jukebox/Screen-to-stage	Movie musical adaptation
Summer: The Donna Summer Musical	2017–2018	288	Jukebox	Single artist: autobiographical
Ain't Too Proud: The Life and Times of the Temptations	2018–2019	488	Jukebox	Single artist: autobiographical
Head Over Heels	2018–2019	188	Jukebox	Single artist: new story
The Cher Show	2018–2019	295	Jukebox	Single artist: autobiographical

Jukebox Musicals and Revues **57**

Show Title	Season	Run	Category(ies)	Jukebox Type
Girl From the North Country	2019–2020	117	Jukebox	Single artist: new story
Jagged Little Pill	2019–2020	171	Jukebox	Single artist: new story
Moulin Rouge	2019–2020	501★	Jukebox/Screen-to-stage	Multiple artists new story/movie musical adaptation
Tina: The Tina Turner Musical	2019–2020	370★	Jukebox	Single artist: autobiographical

★The totals for these musicals, which were running at the time of this writing, represent the show total through May 8, 2022.

TABLE 3.2 Revues in 20 seasons

Show Title	Season	Run	Category(ies)
One Mo' Time	2001–2002	21	Revue
The Look of Love	2002–2003	49	Revue
Chita Rivera: The Dancer's Life	2005–2006	72	Revue
Sondheim on Sondheim	2009–2010	76	Revue
After Midnight	2013–2014	273	Revue
Prince of Broadway	2017–2018	76	Revue

History and Development of the Jukebox Musical

On October 23, 1995, *New York Times* theatre critic Ben Brantley shared his fears that a new musical, *Swinging on a Star: The Johnny Burke Musical*, would just be "yet another jukebox musical,"[1] marking the first time that the term had been used in print to describe a specific genre of Broadway musical.[2] Though the jukebox musical as a distinct genre of musical theatre emerged and developed in the latter half of the 20th century,[3] its roots can be traced back to the 18th century. In 1728, John Gay's *The Beggar's Opera* opened at the Lincoln's Inn Fields Theatre in London and is often cited as a watershed moment in the development of musical theatre. Gay's play, a satirical lampoon of the aristocracy and serious opera, incorporated popular songs, arguably making it the first jukebox musical. *The Beggar's Opera* was the most

58 Jukebox Musicals and Revues

popular play of its time. It played in London for years, had multiple global adaptations, and toured all over the world, including in the United States where it would influence the development of American musical theatre.

Years later, in the early 20th century, Tin Pan Alley composers often utilized existing songs in their musical comedies, examples include Jerome Kern's *Princess Musicals* [4] and works by Cole Porter and the Gershwins. Many early-20th-century musical comedies incorporated music that was not specifically written for a production, but rather, was previously composed and then included in the production. Additionally, composers, especially Cole Porter, would often reuse songs from musicals that were less successful in later productions. For example, Porter's hit song "I Get a Kick Out of You" was originally written for a 1931 musical titled *Star Dust* that was never produced due to financing problems. Porter repurposed the song, which would become one of his best known, in his 1934 musical *Anything Goes*. [5] This recycling of material was common with Porter and his contemporaries and happened both in musical revues and in story-driven musical comedies. Though many songs in early musical comedies and revues were recycled, appearing in multiple productions, the positioning of musical theatre as an incubator for popular music meant that these songs were most often created for musicals and later became popular tunes. Contemporary jukebox musicals are the opposite. The popularity of the music precedes its incorporation into a musical.[6]

The Revue vs. The Jukebox

The jukebox musical and the revue are related but distinct and conform to the following definitions. A jukebox musical is a book musical that utilizes existing songs, sometimes the work of one composer and sometimes the work of multiple composers, to tell a story. A revue is a musical production that utilizes existing songs, sometimes the work of one composer and sometimes the work of multiple composers but does not tell a story. A revue may be organized around a theme or idea, but does not have a plot and/or is not book-driven. The differentiation between the two forms lies in the book. To be a jukebox musical, a show must have a book that includes some sort of plot, whereas a revue does not have a plot-driven book. In the 20 seasons, both jukebox musicals and revues were produced, though jukebox musicals were far more common. Some notable examples of revues are 2010's *Sondheim on Sondheim*, a revue of the music and lyrics of composer Stephen Sondheim and 2013's *After Midnight*, a Jazz Age revue set in Harlem's Cotton Club. The production featured the music of Duke Ellington, Harold Arlen, and Cab Calloway among others, and included prose passages by Langston Hughes. Both productions had a specific thematic focus, but neither had a plot, making them both revues.

Though the practice of incorporating existing music into new musicals is as old as the musical theatre form, the contemporary Broadway jukebox musical didn't appear until 1975 when Harry Chapin's *The Night That Made America Famous* opened on Broadway. The production utilized Chapin's song catalog intertwined with a plot, which separates it from the more common musical revues.[7] The next musical that conforms to the definition would not hit Broadway until 1985[8] when the Ellie Greenwich musical *Leader of the Pack* opened. As *The Night That Made America Famous* had a short run, *Leader of the Pack* is often pointed to as the birth of the jukebox musical as it is known today. *Leader of the Pack* utilizes a familiar jukebox formula, telling the story of a songwriter by utilizing their own music. In this case, the life of Ellie Greenwich is chronicled from the 1950s to the 1980s through music that she wrote or co-wrote. Though by no means a smash hit, the production's 120 performances over four months earn it a place in musical theatre history.[9]

The 1970s through 1990s also saw a renewed presence of the revue on Broadway. Notably, 1978's *Ain't Misbehavin'*, which includes songs associated with Fats Waller. This multi-composer musical falls into the revue category because it does not include a plot. Another notable and often performed revue of this time period is 1997's *Smokey Joe's Cafe*, which showcases popular songs by Jerry Leiber and Mike Stoller. *Smokey Joe's* also has no plot. Additionally, the jukebox musical, *The Who's Tommy*, based on the band's 1969 album of the same name (which is often referred to as a rock opera), opened on Broadway in 1993 and ran for over two years. During this period there were also other jukebox musicals finding success but Off-Broadway and regionally rather than on Broadway. These musicals include 1988's *Always Patsy Cline*, and 1989's *Buddy: The Buddy Holly Story*.

60 Jukebox Musicals and Revues

Though there were sporadic jukebox offerings in the last few decades of the 20th century, the jukebox musical as a Broadway trend did not accelerate until 1999 when *Mamma Mia*, which featured the music of the Swedish pop group ABBA, opened in London. The production was wildly successful, eventually breaking box office records at multiple venues in the city.[10] Soon after its success in the United Kingdom, the musical embarked on a limited US tryout tour before landing on Broadway in 2001. It should be noted that there were two clusters of jukebox musicals that landed on Broadway in the 1990s. The 1992–1993 season included *Crazy for You*, which featured the music of the Gershwins, *Jelly's Last Jam* which told the story of jazz legend Jelly Roll Morton, and the aforementioned *The Who's Tommy*, which staged the iconic 1969 concept album *Tommy*. Though notable, the trend did not pick up momentum until the end of the decade. In 1999, two other jukebox musicals opened on Broadway, *Saturday Night Fever* and *Footloose*. While both productions utilize existing music and feature a plot, both are primarily screen-to-stage musicals that utilize the soundtrack of the film as the score for the musical by transforming the background music from the films into songs that are sung by the characters on stage. 2006's *Tarzan* and 2007's *Xanadu* are also examples of this type of jukebox/screen-to-stage musical.

Prior to *Mamma Mia*, which opened on Broadway in 2001 and ran for fourteen years and 5,758 performances,[11] no jukebox musical had an extended run on Broadway. The success of the show proved the commercial viability of the jukebox form leading to an increasing number of jukebox musicals in the first 20 seasons of the 21st century. In twenty years, an average of approximately three jukebox musicals opened on Broadway each year with six in both the 2005–2006 and 2009–2010 seasons. No year in this period saw a season without a Broadway jukebox musical.

Jukebox Musical Types

Several distinct types of jukebox musicals developed as the form exploded in the early 21st century. These types can first be separated by the number of artists represented in the score (one artist or multiple artists) and then by how the songs are related to the production's subject matter. These distinctions create four types of jukebox musicals:

Jukebox Musicals and Revues **61**

- single artist: autobiographical;
- single artist: new story;
- multiple artists: biographical; and
- multiple artists: new story.

In addition, there is a fifth category, movie musical adaptations, which were frequent in this period. This category contains musicals that are adaptations of films in which the characters sing as a part of the film and in which the majority of the music in the stage production is from the original film.[12]

The single artist: autobiographical jukebox musical utilizes the songs of a single artist to tell the story of that artist. For this type of jukebox musical, the artist might be a performer or a writer. Some notable musicals in this category from the 20 seasons are as follows: *Jersey Boys* (2005), which tells the story of Frankie Valli and the Four Seasons; *Beautiful: The Carole King Musical* (2014), which tells the story of and features songs written by and/or performed by Carole King; *On Your Feet* (2015), which features music by and tells the story of Gloria and Emilio Estefan, including the music and story of Miami Sound Machine; and *Ain't Too Proud: The Life and Times of the Temptations* (2019), which chronicles the Temptations from 1960 to 2019.

The single artist: new story jukebox musical utilizes the songs of a single artist to tell a new story, either a fully original story or a story adapted from another medium. Some notable musicals in this category from the 20 seasons are as follows: *All Shook Up* (2005), which features the music of Elvis Presley and a story inspired by Shakespeare's *Twelfth Night; American Idiot* (2010), which features the music of *Green Day* and tells an original story; and *Girl from the North Country* (2020), which features the music of Bob Dylan and tells an original story.

The multiple artists: biographical jukebox musical utilizes the songs of multiple artists to tell the story of someone involved in the creation of the music, most often a producer. This is the least common type of jukebox musical during the 20 seasons, with only three musicals falling in this category. Two of the three tell the story of a producer: *Motown the Musical* (2013), which uses the music of multiple Motown artists to tell the story of producer Barry Gordy, and *Baby It's You* (2011), which uses the music of multiple Scepter Records artists to tell the story of

62 Jukebox Musicals and Revues

producer Florence Greenberg and Scepter Records. The third is *Million Dollar Quartet* (2010), which tells the true story of the night that Elvis Presley, Jerry Lee Lewis, Carl Perkins, and Johnny Cash came together in a Memphis recording studio for an impromptu recording session and recreates the music that was recorded at that session.

The multiple artists: new story jukebox musical utilizes the songs of multiple artists to tell a new story. Notable examples of this type include *Rock of Ages* (2009), which uses music by various rock artists of the 1980s to tell a new story, *Everyday Rapture* (2010), which utilizes the music of multiple artists to tell the story of Sherie Rene Scott, a Broadway actress and one of the show's writers, and *Disaster!* (2016), which utilizes the music of the 1970s to tell a new story.

Representation and the Jukebox Musical

As was covered in Chapter 1, Broadway has a representation problem. While progress was made during the 20 seasons, the lack of representation of people of color and women on stage and on creative teams was still startling. The jukebox musicals in this period presented an opportunity for better representation, particularly for people of color. Many producers cite the ability to sell a show as a reason not to back shows by and featuring people of color, however, producers also cite the catalog of popular music artists as a reason to program jukebox musicals. This leads to more willingness to back a jukebox musical for Broadway. During the 20 seasons, Broadway saw an uptick in musicals by and about popular music artists of color: *Hot Feet* (2006), *Fela!* (2009), *Motown the Musical* (2013), *Holler If Ya Hear Me* (2014), *On Your Feet* (2015), *Summer: The Donna Summer Musical* (2018), *Ain't Too Proud: The Life and Times of the Temptations* (2019), and *Tina* (2019). Many of these musicals feature casts that are mostly people of color. For example, in 2019's *Tina*, the cast includes nineteen black actors and six white actors, a stark contrast to most Broadway musicals. A white body does not appear on stage until halfway through the first act and a white supporting character is not introduced until the end of the act. The musical, which fits into the one artist: autobiographical category, tells the story of pop superstar Tina Turner utilizing Turner's music.

However, despite the black bodies on stage, the creative team for *Tina* was still mostly white. While the musical's book was written by Black playwright Katori Hall, the director and choreographer were both white. As is the case with many jukebox musicals, the songs, though all performed by a single artist, were written by a variety of songwriters. In the case of *Tina,* there are dozens of artists with song composition or lyrics credits and those artists are a variety of races and genders. The design team for *Tina* is also less diverse than many other productions in the 20 seasons. The scenic, costume, lighting, sound, and projection designers for the production were all white men.

While the bodies on stage in many jukebox musicals in this period may have pushed Broadway forward, the creators of the production are in many cases as or less representative than many other 21st-century productions. Some productions do better, for example, 2015's *On Your Feet* employed Latinx artists in all writing and directing roles except for the director, who was a white male.[13] Additionally, as will be discussed later in this chapter, 2013's *Motown: The Musical* had a mostly Black creative team. However, the disconnect between the bodies on stage and those that created the shows led to questions about what makes a Black musical or a Latinx/Latine musical? Jukebox musicals offer an opportunity to see BIPOC bodies on stage, but are they truly addressing Broadway's representation problem if the people behind the scenes are predominantly white?

What Is the Appeal of the Jukebox Musical?

It depends on who you ask, producers or audiences. For producers, the draw is clear, the potential to earn a lot of money. Broadway musicals are very expensive and the cost of production has been growing exponentially since the 1990s. *Disney's Beauty and the Beast* (1994), an enormous musical full of theatrical magic, cost $12 million to stage.[14] Fourteen years later, that number would double with another behemoth of a production, *Shrek the Musical* opening with a $24 million dollar price tag.[15] In 2011, *Spider-Man: Turn Off the Dark* would take the title for most expensive musical ever staged at $75 million.[16] Though Broadway is often held up as the pinnacle of artistry in the American theatre, money is the bottom line. While many producers

64 Jukebox Musicals and Revues

seek to present shows that are artistically successful, their main goal is to present productions that are financially successful. In order to make money, a show must sell a lot of tickets. In a crowded field, one of the best ways to capture ticket sales is with a known property. Utilizing a known property, in this case, the music of a popular artist, is one way that producers bet on success.

This bet goes hand in hand with the appeal of jukebox musicals for audiences. In his 1996 book *Performing Rites*, Simon Frith explains that because of music's "unique emotional intensity—we absorb songs into our own lives."[17] The combination of words and lyrics fosters deep emotional connections. The connections are also social, Frith continues, "Music … provides us with an intensely subjective sense of being sociable … it both articulates and offers the immediate experience of collective identity."[18] In her 2012 book *Musical Theatre, Realism, and Entertainment*, Mille Taylor ties Frith's assertions about popular music to the Jukebox Musical, noting, "attendance at a [jukebox musical] focusing on a musical genre of performer with whom the audience member identifies can trigger … feelings of transcendence through the reinforcement of social narratives and imaginative identity. Such responses are then augmented by the shared experience …"[19] Here Taylor points to the familiarity of the material and the experience of seeing that material live with others creating a sense of elation for audience members. This phenomenon illuminates why some patrons attend shows multiple times.

Jukebox musicals, like their screen-to-stage cousins, also invoke nostalgia. The use of pre-existing music makes these musicals a prime location for audience members to interact with prior iterations of themselves. When engaging with a jukebox musical, audience members familiar with the music are also able to engage with memories tied to the music in addition to experiencing the musical. In their 2022 book *The Jukebox Musical: An Interpretive History*, Kevin Byrne and Emily Fuchs note that the popularity of the jukebox musical is tied to "nostalgia of the music itself."[20] Attending a jukebox musical is often as much or more about experiencing the music and the nostalgia for past interactions with that music or artist than it is about experiencing the musical.

Jukebox musicals, particularly the biographical jukebox musicals are also appealing because they offer the opportunity for virtuosic performances. The aural spectacle of a high-caliber performer mimicking the vocal and physical mannerisms of a beloved artist is also a draw. Take for example Adrienne Warren's striking performance as Tina Turner in 2019's *Tina*. Peter Marks of the Washington Post titles his review "As rock-star portrayals go, it doesn't get any better than Adrienne Warren as Tina Turner." In the article he notes:

> Any critical assessment of "Tina," the new Broadway musical super-heated by the sizzling essence of Tina Turner, begins and ends with another dazzling entity by the name of Adrienne Warren. Truly, all you need to know about this by-the-book jukebox show, which marked its official opening Thursday at the Lunt-Fontanne Theatre, has to do with Warren's earth-moving gifts. Hers isn't so much a performance as an eruption. Blessed with extraordinary pipes, restless grace and a star's joy of center stage, Warren creates the impression of being as good a Tina Turner as, well, Tina Turner. Yes, that is an illusion, but as illusions go, this one's worth buying into … Warren has that extra something—the rare gene on the E! chromosome, for entertainer, maybe?—that separates a workmanlike portrayal from a great one.[21]

Warren's performance of Turner was remarkable. Not only does she transform physically, capturing Turner's signature dance moves, but she also manages to recreate Turner's unique vocal quality in both singing and speech. This excellent approximation of Turner was noticed by theatregoers as well as is evidenced in some of the show's online reviews. On Yelp Tanesha J. of Bronx, NY, shares, "I thought I was at a real life Tina Turner concert towards the end. Adrienne Warren who plays Tina Turner was absolutely incredible. A truly stellar perfor-mance."[22] Maday M. of Fort Lee, NJ, states in reference to Warren, "That lady did Tina as good as Tina herself."[23] Raoul W. of Queens, NY, explains, "Adrienne Warren did an incredible job. Her voice and timbre is very close to Tina's."[24] Tanesha J. gave the production four stars and Maday M. and Raoul W. each gave the production five stars. Clearly, Warren's ability to capture Turner in her performance was a factor in the audience's enjoyment of the performance.

This recreation of a beloved star is not unique to *Tina*. Many reviews of other productions from both critics and audience members

66 Jukebox Musicals and Revues

mention the performer's ability to capture the performers that they are portraying. In some cases, those portrayals even led to awards recognition, as was the case for Adrienne Warren as Tina Turner, and Stephanie J. Block, who portrayed one of three versions of Cher in 2018's *The Cher Show*. While Jesse Green's review in the *New York Times* is scathing, of Block he says, "Not only does she ace Cher's vocal inflections and physical mannerisms, including the half-mast eyes, the arm akimbo and the dancing-from-the-hair-up hauteur, but she somehow integrates them into a portrait of a woman at odds with the very dream that sustained her."[25] Block's ability to mimic Cher and deliver a moving performance was likely a decisive factor in her win.

With this desire to interact with beloved music and masterful recreations of beloved musicians in a live setting driving ticket sales, it is not surprising that jukebox musicals continue to be produced on Broadway. Like any category, some are of a higher artistic quality than others and some make more money than others. Of the 62 musicals that could be designated jukebox musicals,[26] 42 played for over 100 performances and around one-quarter of the musicals that played over 500 performances during the 20 seasons were jukebox musicals.[27] Clearly, the jukebox musical has become an integral part of the landscape of the 21st-century Broadway musical.

Case Studies

Single Artist: Autobiographical—Jersey Boys

- **Opened: November 6, 2005**
- **Closed: January 15, 2017**
- **Performances: 4642**[28]

Jersey Boys is a 2005 musical with a book by Marshall Brickman and Rick Elice that features the music of and tells the story of Frankie Valli and the Four Seasons. The production utilizes the group's catalog to tell the story of the band and its members through the "four seasons" of their careers. Some scholars call *Jersey Boys* a review because most of the songs are performed concert style. However, the show is held together by a book that tells the story of the band from the perspective

Jukebox Musicals and Revues **67**

of the band members (each season told by a different member), so therefore, despite the fact that many of the numbers are performed concert-style, *Jersey Boys* conforms to this chapter's definition of a jukebox musical.

The creation of *Jersey Boys* was inspired by the success of *Mamma Mia!* In the early 2000s, writer (and then Walt Disney Studios Creative Consultant) Rick Elice got a call from a former client asking if he wanted to do "sort of a *Mamma Mia!* musical?"[29] Elice and his friend and fellow writer Marshall Brickman met with Elice's former client and the two of them decided to write the musical, noting that "there's nothing to lose but [their] own time."[30] Prior to moving forward, the pair secured the blessing and help of Frankie Valli and Bob Gaudio, two of the band's original members. Elice leveraged his connections from his time at the top of a theatrical advertising agency to secure the backing of Dodger Theatricals, one of the major producers of Broadway musicals. Elice remembers, "They said yes really not because we'd written the show yet, but because they understood immediately that if you were one of the 125 million people who bought a record in 1967 you would be right in the sweet spot of people who are the right age for ticket-buying."[31] The Dodgers were not wrong and like *Mamma Mia!* before it, *Jersey Boys* would become one of the longest-running Broadway musicals of all time.[32]

To write the musical, Elice and Brickman interviewed all four of the band members and spent a great deal of time with their families. This research both humbled and inspired the duo as they realized that the band had a fantastic story and that Bob Gaudio, who wrote the majority of the band's songs, is an extraordinary composer worthy of a Broadway musical. The research also led them to a structure for the musical, four seasons, four band members, and therefore four "acts." Elice and Brickman noted that the four men had different versions of the same events and rather than trying to discern which version was the truth, they made the choice for each to tell their version of the story and gave each band member a season.

This narrative device is one of the aspects that contributed to the success of the musical. *Jersey Boys* is not a good musical only because of the music, it is a good musical because it is well-crafted. The storytelling is dynamic and nuanced because the audience is able to see the events through four different lenses. The four viewpoints bring

68 Jukebox Musicals and Revues

perspective and interest to what might otherwise be a generic rags-to-riches story. Elice and Brickman resisted the urge to canonize the four men, and instead portrayed them as the flawed humans that they are. Because of the unique structure, each man is allowed to be both the hero and the antagonist of the story.

The music certainly contributed to the success as well, particularly with the "bridge and tunnel"[33] crowd. Many who had not only experienced the music during their formative years but were also cut from the same cloth as the show's protagonists. Elice observes:

> When audiences started to come, and we saw men, of the age of the guys who were in the group, and we saw their heads, nodding, at places in the show, we realized what we had created for these guys- The guys who were not the cultural elite, the guys who were not made, who got on buses, and went to Washington to protest the war in Vietnam. But the guys who actually went to Vietnam, and fought, and came back, and were disrespected. The guys who saw onstage, four band members, who kind of looked like them, and talked like them, and sounded like them.[34]

Elice and Brickman crafted a musical that was not only structurally sound and an innovative example of the form, but also deeply connected with a specific demographic of audience members, a demographic that was in huge supply. Tourists make up a large part of the Broadway audience, especially for big musicals, but having a local audience base in addition to the tourists certainly helped *Jersey Boys* to succeed and to continue running for an extraordinary 12 years, including through the Great Recession.

Though his review was mixed, which is not surprising given his very vocal disdain of jukebox musicals, Ben Brantley of the *New York Times* also anticipated that the production was "destined to attract" Baby Boomers, noting, "once the Four Seasons classics are rolled out every other pair of shoulders in the house starts a-twitching." He observes that the "mostly middle-aged crowd at the August Wilson Theater ... seem to have forgotten what year it is or how old they are or, most important, that John Lloyd Young is not Frankie Valli." Brantley also comments on

Young's performance as Valli, anointing him a "genuine star in the making." He continues, "Mr. Young has crossed the line from exact impersonation into something more compelling. It's that sort of melting from perfect wax effigy into imperfect flesh."[35] While Brantley also notes that the other three men portraying the Four Seasons also deliver excellent performances, it is Young who earns the most praise.

Brantley's review points to two key factors that contributed to the production's success: the appeal to audience members of a certain age, and the exceptional performances. Unlike a musical with original music, performers in jukebox musicals have the added task of vocally mimicking the often distinctive sounds of the performers they portray. Frankie Valli's voice is unique and instantly recognizable, making an accurate recreation a necessity for a successful portrayal. Young and the many men who came after him executed the recreation with precision and skill, which helped the show to run for 12 years.

One of the most complicated aspects of staging a jukebox musical is the rights. Producers must obtain the rights to use the music, and in the case of biographical musicals, the rights to the story. Though the producers/ creators of *Jersey Boys* did their due diligence in obtaining the rights, in 2007 there was a copyright infringement lawsuit filed against the production, which led to a prolonged court battle. The lawsuit was filed by Donna Corbello, the wife of Rex Woodward, the man who had assisted Tommy DeVito, one of the band members, in writing an autobiography. The book was never published before Woodward's death, but once the musical was successful Corbello asserted that the musical utilized material from the unpublished book. Though DeVito had granted permission to use his autobiography, Woodward registered a Copyright for the book in his own name, so his widow sued the production, seeking a portion of the profits. The case spent ten years in court, and though Corbello at one point was awarded 10% of the show's profits, after several appeals, a judge found only "about 145 creative words to have been copied from the Work into the Play, whether as dialogue or creative descriptions of events ... [which] constitute[s] about 0.2% of the approximately 68,500 words in the Work."[36] The judge also ruled that prior to the production, the book had no market value and that it was the play that increased the value of the book, negating the case's main argument that the play diminished the value of the book. The producers won the lawsuit, which

70 Jukebox Musicals and Revues

was the third Copyright lawsuit in 2017 settled with a decision for the defendant.[37]

Jersey Boys is an excellent example of the single artist: autobiographical jukebox musical. It utilizes the catalog of a single artist, in this case, Frankie Valli and the Four Seasons, to tell the story of that artist. It combines innovative storytelling with virtuosic performances (singing Frankie Valli for eight shows a week is no easy task) and a catalog of well-known and well-loved songs. The show contains another feature that is common to Autobiographical Jukebox musicals, the post-show concert. At the end of many jukebox musicals, typically after the curtain call, the performers and the orchestra will put on a mini-concert for the audience, featuring the greatest hits of the artist, that is designed to get patrons off their feet. Audience members are encouraged to dance and sing along and regardless of how the story of the musical ends, the event of the musical leaves audience members elated. This moment in an autobiographical jukebox musical is the payoff for many audience members who might be instantly transported back to earlier times in their life when they encountered the music or attended a concert by the real artist. The post-show concert is not unique to the jukebox musical, the 1980s trend of the megamix comes to mind as a precursor. However, it has become a staple of the form with most, especially those about major recording artists, ending with a participatory concert.

Though *Jersey Boys* closed on Broadway in 2017, it continues to find success. In November 2017, less than a year after the Broadway show closed, an Off-Broadway production opened at New World Stages opened and ran until May 2022.[38] Prior to the COVID-19 pandemic, the show was also on tour in the United States and the UK, and was performed on Norwegian cruise lines. Additionally, a production opened in London in Spring 2021.[39]

Jersey Boys is an important jukebox musical because it provided a successful model for the autobiographical musicals that would come after it. The production's success showed that there was a large market for musicals with recycled music by artists with a compelling story. Some musicals that were subsequently crafted in the image of *Jersey Boys* include, 2014's *Beautiful the Carole King Musical*, which ran for over five years and was an awards season favorite, and 2015's *On Your*

Feet, which chronicled the rise of Gloria Estefan and ran for over 700 performances. 2019's *Ain't Too Proud: The Life and Times of the Temptations* followed the *Jersey Boys* Formula and played for a total of 488 performances during its run (both before and after the 2020 shutdown). *Tina: The Tina Turner Musical* is another 2019 production that resembles *Jersey Boys.* The show had played 143 performances when shuttered for the pandemic and hit 370 performances as of May 8, 2022. *Tina* also features a vocally distinctive protagonist and Adrienne Warren's startling performance, which earned her a Tony Award for Best Performance by a Leading Actress in 2020. *Jersey Boys* proved that audiences were hungry to engage with beloved music and performers through the vehicle of a live musical and producers took notice.

Single Artist: New Story—American Idiot

- **Opened: April 20, 2010**
- **Closed: April 24, 2011**
- **Performances: 422**

In September 2004, the 1990s pop-punk trio Green Day released *American Idiot,* a concept album/rock opera. The album is described in *Rolling Stone* as "a fifty-seven-minute politically charged epic depicting a character named Jesus of Suburbia as he suffers through the decline and fall of the American dream."[40] In the 2013 documentary, *Broadway Idiot,* Green Day frontman Billie Joe Armstrong explains, "as a band we really wanted to make some kind of concept record, drawing from *Tommy* to *Sergeant Pepper's.*"[41] The album found modest success, peaking on the Billboard Hot 100 at #61 in October 2004. *American Idiot* also had two top 10 hits: "Boulevard of Broken Dreams," which peaked at number 2, and "Wake Me Up When September Ends," which peaked at number 6.[42]

American Idiot's road to Broadway began with director Michael Mayer, who wanted to turn the album into a stage musical from the moment of his first listen. Mayer secured the exclusive rights to the album in 2008 and the band gave him six months to put something together.[43] In *Broadway Idiot,* Mayer explains, "We put the stuff together and you never really knew if Green Day would dig what we were

72 Jukebox Musicals and Revues

gonna do with their material. It was terrifying and incredibly important to get Billy Joe's okay on it. But we didn't see them for quite a while because they were touring in Europe."[44] While the band was away, Mayer and orchestrator/composer Tom Kitt, best known for the 2008 Pulitzer Prize-winning musical *Next To Normal*, collaborated to transform the songs to the stage. For Mayer and Kitt, it was a question of transforming songs sung by one person into multiple stories and characters. As a seasoned musical theatre composer and orchestrator, Kitt was focused on how the music of each song could support the storytelling. For example, during the song "Last Night on Earth" two characters shoot heroin "romantically." To tell the story, Kitt used choral harmonies to fit the song to the moment, which he notes were inspired by the music of the Beach Boys.[45] *Broadway Idiot* captures the first time that the band heard Kitt's version of the song. In response, Armstrong exclaimed, "that was fucking sick." He reflects, "I was floored. As soon as I heard it that way, I could visualize it. I was like, this can work."[46]

American Idiot was not Armstrong's first experience with musical theatre. As a child, he took voice lessons and sang a lot of musical theatre and Tin Pan Alley music. Kitt recognized the influence of musical theatre in Armstrong's music:

> You take a song like "Wake Me Up When September Ends", which is in the penultimate moments of the show and the penultimate moments of the album and [the chord] progression, which is so beautiful, and feels to me like *Chorus Line* "What I Did For Love," and you have this major to minor [modulation]. It is, it's melodic and it comes certainly from this whole [musical theatre] tradition.[47]

The connection between Armstrong's songs and a musical theatre sensibility may be attributable to his writing process. Armstrong shares, "I think album making, the art of it for me is that it takes you on a ride and the songs speak to each other."[48] Just like in a musical, the songs in the *American Idiot* album relate to each other and connect to create a cohesive whole. The combination of this holistic approach to the album and the influence of musical theatre in the songs made *American Idiot* a prime candidate for adaptation.

Jukebox Musicals and Revues **73**

Though Armstrong shares that the album is "90% sort of based on [his] life,"[49] for the musical, the story was expanded to include three main characters and a cast of nineteen actors. This lands the production squarely in the New Story: Single Artist jukebox musical category. However, Armstrong's close connection to the material and the emotion he infused into the album helped to drive the stage production. In *Broadway Idiot*, Armstrong shares that he put more emotion into the "American Idiot" album than any other and that the song "Wake Me Up When September Ends" was "the first time [he] ever wrote about [his] father dying."[50] While based on experiences that Armstrong had growing up in suburbia in the 1980s and early 1990s, the show follows three disaffected young men living in suburban Jingletown USA in the recent past (the early 2000s during the George W. Bush presidency). The three, Johnny, Tunny, and Will each go their separate ways in search of something more, Johnny and Tunny move to the city, where Johnny ends up addicted to drugs and Tunny enlists in the army. Will, who plans to go with them, finds out that his girlfriend, Heather, is pregnant and stays in Jingletown. Johnny falls in love with a girl, Whatsername, but chooses his dealer St. Jimmy and drugs over her. Tunny is injured in combat and loses a leg. While he's in the hospital he meets the Extraordinary Girl and returns home with her. Will neglects Heather and his child and they leave him. Tunny and Johnny return home and the three reconnect. The show ends hopefully with each recognizing what they've lost but also what they've gained.

The story, like the album, is closely tied to the early 2000s, and not just because of specific references to George W. Bush peppered throughout. The story captures the experience of many young people who were teenagers when 9/11 happened and who watched their entire world change in a day. This experience and connection, in addition to the popularity of the band *Green Day*, made the musical appeal to a large audience, which included many who were not typically Broadway theatregoers. In *Broadway Idiot* Armstrong notes the variety of people on opening night, he shares, "the reaction was amazing, one hardcore Green Day fan said, 'Oh My God' and I said, 'It's not what you thought it was going to be,' and he said 'not at all.'

74 Jukebox Musicals and Revues

And then I heard someone say, 'I guess this was inspired by a rock band or something.'"[51]

The reviews for the production were mixed. Charles Isherwood of the *New York Times* praised the production, calling it "thrillingly raucous and gorgeously wrought."[52] Chris Jones of the *Chicago Tribune* shares, "the show delivers a thick, gorgeous head rush of a musical soundscape without current Broadway parallel. It turns out to offer the kind of sensual lushness that a lot more traditional musicals would kill to emulate."[53] As often as the music was praised, the book was denigrated. Frank Scheck of the *Hollywood Reporter* notes that "in terms of dramatic impact, it falls far short of predecessors like 'The Who's Tommy.'" He continues, "Although the original concept album is reasonably cohesive, it's a thin premise on which to base a musical, and the show's book doesn't manage to flesh it out sufficiently. [It] never manages to make us care about the fate of its thinly drawn characters."[54]

Scheck was not wrong about the book, it is thin and became even thinner between its tryout and Broadway opening. This is a frequent challenge with jukebox musicals that tell new stories because the music already exists, the book must be written around them. Sometimes this leads to songs feeling out of place or wedged in and sometimes, like with *American Idiot*, leads to an underdeveloped plot. In *Broadway Idiot*, Director Michael Mayer addresses this challenge noting, "Because all the material has already been written and is being sung, we can't change what they're saying. So we had to figure out how to plot out a real story and make them three-dimensional characters."[55] While the three main characters begin to come to life, the secondary characters remain flat, two of the main women in the show don't even have names.

Despite the justified criticism, the show did receive several Tony nominations, including Best Musical, Best Scenic Design for Christine Jones[56], and Best Lighting Design for Kevin Jones. The show won the two design awards and there was talk of Tom Kitt being snubbed for his orchestrations. The two wins for design point to another important aspect of the production, its innovative scenic design. Rather than attempting to move between the multiple different locations in the production, scenic designer Cristine Jones created a unit set that allowed the action to fluidly move from place to place during the show's frenetic 90-minute run time. The set featured dozens of flat-panel televisions embedded in walls papered with newspapers, flyers, and other paper media, which could be accentuated or made to disappear depending on the lighting. Jones's use of televisions in the set was a part of a larger trend of the use of LCD/LED technology on Broadway that gained momentum in the middle of the 20 seasons. The show's recognition for its use of the technology was a harbinger of things to come as by the end of the 20 seasons, digital scenery would become ubiquitous on Broadway in all types of musicals.

Multiple Artists: New Story/ Movie Musical Adaptation—Moulin Rouge

- **Opened: July 25, 2019**
- **Closed: Still running at the time of publication**

Moulin Rouge is based on the 2001 film of the same name. Though this production fits into both the screen-to-stage category and the jukebox musical category, the adjustments made to the music in the transition from screen-to-stage make it best suited to the jukebox category and the way that music is used in the production is representative of an evolution of the jukebox form. *Moulin Rouge* is also an excellent example of the multiple artists: new story category as it uses the music of dozens of artists to tell its story as most musical numbers in the production are medleys of multiple songs.

Since the success of Baz Luhrmann's 2001 film, fans have been calling for a stage adaptation of *Moulin Rouge*, however, the adaptation was actually set in motion at a dinner party hosted by a mutual friend of Luhrmann and Alex Timbers, the production's director.[57] In an interview with *Variety*'s Gordon Cox, Luhrmann notes of Timbers, "if theatrical language were people, we might have been relatives."[58] that chance meeting eventually led to a collaboration which led to the production.

while certainly an adaptation of the film, the musical takes the style and format of the original source material and expands it, incorporating a much wider variety of popular music. Like the film, rather than utilizing entire songs the production utilizes a mixture of short snippets

76 Jukebox Musicals and Revues

and longer passages from recognizable pop songs to tell its story. These sections get stitched together to create musical numbers that are often centered on a particular idea or theme. In an interview with *Entertainment Weekly*'s Maureen Lee Lenker, the production's music supervisor Justine Levine discussed the "Elephant Love Medley," a number that in its original iteration sampled several love songs including "I Will Always Love You," "Heroes," and "Silly Love Songs," pop culture touchstones that predated the film. He explains, "I wanted to make sure it felt robust without feeling schizophrenic. Ultimately, the goal was you stop thinking of it as a medley of songs, but [instead], it's this epic treatise on love."[59] For the musical, the catalog of songs was expanded to include dozens of songs from the later 20th and early 21st century, each song contributing a phrase or two to the final creation. The song as it appears in the Broadway production becomes a call and response between contemporary pop songs where, for example, A-ha's "Take on Me" (1985) is answered with Natalie Imbruglia's "Torn" (1997). This approach mitigates some of the challenges of the jukebox format. Whereas the existing songs were sometimes a liability for *American Idiot* as the book had to be written around them, in the case of *Moulin Rouge*, the use of small sections of many songs allowed the creators a greater amount of flexibility that was limited only by the breadth of the canon of popular music.

Though some parts of the production do feature longer sections of music, for example, in both the film and the stage production the Police's "Roxanne" is rearranged as a tango and becomes a showstopping number, the production's use of musical pastiche throughout is a new approach to the jukebox musical. It reminds one more of a dance team competition (where this type of musical surgery is commonplace) than a Broadway musical. The construction of the songs becomes a tool for storytelling in a new way. Levine notes:

> In translating Baz's style to the stage, there were certain cinematic tools we didn't have at our disposal, like jump cuts, zooming in, crane shots. We felt that music was a great way to translate that bombastic style … We already had this iconic love story, and so in searching for the right music, we're not starting so much from a place of style, but of content.[60]

The songs are constructed to move the plot forward and to speak to character like they would be in a production with original music, but the phrases of that music are drawn from preexisting material.

Though the approach to the music was copied from the film, which premiered in 2001, the music is well suited to a young contemporary audience. This is not only because it is stuffed with recognizable pop tunes, but because the rapid-fire pace of the music and its sampled quality speaks to an audience saturated by social media. Like scrolling through a TikTok or Instagram Feed, the musical references fly past a breakneck speed, never lingering long enough for boredom to set in. This aural spectacle combined with the sensory overload of the production's design, staging, and choreography makes experiencing the production akin to living inside the TikTok algorithm for 2.5 hours.

This approach is jarring and might have failed, but as with the original film, the artistry with which the songs are put together and the fact that the frenetic energy of the "jump cut" score matches the energy of the narrative and the production, so somehow it works. In his review of the production Ben Brantley observes that the show "walks a tightrope between archness and sincerity, sophistication and gee-whiz wonder, without ever stumbling."[61] He finishes his review by noting:

> In "Moulin Rouge," life *is* beautiful, in a way reality never is. All is permitted, and forgiven, in the name of love. Bohemian poverty is exquisitely picturesque. Stardom is around the corner for the gifted and hungry. And even songs you thought you never wanted to hear again pulse with irresistible new sex appeal. What this emporium of impure temptations is really selling is pure escapism. You may not believe in it all by the next morning. But I swear you'll feel nothing like regret.[62]

Brantley's high praise, which is a far cry from his 1995 concerns about the jukebox genre, points to the production's ability to successfully meet the expectations for a splashy musical and push the form of the jukebox musical into new territory. At the time of this writing, the production has reopened following the 2020 shutdown with no sign of closing and launched a national tour in March 2022. Like the film on which it was based, *Moulin Rouge* may be an anomaly and other productions may not

78 Jukebox Musicals and Revues

copy its musical style, but it may also open the door for other reimaginings of the jukebox formula and it may push the form in new directions.

Multiple Artists: Biographical—Motown: The Musical

- **Opened: April 14, 2013**
- **Closed: January 18, 2015**
- **Reopened: July 12, 2016**
- **Closed: July 31, 2016**

Motown: The Musical is one of the few multiple artist biographical jukebox musicals in the 20 seasons. Rather that following the story of one artist, *Motown* follows the story of Berry Gordy who founded the Motown Record Corporation (also known as Hitsville) in Detroit in 1959. The company gave its name to a wildly popular music style that swept the United States in the 1960s and launched the careers of some of the greatest music artists of the 20th century including Michael Jackson, Diana Ross, and Stevie Wonder, among many others.

The musical tells the story of the birth of Motown, and its rise to become one of the most influential record labels of the 20th century through the eyes of its founder, Berry Gordy. The musical is based on Gordy's 1994 autobiography, *To Be Loved: The Music, The Magic, The Memories of Motown*. The book was written after Gordy sold *Motown* and chronicled the company's journey and his personal relationships with many of the artists he discovered. However, the book was a sanitized version of the company's history and Gordy himself admitted that part of the purpose of writing it was to respond to the criticisms that he treated his artists poorly and didn't pay them fairly.[63] Gordy was also a producer on the musical, so its perspective is skewed. Michael Billington of *The Guardian* sums up the problem nicely in the opening to his 2016 review of the London production. He notes, "Given that Berry Gordy has written, co-produced and is the lead character … it is clear that the ego has landed. But, eager as I am as the next person to learn more about the Motown mogul, I was disappointed at how little I discovered."[64] The production traded story for aural spectacle, diving deeply into the Motown Records catalogue at the expense of a compelling or truthful narrative.

Jukebox Musicals and Revues 79

What the show lacked in storytelling, it made up in music, featuring over 60 songs from the Motown catalogue and a cavalcade of 20th-century musical legends, the production did what most audiences expect from a jukebox musical, it provided an evening of nostalgia. In his review for *Backstage*, Erik Haagensen observed:

> If you are looking to bathe in nostalgia evoked by beloved tunes while watching talented and committed professionals do their industrious best to locate the magic of legendary performers, this is the show for you. If you prefer a well-written story with multi-dimensional characters that digs beneath the surface and uses song with dramatic acumen, then steer clear.[65]

The musical presented Gordy and his story in a glossy haze while it rapidly ticked through the Motown catalogue and paraded a who's who of the music industry in the second half of the 20th century. This approach meant that the show was incredibly expensive. It was rumored to have cost $17 million to mount with its cast of 36 and 20-piece orchestra.[66] While this approach lacked depth and nuance, it gave audiences what they wanted, a fact noted by many of the reviews.

The enormous price tag meant that it was expensive to run and after playing on Broadway for almost two years and 738 performances, the production closed. However, a national tour launched a year into the show's Broadway run and the producers planned to remount the production on Broadway after the tour concluded. The musical was streamlined for the tour, with changes made to its structure and its book, and a limited 18-week run on Broadway was planned as the tour's last stop. *Motown*'s return engagement is one of the few examples of a remount in the 20 seasons as even though the production was adjusted, it was the same production that originally opened rather than a new production of the title. Therefore, it is a remount not a revival. Though hopes were high that the musical would draw a crowd for its return to Broadway, it closed after only three weeks of the planned 18 as it was only earning a third of its potential and running at a loss.[67]

Though *Motown: The Musical* is not particularly interesting for its form or content, it is important for its representation. Unlike most

80 Jukebox Musicals and Revues

musicals in the 20 seasons, there were multiple artists of color on the creative team. The book was written by a Black man, Berry Gordy (who was also one of the show's lead producers), it was directed by a Black man, Charles Randolph-Wright, and one of its two choreographers, Warren Adams, was also Black, and it featured a catalogue of tunes originally written and recorded by Black artists.[68] *Motown* was one of two productions to open in the 2012–2013 season that featured a mostly black creative team. The other, a remount of the 2009 jukebox musical *Fela!*, also had at least one Black artist in each role on its directing and writing team and featured a large cast of Black performers. In addition, 32 of the 36 performers listed in the original cast of *Motown*, and all but one of the swings and understudies were Black. Though the musical may not have been of exceptional quality, it employed more Black performers than any other musical that season, and because of its large cast, more than most other musicals in the 20 seasons. As mentioned earlier in this chapter, jukebox musicals present an opportunity for BIPOC representation both on and off stage. Unlike many jukebox musicals in this period that provide onstage opportunities for actors of the global majority, *Motown* also employed Black artists to write, direct, and choreograph.

Reading Questions

1. What are the antecedents of the jukebox musical?
2. What is the difference between a jukebox musical and a revue?
3. What are the four types of jukebox musicals?
4. How does the jukebox musical fit into discussions of representation on Broadway both on and off the stage?
5. How are each of the jukebox musicals case studied in the chapter good examples of the genre?

Notes

1 Ben Brantley, "Theatre Review; Tribute to a Jazz Age Lyricist," review of *Swinging on a Star: The Johnny Burke Musical*, Music Box Theatre, New York, NY, *New York Times*, October 23, 1995, sec. c, accessed December 28, 2020, www.nytimes.com/1995/10/23/theater/theater-review-tribute-to-a-jazz-age-lyricist.html.

2 Charles D. Adamson, "Defining the Jukebox Musical through a Historical Approach: From The Beggar's Opera to Nice Work if You Can Get It" (PhD diss., Texas Tech University, 2013), 7.

3 The term was used frequently in the 1940s and 1950s in Hollywood to describe musical films that utilized previously published music.

4 The "Princess Musicals" are seven musicals written for the Princess Theatre between 1915 and 1918 that are often cited as an important development toward the codification of American musical theatre.

5 Stephen Citron, *Noel and Cole: The Sophisticates* (New York: Oxford University Press, 1993), 133–34, accessed December 28, 2020, https://archive.org/details/unset0000unse_a7u7/.

6 Millie Taylor, "I've Heard That Song Before: The Jukebox Musical and Entertainment," in *Musical Theatre, Realism and Entertainment* (Farnham: Ashgate, 2012), 150.

7 Adamson, "Defining the Jukebox," 23.

8 A short-lived 1978 production titled *Elvis: The Legend Lives* is sometimes cited as a jukebox musical, however, the Broadway League categorizes the production as a special and not a musical. As this volume utilizes the Broadway League's categorizations, this production is not included here.

9 Broadway League, The Internet Broadway Database, www.ibdb.com/.

10 "Facts and Figures," Judy Cramer, accessed December 28, 2020, www.judycraymer.com/press-centre/facts-and-figures.php.

11 Broadway League, The Internet Broadway Database.

12 It should be noted that there are several jukebox musicals in this period that belong both to the movie musical adaptation category and one of the other categories.

13 The production also had a Black male costume designer, but all other designers were white.

14 Amy Sara Osatinski, *Disney Theatrical Productions: Producing Broadway Musicals the Disney Way* (New York: Routledge, 2019), 32.

15 David Rooney, "Shrek the Musical," review of *Shrek the Musical*, accessed January 7, 2021, https://variety.com/2008/film/awards/shrek-the-musical-4-1200472752/.

16 Kevin Flynn and Patrick Healy, "How the Numbers Add Up (Way Up) for 'Spider-Man,'" *New York Times*, June 23, 2011, sec. A, [Page #], accessed January 7, 2021, www.nytimes.com/2011/06/23/theater/spider-man-by-the-numbers-breaking-down-its-costs.html.

17 Simon Frith, *Performing Rites: On the Value of Popular Music* (Cambridge, MA: Harvard University Press, 1996), 273.

18 Frith, *Performing Rites*, 273.

19 Taylor, "I've Heard," 155.

20 Kevin Byrne and Emily Fuchs, *The Jukebox Musical: An Interpretive History* (Abingdon: Routledge, 2022), 14.

21 Peter Marks, "As Rock-Star Portrayals Go, It Doesn't Get Any Better than Adrienne Warren as Tina Turner," review of *Tina, Washington Post* (Washington, DC), November 7, 2019, accessed February 8, 2021, www.

82 Jukebox Musicals and Revues

washingtonpost.com/entertainment/theater_dance/as-rock-star-portraya
ls-go-it-doesnt-get-any-better-than-adrienne-warren-as-tina-turner/2019/
11/07/79ee6c4c-0179-11ea-8bab-0fc209e065a8_story.html.

22 Tanesha J., *Yelp* Review, December 14, 2019, www.yelp.com/biz/tina
-the-tina-turner-musical-new-york-4.

23 Maday M., *Yelp* Review, November 14, 2019, www.yelp.com/biz/tina
-the-tina-turner-musical-new-york-4.

24 Raoul W., *Yelp* Review, December 15, 2019, www.yelp.com/biz/tina
-the-tina-turner-musical-new-york-4.

25 Jesse Green, "Review: In 'The Cher Show,' I Got You, Babe. And You.
And You.," review of *The Cher Show*, New York, NY, *New York Times*
(New York, NY), December 4, 2018, sec. C, 1, accessed February 8, 2021,
www.nytimes.com/2018/12/03/theater/the-cher-show-review.html.

26 Many shows can be attributed to multiple categories, this number represents all the productions that fit the definition of a jukebox musical, even if
primarily categorized in another category.

27 It should be noted that there are four jukebox musicals from 2019 and
2020 that were still running when Broadway shut down and that may cross
this mark after they reopen.

28 Broadway League, The Internet Broadway Database.

29 Rick Elice, "As Jersey Boys Prepares for Its New Jersey Premiere, Tony-
Nominated Book Writer Rick Elice Shares the Oral History of the Tony-
Winning Musical.," interview by Ruthie Fierberg, *Playbill.com*, last modified October 11, 2017, accessed January 7, 2021, www.playbill.com/a
rticle/how-the-story-of-frankie-valli-and-the-four-seasons-went-from-jers
ey-lore-to-broadway-hit.

30 Elice, "As Jersey," interview, *Playbill.com*.

31 Elice, "As Jersey," interview, *Playbill.com*.

32 As of March 2020, *Jersey Boys* is the 12th longest running musical in
Broadway history. *Mamma Mia!* Is the 9th.

33 Bridge and tunnel is an often derogatory term used to describe people who
live outside of Manhattan (outer boroughs or New Jersey) who drive over
a bridge or through a tunnel to get to Manhattan.

34 Elice, "As Jersey."

35 Ben Brantley, "From Blue-Collar Boys to Doo-Wop Sensation: A Band's
Rise and Fall," review of *Jersey Boys*, *New York Times* (New York, NY),
November 7, 2005, accessed January 9, 2021, www.nytimes.com/2005/
11/07/theater/reviews/from-bluecollar-boys-to-doowop-sensation-a-band
s-rise-and-fall.html.

36 Eriq Gardner, "Judge Overturns Jury's Verdict That 'Jersey Boys' Is a
Copyright Infringement," *Hollywood Reporter*, June 14, 2017, accessed January 9, 2021, www.hollywoodreporter.com/thr-esq/judge-overturns-jur
ys-verdict-jersey-boys-is-a-copyright-infringement-1013558.

37 Gardner, "Judge Overturns."

38 The production closed during the COVID-19 pandemic and reopened in
December 2021.

Jukebox Musicals and Revues 83

39 "Jersey Boys," Jersey Boys, accessed January 9, 2021, www.jerseyboysinfo.com/.

40 Rob Sheffield, "American Idiot," review of *American Idiot, Rolling Stone*, September 30, 2004, ProQuest.

41 *Broadway Idiot*, directed by Doug Hamilton, FilmBuff, 2013.

42 "Chart History: Green Day," Billboard, accessed January 9, 2021, www.billboard.com/music/green-day/chart-history/hot-100/song/458528.

43 Patrick Healey, "Finding the Musical Hidden in a Punk Album," *New York Times* (New York, NY), April 1, 2010, sec. C, accessed April 1, 2010, www.nytimes.com/2010/04/02/theater/02greenday.html

44 Quoted in *Broadway Idiot*.

45 *Broadway Idiot*.

46 *Broadway Idiot*.

47 *Broadway Idiot*.

48 *Broadway Idot*.

49 *Broadway Idiot*.

50 *Broadway Idiot*.

51 *Broadway Idiot*.

52 Charles Isherwood, "Stomping Onto Broadway With a Punk Temper Tantrum," review of *American Idiot, New York Times*, April 21, 2010, sec. C, 1, accessed January 16, 2021, www.nytimes.com/2010/04/21/theater/reviews/21idiot.html.

53 Quoted in "American Idiot Broadway Reviews," Broadwayworld.com, accessed January 16, 2021, www.broadwayworld.com/reviews/American-Idiot.

54 Frank Scheck, "Green Day's American Idiot a Tough Sell on Broadway," *Hollywood Reporter*, April 10, 2010, accessed January 16, 2021, www.reuters.com/article/us-stage-idiot/green-days-american-idiot-a-tough-sell-on-broadway-idUSTRE63J6IO20100420.

55 *Broadway Idiot*.

56 Jones is one of only a few women to win or be nominated a Tony for scenic design. She won a second Tony in 2018 for her work on *Harry Potter and the Cursed Child*.

57 "'Moulin Rouge!' Director Baz Luhrmann on Turning the Film into the Tony-Nominated Broadway Musical," video, 59:45, YouTube, accessed May 12, 2022, www.youtube.com/watch?v=pGE9efj6b2I.

58 "'Moulin Rouge!,'" video.

59 Maureen Lee Lenker, "How Moulin Rouge! The Musical Turned a Smash Soundtrack into a Broadway Show," *Entertainment Weekly*, July 23, 2019, accessed May 12, 2022, https://ew.com/theater/2019/07/23/moulin-rouge-the-musical-behind-the-music/.

60 Lenker, "How Moulin,"

61 Ben Brantley, "Review: 'Moulin Rouge! The Musical' Offers a Party, and a Playlist, for the Ages," review of *Moulin Rouge: The Musical*, New York, NY, *The New York Times*, July 25, 2019, accessed May 12, 2022, www.nytimes.com/2019/07/25/theater/moulin-rouge-review.html.

84 Jukebox Musicals and Revues

62 Brantley, "Review: 'Moulin," review.

63 Barry Koltnow, "Berry Gordy, the Father of Motown, Sets Record Straight," *Orlando Sentinel* (Orlando, FL), December 19, 1994, accessed December 28, 2022, www.orlandosentinel.com/news/os-xpm-1994-12-2 0-9412170897-story.html.

64 Michael Billington, "Motown the Musical Review - Berry Gordy Show Is a Ball of Confusion," review of *Motown the Musical*, London, UK, *The Guardian*, March 8, 2016, accessed December 28, 2022, www.theguardian.com/stage/2016/mar/08/motown-the-musical-review-berry-gordy-shaftes bury-theatre.

65 Erik Haagensen, "'Motown: The Musical' Bathes Us in Nostalgia," review of *Motown: The Musical, Backstage*, accessed December 28, 2022, www.backstage.com/magazine/article/motown-musical-bathes-us-nostalgia-15186/.

66 Marilyn Stasio, "Legit Review: 'Motown,'" review of *Motown: The Musical, Variety*, accessed December 28, 2022, https://variety.com/2013/legit/reviews/legit-review-motown-1200364348/.

67 Michael Paulson, "'Motown: The Musical' to Close for Second Time on Broadway," *The New York Times*, July 23, 2016, sec. C, 3, accessed December 28, 2022, www.nytimes.com/2016/07/23/theater/motown-the-musical-to-close-for-second-time-on-broadway.html.

68 Not all the music in the production was written by Black artists, but much of it was.

4

SCREEN-TO-STAGE MUSICALS

TABLE 4.1 Screen-to-stage musicals in 20 seasons

Show Title	Season	Run	Category(ies)	Screen-to-Stage Adaptation Type
The Full Monty	2000–2001	770	Screen-to-stage	Independent/foreign film
The Producers	2000–2001	2502	Screen-to-stage	Cult classic
The Rocky Horror Show	2000–2001	437	Screen-to-stage	Cult classic
Sweet Smell of Success	2001–2002	109	Screen-to-stage	Classic film
Thoroughly Modern Millie	2001–2002	903	Screen-to-stage	Classic film
Dance of the Vampires	2002–2003	56	Screen-to-stage	Independent/foreign film
Hairspray	2002–2003	2642	Screen-to-stage	Cult classic
Urban Cowboy	2003–2003	60	Screen-to-stage	Blockbuster
Never Gonna Dance	2003–2004	84	Screen-to-stage/ Jukebox	Classic film

DOI: 10.4324/9781003139171-5

86 Screen-to-Stage Musicals

Show Title	Season	Run	Category(ies)	Screen-to-Stage Adaptation Type
Chitty Chitty Bang Bang	2004–2005	285	Screen-to-stage/Jukebox	Animated/family film
Dirty Rotten Scoundrels	2004–2005	627	Screen-to-stage	Blockbuster
Spamalot	2004–2005	1575	Screen-to-stage	Cult classic
Tarzan	2005–2006	486	Screen-to-stage/Jukebox	Animated/family film
The Color Purple	2005–2006	910	Screen-to-stage/Original	Blockbuster
The Wedding Singer	2005–2006	285	Screen-to-stage	Blockbuster
Grey Gardens	2006–2007	307	Screen-to-stage	Cult classic
High Fidelity	2006–2007	14	Screen-to-stage	Blockbuster

*The totals for these musicals, which were running at the time of this writing, represent the show total through May 8th, 2022.

History and Development of the Screen-to-Stage Musical

Contrary to the belief that musicals based on films are a new phenomenon, screen-to-stage musicals have been around almost as long as the Broadway musical. The history of the screen-to-stage musical begins before movies could even talk[1] with 1919's *The Little Whopper*, which was based on the 1916 silent film, *Miss George Washington*.[2] The production, with a book by Otto Harbach, music by Rudolf Friml, and Lyrics by Otto Harbach and Bide Dudley, ran for 204 performances. Though relatively successful in its day, it was not particularly memorable, is rarely discussed, and was never revived. The most famous of its creators, Otto Harbach, is known more for his mentorship of Oscar Hammerstein than for his own work. Harbach was an early proponent of integrating the songs in a musical comedy into the plot, a practice that Hammerstein, along with Richard Rodgers, would solidify during the Golden Age of musical theatre in the 1940s–1960s. *Whopper* came and went without much attention or fanfare. Though the *New York Times* review calls the production "a musical comedy above the average" it also notes that the book neither "reaches the high spots" nor "comes down to the too utterly inane."[3]

After *The Little Whopper*, Broadway would not see another screen-to-stage musical until 1951, 32 years later.[4] In the 1950s, there were four musicals based on films that played on Broadway. According to musical theatre scholar Ronald Zank, in the 1960s 5% of musicals were based on films, conversely, in the 2010s, 41% of musicals were based on films.[5] In the first decade of the 21st century, there were 27 screen-to-stage musicals that opened on Broadway. Though musical adaptations of films are not new, the increase in number in the 2000s was noticed, and not in a good way. The influx of movie-based properties on Broadway led to many complaints and a great deal of criticism as captured by James Wolcott in his 2011 *Vanity Fair* article, *Pop Goes the Great White Way*. He comments, "Broadway purists may deplore the influx of movie-spinoff musicals in recent years, wishing someone would turn off the popcorn machine and let more imaginative brainstorms blow through."[6] Wolcott continues:

> Pop culture has assimilated—Borg'd—every entertainment field into a prismatic present where everything refracts everything else, gets pumped nonstop into media feeds, and is pooped out the other end of the Huffington Post. Hairspray was a movie turned Broadway musical turned Hollywood remake, and that is the Lion King circle of life as we know it in Times Square, the creative loop that swings for the stars and sometimes crashes into the upper deck.[7]

Wolcott's comments capture the prevailing sentiment among the "Broadway establishment" that the influx of screen-to-stage musicals is a bad sign for Broadway. A death knell for creativity and original works on the Great White Way. However, just like any other category of Broadway musical, there are artistically successful screen-to-stage musicals and there are creative misses. Why then was there such a huge backlash against the screen-to-stage musicals in the twenty seasons?

Types of Screen-to-Stage Musicals

Before answering the question of why, first, let's examine the types of screen-to-stage musicals that opened on Broadway during the 20

88 Screen-to-Stage Musicals

seasons as some were more prone to controversy than others. During this period there were five categories of screen-to-stage musicals which are determined by the source film: animated/family film musicals, blockbuster film musicals, cult classic film musicals, classic film musicals, and independent/foreign film musicals.

The first category, animated/family film musicals are musicals based on animated films or films that are aimed at children and families. As would be expected, this category was dominated by Disney properties during the 20 seasons. Disney opened six musicals in this period and had three others that opened prior to the 20 seasons that were still running, including *The Lion King*, which at the time of this writing, is the third longest-running musical in the history of Broadway.[8] Though Disney started the trend of turning animated and family films into Broadway musicals with *Beauty and the Beast* in 1994, and produced many adaptations in the 20 seasons, after the success of the early Disney properties, other producers followed suit. Some examples include *Shrek, Anastasia,* [9] and *SpongeBob SquarePants.*

Blockbuster film musicals are musicals based on major motion pictures. These are films with name recognition that were box office hits when released and/or had a huge presence on television or home video. These musicals are often very big and very expensive. Examples include *Ghost, Rocky, Pretty Woman*, and *Mean Girls.* Cult classic film musicals are musicals based on films that were not particularly successful in their theatrical release, but have since acquired a cult following and have been present in popular culture in the few decades before their musical adaptations. Examples for this category include *Xanadu, American Psycho*, and *Cry-Baby.* Classic film musicals are those based on films that would be considered "classics" including *An American in Paris* and *White Christmas.* The Independent/Foreign film category includes musicals based on small, domestic, independent films, or foreign films. This category often includes musicals that many do not even realize are based on a film. This group includes *The Full Monty, Kinky Boots, Once*, and *The Band's Visit.*

Of these five categories, the musicals that most often draw criticism for merely existing (regardless of their quality) is the blockbuster category. As soon as one of these big movie properties is announced, there is often a backlash, for example, in his review of 2018's *Pretty Woman:*

The Musical, which is based on the hit 1990 film, Ben Brantley of the *New York Times* asserts that the production "lowers the already ground-scraping bar for literal-minded adaptations of film to stage."[10] While this author does not disagree with Brantley's assessment of the production, as it can certainly be tossed in the pile of artistically unsuccessful adaptations, the assertion of a "low bar" for movie adaptations is indicative of a wider dismissal of stage musicals based on big films. Another production that received Brantley's ire is 2015's *Finding Neverland*, based on the 2004 film of the same name. Brantley seems most offended by the celebrity casting of Matthew Morrison and Kelsey Grammer, in fact, the review is titled: "*Finding Neverland*: A Musical With Matthew Morrison."[11] What Brantley misses about the adaptation is that it is well-constructed, reminiscent of the musicals of the mid-20th century that continue to be revived to great acclaim. The production did not rely on flashy special effects, with the exception of a stunning moment in the second act (that this author refers to as the glitter tornado), but rather utilized more traditional theatrical storytelling devices. Despite the scathing reviews that the production received, it ran for 565 performances and spawned a national tour that began when the show closed and a second tour in 2018. There are two possible reasons for the disparity in response between the critics and audiences. First, by 2016 there was a noted bias against any musical based on a major film, and second, a difference in taste between New York audiences (including critics) and audiences in other parts of the country, including the tourists who make up a large portion of Broadway ticket buyers.

The divide between New York audiences and tourists points to the first reason for the bias against screen-to-stage musicals. Broadway is commercial theatre, meaning that the main purpose of mounting a production is to make money. Opening a musical on Broadway is not cheap. In the 2010–2011 season the average cost of a new musical on Broadway was \$9,660,000.[12] However, it is not only the initial cost of the production that impacts the profit margin, there is also a weekly cost for running a production that must be met before a show will make any money. In the 2010–2011 season the average running cost for the musicals running on Broadway was \$589,754.[13] These numbers, while large, are also only the averages. Bigger musicals can cost

90 Screen-to-Stage Musicals

significantly more. This period saw the most expensive production ever mounted on Broadway: *Spider-Man: Turn Off the Dark* (2011), which cost \$75 million.[14] After *Spider-Man* announced its closing in late 2013, *Vulture.com* published a "postmortem" of its financials that reported the show's investors were poised to lose \$60 million when the show closed. The article also reported the following budget items for the production: \$9,662,885 for sets and costumes, \$4,373,375 in rental fees for the Foxwoods theatre before performances even started,[15] \$438,389 for props, \$370,074 for Puppets, \$2,215,047 for flying rigs and harnesses, \$189,889 for musical instruments, \$92,000 in fees for the show's authors (including Bono and the Edge of U2), \$125,000 to Julie Taymor for directing and an additional \$9,750 in royalties paid to her after she was fired from the production in March 2011. In addition, the production cost \$1.3 million to run each week and the gross for the last week of September 2013 was only \$621,960.[16] Breaking out these costs clearly shows the need for properties on Broadway to make money. *Spider-Man* is certainly an outlier in its exorbitant expenses, but even smaller musicals are expensive. For example, 2017's *The Band's Visit*, an intimate screen-to-stage musical that won the Tony Award for Best Musical, cost \$8.75 million to mount on Broadway and ran for 10 months (and won multiple Tony awards) before recouping that investment.[17]

Given these staggering numbers, it is no surprise that producers aim their expensive productions at tourists. In *Stage Money: The Business of the Professional Theatre*, Tim Donahue and Jim Patterson note, "The top twenty earners between June 1999 and May 2008 account for more than 60 percent of Broadway's total take over a nine-season period. To put that another way, well over half the revenues during this period came from less than 7 percent of productions."[18] With two-thirds of productions on Broadway failing to ever recoup their investment, there is no surprise that producers are chasing that 7%. To compete with the long-running productions (*Phantom of the Opera, Chicago, The Lion King*) for tourist dollars, producers turn to known properties to try and entice tourists to choose their production. According to the Broadway League, in the 2018–2019 season, an average Broadway theatregoer saw 4.4 productions on Broadway a year. This breaks out into 7.5 for those living in the New York area and 3 for tourists, with a 4 show average for domestic tourists and a 2 show average for international tourists.[19] In 2018 an estimated 8 million people lived in New York City and an estimated 65 million people visited New York City, It makes sense that commercial producers would go after the out-of-town crowd. With only four chances to capture the attention of the millions of tourists who attend Broadway productions, producers often turn to adaptations with name recognition.

However, just because a production has name recognition and is based on a film does not automatically make it of lesser quality. Though the properties chosen for Broadway may at times, like *Finding Neverland*, be more palatable for audiences in other parts of the United States (rather than New York audiences), that does not make these productions "bad." Like any other subset of Broadway musicals, there are good screen-to-stage musicals and there are bad ones. Which category a show inhabits most often comes down to the skill of the artists crafting the adaptation. An excellent example of this is 2017's *SpongeBob SquarePants: The Musical* which will be discussed in detail later in this chapter.

Though the elitist perception that screen-to-stage musicals are "for the tourists" is one explanation for the outrage often aimed at them, it is not the only one. These musicals are often accused of only being created to make money. While in many cases, this is true, isn't it also true of the other non-cinematic properties on Broadway? As mentioned above, Broadway is commercial theatre. the goal of productions that play on the Great White Way is to make money. The assertion that screen-to-stage musicals are not worthy of attention or praise because they are only out to make money is inherently flawed, as if this is true, then no production on Broadway is worthy.

There is also an outdated notion of "high" and "low" art at play in the discourse surrounding screen-to-stage musicals. "High" art is the art that is for those with discerning taste, the cultural elite. "Low" art is for the masses. In his 2003 Book, *A Queer Sort of Materialism: Recontextualizing American Theatre*, Theatre scholar David Savran asserts that the American theatre (including musical theatre) is "middlebrow" a category that he acknowledges "has derived historically less from its innate characteristics than from the determination of the arbiters or taste to use the category to secure their own intellectual authority."[20] He discusses the ways in which the "unstable, unpredictable, and anxious relationship between art

92 Screen-to-Stage Musicals

and commerce" allows the designation to "provide a key to understanding the histories of American theatre."[21] While the concept of "middlebrow" is useful to understanding the history of American theatre and musical theatre, the categorization of cultural objects as "high" "middle" or "low" art also reinforces outdated and positivist critical structures that have historically placed the works of white, western, male creators over the works of women and global majority artists and art from outside of the United States and Europe. Additionally, these designations simply don't apply in the 21st century because the Internet has democratized the dissemination, consumption, and creation of a variety of media and cultural objects. The value of art is in the eye of the beholder. Take for example the phenomenon of nonfungible tokens, or NFTs in this period. An NFT is a "unique digital asset, individually identified on a blockchain."[22] In other words, digital "things" that have a unique identifier on a blockchain, which is a ledger of cryptocurrency transactions. The value of this digital art resides in how much someone will pay to "own" it. As of March 2021, the most expensive NFT to be sold was the artist Beeple's *Everydays—The First 5000 Days*, which fetched $69 million at auction. The piece was a digital collage of the artist's daily drawings beginning in May 2007.[23] However, it is not only digital "art" that is sold as NFTs, tweets have been turned into NFTs. For example, in March 2021, Twitter founder Jack Dorsey sold his first-ever tweet (and the first on the platform), "just setting up my twitter," for $2.9 million.[24] The value of an NFT is what someone will pay for it, which is not tied to any traditional idea of artistic legitimacy, quality, or value.

This is the world that 21st-century screen-to-stage musicals exist within. The argument that many of the films that serve as source material are "low" art, and therefore not worthy of adaptation is outdated and invalid. Additionally, even if one were to buy into the idea that these films are "low" art or even "middlebrow" art, the argument is still derailed by the fact that musical theatre has never been seen as "high" art. While today theatre elitists may decry screen-to-stage musicals, it was not long ago that all musical theatre was called "popular entertainment" and dismissed as being of little value. While opera and non-musical theatre were seen as legitimate "high" artforms, musicals were always for the masses.

Despite the ire often aimed at screen-to-stage musicals, they have been a site of innovation, particularly in their technical elements. In the first twenty years of the 21st century, digital scenography and the use of projection/video advanced rapidly. Around the midpoint of this period, Broadway musicals employing a projection/video designer became the norm and digital scenic elements (both subtle and over the top) became ubiquitous. While digital scenery appeared across all categories of musicals, it was particularly prevalent in screen-to-stage musicals. In the 2017 chapter "Ghosts in the Machine: Digital Technology and Screen-to-Stage Musicals," this author observes, "advances in digital scenography have led to stage productions that can both literally and figuratively evoke the material on which they are based. It is not only easier to create multiple locations on stage by utilizing light-emitting diode (LED) screens; it also adds a cinematic quality to the projected locations, blurring the line between stage and screen."[25] Film adaptations lend themselves to cinematic scenography, allowing audiences an experience as close to live interaction with the source material as is possible in the theatre. This had led to innovative uses of the technology, like the set for *Ghost: The Musical*, which utilized LED walls to evoke the various locations in the production and to support the staging with the use of digital "ensemble members," apparitions that mirrored the moves performed by their live counterparts. Another example is the scenery for *Mean Girls*, which utilized a curved wall of high-powered digital screens to quickly shift the action to the production's various locations. The creators chose video as the primary mode of scenery for several reasons, first because of the fast pace of the book, "in which the stage environment rapidly changes."[26] Additionally, in an interview with Broadwayworld.com, scenic designer Scott Pask explains, "New (and evolving) media is so often the chosen 'language' of communication between teenagers, and to use that vocabulary in a transformative and humorous way felt like the perfect solution for our production."[27] The ability to "jump cut" between scenes lends to the cinematic feel of *Mean Girls* and the use of digital media mirrors the tone of the production and reflects the world of the characters.

In addition to advances in LED technology and the rise of cinematic scenery, screen-to-stage musicals in this period also led to other spectacular scenic innovations. Two prominent examples are *Rocky: The*

94 Screen-to-Stage Musicals

Musical and *King Kong: The Musical*. While both of these productions were not particularly successful on Broadway, both contained innovative elements unlike anything attempted on Broadway before them. First, 2014's *Rocky*. The majority of the production exemplified the tendency of blockbuster screen-to-stage musicals to pander to the fans of the property. For example, Rocky drinks raw eggs in the kitchen, punches a side of beef, and shouts "ADRIAN" in a tone reminiscent of the film's star, Sylvester Stallone. But, the last twenty minutes of the production were unlike anything this author had ever seen before and created a hybrid theatrical/athletic experience that altered the relationship between the production and its audience in a groundbreaking way. When the production arrived at the final fight between Rocky Balboa and his nemesis, Apollo Creed, ushers moved into the orchestra and directed patrons seated in the center, front orchestra to get out of their seats and walk up onto the stage where bleachers appeared. Once the audience cleared, a boxing ring was lowered into the space and placed over the seats of the front orchestra. Once the ring was in place, the patrons seated in the side and rear orchestra were encouraged to stand up and surround the ring. Thus, in the space of a few minutes, the theatre was transformed into a boxing venue. Then they fought. Rocky and Creed boxed each other in a choreographed fight that was so real that members of the audience were on their feet cheering and shouting. The experience of those final twenty minutes was more akin to a sporting event than a theatrical one and elicited the same rush of adrenaline that one experiences sitting ringside at a boxing match. Though many aspects of the production may not have been noteworthy, the innovation on display in this immersive ending was unforgettable.

Another production that exemplifies this type of innovation is 2018's *King Kong*. The production reportedly cost \$35 million to stage[28] and that cash was on display in both the scenery and the title character. The scenery utilized an enormous, curved LED wall that provided both location and action. For example, when Carl Denham and his crew travel to Skull Island, the screen fills with the crashing waves of the ocean while the stage floor rises to a point to evoke the prow of a ship. In the climactic scene when Kong scales the Empire State Building, the screen is used to show his ascent from multiple perspectives, heightening the excitement. Though the screen was massive and the video design captivating, the star of the production was Kong himself. The puppet was 20 feet tall, weighed 1.2 tons, and required fifteen people to operate.[29] in an interview with NPR's Jeff Lunden, Jacob Williams, whose title on the production was "Kong Captain," explains the mechanics of bringing the beast to life. He describes it as a blend of "old-school and new-school puppetry."[30] There were ten puppeteers, referred to as the "King's Company," who move Kong's wrists and elbows with ropes. Puppeteer Khadija Tariya explains:

> To be Kong, we are one with Kong … We wear these black hoodies, and we're all in black outfits, and we're for the most part quite hidden. And we—we're in a crouch position, so you don't necessarily always see us—we're almost like his shadows. And then there also moments in the show where we are able to come out and almost express his feelings, like when he's curious about something, we do have a little appearance.[31]

In addition to the on-stage puppeteers, there were three operators in a booth in the balcony of the theatre who controlled the puppet's "face, head, neck and shoulders remotely" utilizing foot pedals and a joystick. The head and neck operator, John Hoche, also provided the voice of Kong, which was modulated through a processor to provide its beastly timbre.[32] The effect is stunning and visceral. The gasps and jumps exhibited by audience members, including this author, were more like the reaction of an audience in a movie theatre than a Broadway house. With the exception of the choreography, which utilized modern dance rather than traditional musical theatre forms to evoke the feeling of each moment, there was little to remember in the book or score. However, a 20-foot-tall gorilla descending from the ceiling and roaring in one's face is unforgettable. Screen-to-stage musicals, and the money that backs them, often because of their name recognition and potential for capturing tourist dollars, make these innovative and unforgettable experiences possible, even when the song and dance aren't the main attraction.

Though blockbuster screen-to-stage musicals have often elicited rolling eyes and elitist anger, there are screen-to-stage musicals whose

96 Screen-to-Stage Musicals

success and presence on Broadway was celebrated. Nine of the musicals that won the Best Musical Tony award in the twenty seasons were screen-to-stage musicals: *The Producers* (2001), *Thoroughly Modern Millie* (2002), *Hairspray* (2003), *Spamalot* (2005), *Billy Elliot* (2009), *Once* (2012), *Kinky Boots* (2013), *The Band's Visit* (2018), and *Moulin Rouge: The Musical* (2020). With the exception of *Thoroughly Modern Millie*, which is based on a classic film, and *Moulin Rouge* which might best be called a blockbuster, but doesn't fully conform to the category, all of these musicals fall into either the "cult classic" category (*Hairspray, The Producers, Spamalot*) or the "independent/foreign film" category (*Billy Elliot, Once, Kinky Boots, The Band's Visit*). The independent/foreign film-based properties are especially interesting as their connection to the original source material is often less pronounced. This allows these musicals to be judged on their own merits rather than in comparison to their celluloid predecessors and leads to less establishment backlash against them. It should be noted that all four of the Tony winners in this category were exceptional musicals and well-deserving of the award, which also points to the previous argument that like any other type of musical, there are high-quality examples of screen-to-stage musicals and less successful examples.

The other category of screen-to-stage musical that has come to be widely accepted is the animated/family musical. This genre took off in the 1990s after the success of two of Disney's animated screen-to-stage musicals, *Beauty and the Beast* (1994) and in particular, *The Lion King* (1997). While *Beauty* was successful financially, it drew much ire from the critics who compared it to a theme park ride and railed against Disney's presence on Broadway, *The Lion King* was more successful in its artistry in addition to its finances. Disney's decision to hire Julie Taymor to direct it and to allow her complete creative control led to it becoming in the words of critic John Lahr, "the ultimate business art."[33]

Once *The Lion King* was anointed, Disney Theatrical Productions was legitimized and the presence of family-friendly, screen-to-stage adaptations on Broadway was normalized although not altogether accepted. While Disney Theatrical Productions has been responsible for many of these musicals, they are not alone as other non-Disney animated films also became Broadway musicals during the 20 seasons including *Shrek,* a DreamWorks property, *Anastasia*, which was released by 20th Century Fox, and *SpongeBob SquarePants: The Broadway Musical* from Nickelodeon, which is the subject of the first case study in this chapter.

Case Studies

SpongeBob SquarePants

- **Opened: December 4, 2017**
- **Closed: September 16, 2018**
- **Performances: 327**

An excellent example of a screen-to-stage musical that was artistically successful despite its recognizable source material is 2017's *SpongeBob SquarePants: The Musical*. The stage show is based on the quirky Nickelodeon cartoon, *SpongeBob SquarePants*, which was created in 1999 by Stephen Hillenburg. The musical was able to successfully translate a multi-billion-dollar franchise to the Broadway stage in a way that pleased both audiences and critics. While the very idea of a SpongeBob musical raised many eyebrows and induced many eye rolls, the production's adherence to the original cartoon's "indie" spirit combined with ingenious design and staging led to a successful Broadway run including twelve Tony Award nominations.

Rather than recycling a storyline from one or more episodes of the show or one of the films, the book writer, Kyle Jarrow, and the show's director, Tina Landau, opted to create a new storyline that felt a part of the world of SpongeBob. In the musical:

Bikini Bottom[34] is threatened by impending doom from a foreboding volcano named Mount Humongous. With the city desperate for a way to save themselves, Plankton and Karen[35] craft a plan to take advantage of this fear by convincing the citizens of Bikini Bottom to enter an escape pod. Unknown to the citizens, the escape pod is actually a device that will hypnotize them into liking the Chum Bucket.[36] SpongeBob won't buy it though and with the help of Patrick and Sandy the three decide to scale the volcano to stop it from erupting by using an Eruptor Interrupter.[37]

98 Screen-to-Stage Musicals

While original, this plot includes many hallmarks of the cartoon including some of the locations and the very silly conventions of the source material. The show also includes several moral lessons and comments on social issues much like the cartoon.

But how did SpongeBob make his way to Broadway? Of all the properties for children and families, SpongeBob seems like an odd choice. However, Nickelodeon made some very savvy decisions that allowed the production to succeed. Though the title seems like a bizarre choice for a live musical, the SpongeBob brand has a staying power unlike most other properties of its era. The cartoon had its first season in 1999 and unlike many of its late 1990s counterparts, it is still going strong. As of March 2022, the show has been renewed for a 14th season and has spawned several spin-offs,[38] while many other shows from the same era have run their course. SpongeBob is a staple in theme parks and SpongeBob merchandise and clothing are everywhere. In fact, as of 2019, the SpongeBob IP had brought in over 13 billion dollars worldwide.[39] Therefore, while a SpongeBob musical may have appeared to be an absurd choice, it actually made a lot of financial sense.

When first exploring the possibility of a SpongeBob musical, the cartoon's creator and animator, and former marine biologist, Stephen Hillenburg, was not a fan of the idea. He was afraid that a musical would focus too much on "spectacle and fluff, which went against everything that he felt SpongeBob represented."[40] But Nickelodeon had no intention of giving the title the theme park treatment like SpongeBob Live, the live-action show at the Nickelodeon Hotel in Orlando, which utilized actors in foam suits impersonating the characters from the cartoon. Instead, Hillenburg made it clear that he was only interested in giving his blessing to a musical if it captured the same "indie spirit" as the first few seasons of the cartoon for which he served as showrunner.[41] Nickelodeon listened and made the wise decision to hire a director who could do just that, Tina Landau.

Prior to *SpongeBob*, Landau helmed two productions on Broadway the 2001 revival of *Bells are Ringing*, and the 2009 Broadway outing of Tracy Letts's play *Superior Donuts*. Landau more often works Off-Broadway and at the Steppenwolf Theatre in Chicago where she is a company member. She is also known as one of the creators of Viewpoints, a movement-based actor training and composition technique that has become ubiquitous in the American Theatre. A large, commercial musical based on a cartoon was not something that Landau had considered, in fact, when first approached about working on *SpongeBob* she said no. In an interview with Victoria Myers at *The Interval*, Landau remembers, "I just couldn't imagine anything other than a big theme park show with giant mascot heads."[42] After her initial rejection of the project, Landau's agent, Patrick Herold, shared Hillenburg's demand that in order to happen with his blessing, the production would have to capture the "indie spirit"[43] of the original. Landau found freedom in that idea and started watching the cartoon. After diving into the world of the Bikini Bottom, Landau was intrigued. She explains, "It's so frigging surreal and wacky and full of non-sequiturs and upside down logic and it was instantly screaming, for me, to put it on stage—because it's the kind of thing that can't be put on stage. You look at it and you're like, 'Um, I would have no idea how to do that. I want to do that.'"[44] After exploring the cartoon, Landau said yes with the stipulation that it had to be done her way. In an interview with *Playbill's* Ryan McPhee, Landau informs, "I thought if I could pitch exactly the kind of show that I want to do and would be interested in seeing, why not give it a whirl?"[45]

Landau began the process of creating the production with a few ideas. First, the characters had to appear in human form, not in full foam costumes as they would at a theme park. Landau notes, "I think we go to the theatre to identify with and relate to and care about and cheer for folks or beings we identify with…if the cast was too concealed or too theatrical, it would put a barrier between us and the show."[46] Landau also wanted the production to be semi-immersive, she wanted audiences to enter the world of Bikini Bottom when they stepped into the theatre. She credits her childhood desire to be an oceanographer for the creation of the world which she wanted to feel "part underwater, part carnival, part party, part junkyard."[47] Finally, Landau determined that the world would be made of found objects, which to Landau "felt completely true to *SpongeBob*"[48] as in the cartoon, the entire world of Bikini Bottom is made from objects that fell to the ocean floor. Last, Landau wanted to enlist a "variety of pop and rock and hip-hop and country artists to each write a song for the show" in order to craft a score that captured the spirit of the cartoon.[49]

With the green light from Nickelodeon, Landau enlisted designer David Zinn to collaborate with her on the project and jumped into finding the vocabulary of Bikini Bottom on Broadway, both in movement and in design. The first year of development consisted of a series of workshops that aimed to discover how Bikini Bottom moved. Landau worked with a variety of actors who she brought in to discover the visual and physical setting. She would begin each workshop by telling the actors "we're going to make a lot of [stuff] and no one owns anything. It's all going into a giant pile in the middle of the room and we're going to pick out the best of the best."[50] This approach is in line with Landau's process as a director for any production. In a 2018 interview with *Playbill*'s Mervyn Rothstein, Landau explains her approach to working with actors. She notes:

> I will say, "Play. Explore." It goes back to that idea that I am there to respond to and sift through what comes up. I will also do work early on with Viewpoints training, which is a technique I use in rehearsal. It involves the actors working physically with their bodies, a whole bunch of exercises to have actors connect with not only what they're thinking or what they're analyzing in the text but also working from their bodies and their instincts.[51]

Landau's approach to creating theatre, which encourages actors to create through play, was perfectly suited to the creation of *SpongeBob* and was absolutely evident in the creative staging in the final piece.

The musical was also remarkable for its approach to gender as the show employed a non-binary sensibility throughout. Musical Theatre scholar Barrie Gelles explains, "SpongeBob redefines gender to be outside of the binary and is mutable and flexible from the beginning … And so [audiences are asked] to think about how multiple versions of gender, multiple permutations of gender, multiple expressions of gender can all exist all at once at the same time."[52] This flexibility was by design and a part of Landau's vision for the show. In her Ted Talk "Everything All at Once: A SpongeBobian Approach to Art and Life," Tina Landau explains, "I started conceiving of the music not as a musical, but as a rock concert, and a party, and a runway show, and an aquarium, and a carnival. And not just as one of these things in the

Screen-to-Stage Musicals **101**

space but all of them, all together, and all at once."[53] Gelles explains that this approach also connects to gender because "none of the characters are defined by their gender, including the ensemble, but who plays the character adds a layer of characterization and definition with their own personal gender."[54] The characters gender are all of these things, all together, all at once.

All aspects of the production from the design to the staging and choreography are flexible in their portrayal of gender. Of David Zinn's costumes, Gelles informs, "It's not just that there aren't rules about the costumes and that the costumes aren't gendered, but it's specifically a pushback and a deconstruction of gender rules in terms of costumes."[55] An example of this deconstruction is in the costuming of the ensemble in Squidword's showstopping number, "I'm Not A Loser," who Gelles refers to as "gender non-binary bedazzled, besequinned queer sea anemones."[56] The tap-dancing ocean dwellers are costumed in a way that quotes a traditional Broadway kickline number but the costumes are not gendered. All performers wear the same costume and that costume defies tradition. Gelles shares, "Where you typically say 'ah, these chorus of tap dancers will all be in unisex costumes,' what it really is is the 'male version' of a tuxedo when in this one it's not, it skews more to the 'femme version' of a tuxedo, à la a chorus line, and then puts it on all genders, on all bodies."[57] The production pays homage to many Broadway traditions in the number while simultaneously subverting the often strict gender conventions of musical theatre.

The production's playfulness extends to its expressions of gender and even in licensing encourages those who produce the show to engage in the same play. In a director's note in the beginning of the version of the script available for productions, Landau asks directors to think more broadly about casting:

> I would love to see a woman play SpongeBob or an Electric Skate, a trans actor play Patchy, etc. ... My dream would be that you mix it up and give some of the 10 "male" tracks to actors who are not cisgender men, and instead give these roles to cisgender women or actors who identify as transgender, genderqueer, or non binary ... The most important thing to consider in casting is diversity. After all, this is one of the main themes in the show.

102 Screen-to-Stage Musicals

> Find and celebrate diversity in body type, color, race, gender, age. That's what an ocean habitat looks like, that's how our world is, and that's the Bikini Bottom Way.[58]

Landau encourages potential directors to move past any preconceived notions of gender in the production and remember that in the ocean, gender really isn't a thing.

SpongeBob SquarePants was able to evoke the beloved characters of a beloved franchise through a new, playful vocabulary that was rooted in the theatre while also crafting a world in which gender is flexible and fluid in a way that Broadway had not previously seen. The production would go on to be nominated for twelve Tony Awards winning for its scenic design, and when it closed in September 2018, a national tour was launched that sent it all over the United States. The title was also made available for licensing for local productions and has since been seen all over the country in professional, community, and educational theatres.

The success of the musical can be attributed to Nickelodeon's decision to hire the right director and to let that director have creative control of the production. In hiring Landau, Nickelodeon took a play out of the Disney Theatrical Productions' playbook. For the 1997 smash-hit adaptation of *The Lion King*, Disney brought in theatre and opera director Julie Taymor and allowed her to create the musical her way, leading to critical acclaim and one of the longest runs in the history of Broadway. As of May 15, 2022, the production has played 9569 performances[59] and spawned resident productions and tours all over the globe. The success of *The Lion King* can be attributed to Taymor's vision and the fact that Disney executives got out of her way. The same is true for Nickelodeon and *SpongeBob*.

Newsies: The Musical

- **Opened: March 29, 2012**
- **Closed: August 24, 2014**
- **Performances: 1004**

Newsies was the sixth Disney film adapted for Broadway by Disney Theatrical Productions,[60] the theatrical producing arm of the Walt

Disney Corporation. The show is based on the 1992 film of the same name, which was a box office disaster. The film cost an estimated $15 million to make and only grossed $2.8 million.[61] However, despite its lack of success at the box office, the film amassed thousands of fans in the 1990s and early 2000s. In a 2011 interview with *DanceOn* the film and show's composer, Alan Menken, shares:

> We became aware over the years, ever since the movie just sort of crash-landed at the box office, that a whole generation had quietly adopted this as their own. And it was everybody's sort of secret pleasure. And, at a certain point, that secret pleasure began to surface and there were pirated production of the movie. And it became apparent that this was going to happen. And if we weren't going to write it, somebody was going to write it. And we should be the ones to do it.[62]

For many children who grew up in the late 1990s and early 2000s, *Newsies* was an important fixture in their childhood. In Former Disney Theatrical Productions Dramaturg and Literary Manager Kenneth Cerniglia's book *Newsies: Stories of the Unlikely Hit*, Noni White, the film's co-screenwriter reports, "Whenever Bob [Tzudiker] and I are asked to speak at colleges, people tell us that we wrote their favorite movie. The people that *Newsies* reached, it touched deeply."[63] Alan Menken has also shared that when he visited colleges in the early 2000s, the question he was most often asked was when *Newsies* would be adapted for the stage. Thomas Schumacher, President of Disney Theatrical Productions admits that *Newsies* was the title for which he most often received requests. Clearly, *Newsies* had fans and those fans wanted to see *Newsies* on stage. It was these fans, lovingly known as "fansies," who ultimately convinced DTP to go ahead and develop a live version of *Newsies*. There was a market for a stage version of the film and Disney wanted to capitalize on the demand. In an interview on *The Graham Show*, Schumacher remarked:

> We knew that the audience wanted *Newsies* to be performed because if you went to YouTube, if you went anywhere, to Facebook sites, people were endlessly performing numbers from

104 Screen-to-Stage Musicals

> the film *Newsies*. We began developing it for that audience, thinking, we'll develop *Newsies*, and then we'll make it available to every high school in America, and every college to go perform.[64]

Initially, the title was destined for licensing rather than a Broadway production. The plan was to create the show, test it with what Disney Theatricals refers to as a "pilot production," a production in partnership with a professional theatre company to test the quality and viability of the libretto,[65] and then release it so that every high school, college, and children's theatre company in the United States could produce the official version, rather than the unauthorized version they were already performing.[66] Disney partnered with the Papermill Playhouse in New Jersey to produce a professional-quality production. Disney Theatricals knew that the fansies would be excited to see it, but they wanted to see if it would resonate with more traditional theatre audiences who were represented in the subscriber base at the Papermill. Both the fansies and non-fansies responded positively to the production, so much so that Disney began to think about moving the production to Broadway.

There were two factors that more than any other led the production to Broadway rather than straight to licensing. First, the availability of the Nederlander Theatre at short notice, which is not often the case for Broadway houses. Second, during the production process Associate Producer and then Disney Vice President of Production Ann Quart had an idea about the set. Scenic designer Tobin Ost had designed a remarkable three-tower moving set that served the production perfectly but was over budget. Quart suggested that if they spent the extra money, they could construct the set so it could tour. Then, that money could be made back by renting it out to other professional companies who produced the show.[67] This decision meant that the entire set could be quickly disassembled, loaded out, loaded into another theatre, and reassembled. Therefore, when discussions began about a Broadway transfer, the logistics of moving the production were already handled and did not present a barrier to the move.

After a wildly successful run at the Papermill, Disney decided to go ahead and move the production to The Nederlander on Broadway. Initially, the plan was to do a limited, twelve-week run in order to launch a national tour. But as soon as tickets went on sale, they sold out. So, the run was extended another ten weeks, which also quickly sold out. At that point, Disney surmised they had a potential hit on their hands and decided to open up the run and see how far it could go.[68] The production ended up running for 1004 performances before closing in order to provide momentum for a national tour. It would not be until March 2018 that the rights were made available for high schools and colleges to perform the title.[69]

In addition to its unorthodox road to Broadway, *Newsies* is also significant for its innovative use of social media. As the fansies were Millennials, most of who were digital natives, once word got out that the stage production was happening, it began to appear on the Internet. Disney on Broadway's first YouTube video about *Newsies* had 135,000 views and by March 2012, the production had 100,000 fans on Facebook. David Schrader, Disney Theatrical's Executive Vice President and Managing Director remembers, "At one point, '*Newsies* Broadway' was trending on Yahoo. To be relevant at that level means that many people are suddenly talking about a stage show—a lot!"[70]

The team at Disney Theatricals had never sold a show like *Newsies* before and social media was becoming an increasingly popular way to reach fans, so the marketing campaign for *Newsies* utilized new strategies. As mentioned in Chapter 1, in 2011, just prior to the launch of *Newsies* at the Papermill, Disney Theatricals hired their first Social Media Coordinator who led a new approach to digital marketing that included cast-created content and sharable "bumpers," which were memes created from production photos that included quotes from the show.[71] This new approach to marketing a production on social media would have wide implications for Disney's marketing of its future productions as well as the marketing of other non-Disney Broadway productions to come.

In addition to the innovations that happened in digital marketing, another novel feature of *Newsies* was its reviews. Prior to its premiere in 2011, Disney properties on Broadway had been subject to a great deal of scrutiny and sometimes even unfair criticism. For example, *The Lion King*, which is arguably one of the greatest artistic successes to ever play on Broadway, received mixed reviews. *Newsies*, on the other hand, was widely praised and signaled a new era for the criticism of not only Disney musicals, but screen-to-stage musicals in general. The production was evaluated on its merits rather than its source material.

106 Screen-to-Stage Musicals

While there are certainly still critics who will immediately dismiss a production because of its connection to a well-known or well-loved film, in the latter part of the 20 seasons, critics began to evaluate screen-to-stage musicals more fairly. The positive critical response to 2012's *Newsies* is an indication of that shift.

Stage-to-Screen Musicals

In concert with the influx of Broadway musicals based on films in the twenty seasons, there was also a rise in film versions of stage musicals. These films included Hollywood films that premiered in movie theatres, professionally shot recordings of live productions for television and streaming platforms, and musicals performed live on television. Though film adaptations of stage musicals are not new, the practice fell out of fashion in the late 20th century but saw a resurgence during the 20 seasons. Interestingly, because of the proliferation of screen-to-stage musicals, there were even several properties that made the journey from screen to stage to screen, including *Hairspray* and *The Producers*.

The contemporary trend of turning stage musicals into film musicals started in 2002 with the film version of *Chicago*. The film starred several Hollywood heavyweights including Richard Gere and Renee Zellweger and received high praise from the critics. It was successful at the box office and was nominated for thirteen Academy Awards, winning six, including Best Picture.[72] The success of the *Chicago* film showed producers that there was a market for film adaptations of stage musicals when they were done well and the number of movie musicals based on Broadway began to rise. 2004 saw *Phantom of the Opera* adapted and in 2005 *The Producers* returned to the movie house in musical form. *Dreamgirls* premiered in 2006 and 2007 saw both *Hairspray* and *Sweeney Todd* hit the silver screen. All of these films were at least modestly successful and with the exception of *The Producers*, all of these films were nominated for multiple academy awards. The trend continued into the latter half of the 20 seasons with titles like *Into the Woods, Les Misérables*, and *Cats* which had varying degrees of artistic and box office success. At the time of this writing, more stage-to-screen transfers are in the works including the long-awaited film adaptation of the Broadway mainstay *Wicked*.

Another interesting development in this period was the return of the live musical to the small screen. Musicals featured prominently on TV in the 20 seasons in a way that had not been seen since the early days of television. While *Great Performances* and *Live from Lincoln Center* on PBS have continually broadcast pro shots of Broadway musicals (in addition to a variety of other performances) since the 1970s, offerings from other networks, though not entirely absent, were sparse. That began to change in the first decade of the 20 seasons, with about a dozen productions aired on a variety of networks.[73] One of the early examples in the period was MTV's broadcast of *Legally Blonde the Musical* in 2007 as the culmination of the reality series, *Legally Blonde: The Search for Elle Woods*, which turned the audition process for replacing Laura Bell Bundy as Elle on Broadway into a reality tv competition. The show's winner, Bailey Hanks, started her run as Elle Woods on Broadway on July 23, 2008, just two days after the conclusion of the television show. Hanks would stay in the role until the production closed only three months later. Therefore, the reality show likely did more for the national tour than the Broadway production. In addition to Hanks, one of the other contestants, Autumn Hurlburt, joined the company as Hanks's understudy and two of the other contestants, Lauren Zakrin and Rhiannon Hansen, were invited to join the national tour.[74] Elle Woods was not the first actor cast on Broadway by way of reality TV. A year earlier, *Grease: You're The One That I Want* on NBC cast Sandy and Danny for the 2007 Broadway revival of *Grease* leading to the Broadway debuts of Max Crumm and Laura Osnes. That show was modeled after a show produced by Andrew Lloyd Webber on the BBC in the UK a year earlier, *How Do You Solve a Problem Like Maria?*, which cast the lead for the West End revival of Rodgers and Hammerstein's *The Sound of Music*.

Though only a few productions received the reality tv treatment, there were many examples of pro shots of live Broadway musicals ending up on television and more commonly, on streaming platforms. This trend started slowly with productions like *Shrek* the musical in 2016 which was released on Amazon Prime, *Newsies* in 2017 on *Netflix* [75] and *SpongeBob SquarePants* on Nickelodeon in 2019. However, it accelerated during the pandemic in 2020 and 2021, with titles like *Hamilton* on Disney+, *Come from Away* on AppleTV+, and the much-maligned cult favorite *Diana: The Musical* on Netflix.

108 Screen-to-Stage Musicals

In addition to these professionally shot stage musicals, the major television networks also began to produce live television musicals during the 20 seasons. In her book *Broadway in the Box: Television's Lasting Love Affair with the Musical*, Kelly Kessler informs, "Between 2013 and 2019, NBC and Fox aired eight musicals: seen live … one combination of live and taped content … and one fully pre-filmed [musical]."[76] Though certainly driven by a rise in the popularity of musical theatre in mainstream culture, Kessler points out that these productions "decentered the theatrical," having more in common with their early TV counterparts than with live Broadway musicals.[77] Still, their very existence points to a re-emergence of musical theatre in popular American culture, particularly given the viewership for the productions. Kessler shares, "NBC landed respectable numbers, with *The Sound of Music Live!* Scoring 18.5 million viewers and a 4.6 Nielsen rating, and *Peter Pan Live!* 9.2 million viewers and a 2.4 rating."[78]

By the end of the 20 seasons, the Broadway musical was finding success on the small screen. From its release on Disney+ on July 3, 2020, to July 13, 2020, *Hamilton* was viewed by 2.7 million households.[79] Though this extraordinary number was likely due to the global COVID-19 pandemic, as much of the world was still in lockdown in July 2020, the number is still staggering. In ten days of streaming availability, more people saw *Hamilton* on Disney + than had ever seen the show live at any venue.[80] Only time will tell if Broadway will continue to inhabit the small screen.

Reading Questions

1. Why did screen-to-stage musicals become far more popular in the 20 seasons than they had been in the 20th century?
2. Why was there a backlash against screen-to-stage musicals from the "Broadway Establishment"? Do you agree with them? Why or why not?
3. What does the rise of stage-to-screen musicals say about the musical in the 20 seasons? What does it say about 21st-century popular culture?
4. How are each of the musicals case studied in the chapter good examples of the genre?

Notes

1 The first "talkie" or motion picture with sound was *The Jazz Singer* in 1927.
2 Curtis Russell, "Screen-To-Stage Musicals Database," last modified 2020, accessed June 8, 2021, www.documentabarbarism.com/academia-new.
3 "'Little Whopper' Welcome; New Play at the Casino a Good Farce, with Tuneful Music.," unsigned review of *The Little Whopper*, New York, NY, *The New York Times*, October 16, 1919, accessed June 8, 2021, www.nytimes.com/1919/10/16/archives/little-whopper-welcome-new-play-at-the-casino-a-good-farce-with.html.
4 Russell, "Screen-To-Stage Musicals."
5 Alexis Soloski, "'Hamilton' Was Just the Beginning. Hollywood Loves Broadway, Again.," *New York Times*, November 4, 2020, accessed June 15, 2022, www.nytimes.com/ 2020/11/04/movies/broadway-movie-adapta tions-prom.html?searchResultPosition=1
6 James Wolcott, "Pop Goes the Great White Way," *Vanity Fair*, July 1, 2011, accessed June 8, 2021, www.vanityfair.com/culture/2011/07/musica ls-201107.
7 Wolcott, "Pop Goes."
8 "Longest-Running Shows on Broadway," last modified March 9, 2020, accessed June 9, 2021, www.playbill.com/article/long-runs-on-broadwa y-com-109864.
9 At the time that *Anastasia* premiered on Broadway, 20th Century Fox had not yet been acquired by Disney, and as such, the stage production was not affiliated with Disney Theatrical Productions.
10 Ben Brantley, "Review: Chasing Shopworn Dreams in 'Pretty Woman: The Musical,'" review of *Pretty Woman: The Musical, The New York Times*, August 17, 2018, sec. C, [Page 8], accessed June 9, 2021, www.nytimes.com/2018/08/16/theater/review-pretty-woman-the-musical-broadway.html?rref=collection%2Fdu-guide-theater%2Ftheater-guide&action=click&contentCollection=undefined®ion=stream&module=stream_unit&version =latest-stories&contentPlacement=1&pgtype=collection.
11 Ben Brantley, "Review: 'Finding Neverland', a Broadway Musical With Matthew Morrison," review of *Finding Neverland, The New York Times*, April 16, 2015, sec. C, [Page 1], accessed June 9, 2021, www.nytimes.com/2015/04/16/theater/review-finding-neverland-a-broadway-musical-with-matthew-morrison.html.
12 Ken Davenport, "What's the Average Cost of Putting on a Broadway Show? (Updated 2018).," *The Producer's Perspective* (blog), entry posted June 7, 2012, accessed June 14, 2021, www.theproducersperspective.com/my_weblog/2012/06/whats-the-average-cost-of-putting-on-a-broadway-show.html.
13 Davenport, "What's the Average," *The Producer's Perspective* (blog).
14 "A Monetary Autopsy of Spider-Man: Turn Off the Dark," last modified November 24, 2013, accessed June 14, 2021, www.vulture.com/2013/11/spider-man-leaves-behind-broadways-biggest-bill.html.

110 Screen-to-Stage Musicals

15 *Spider-Man* had a notoriously long development and preview period in the theatre prior to opening. The production also opened, and then closed again for more development. Most productions only spend a few weeks in the theatre prior to their official opening.

16 "A Monetary."

17 Olivia Clement, "The Band's Visit Recoups on Broadway," last modified September 10, 2018, accessed June 14, 2021, www.playbill.com/article/the-bands-visit-recoups-on-broadway.

18 Tim Donahue and Jim Patterson, *Stage Money* (Columbia, SC: University of South Caroline Press, 2010), 31.

19 "Who's Going to the Theatre: Stats and Facts from Broadway," accessed June 14, 2021, www.theaterseatstore.com/blog/broadway-data.

20 David Savran, *A Queer Sort of Materialism: Recontextualizing American Theater* (Ann Arbor, MI: University of Michigan Press, 2003), 17.

21 Savran, *A Queer*, 17.

22 Sarah Cascone, "Here Are the 10 Most Expensive NFT Artworks, From Beeple's $69 Million Opus to an 18-Year-Old's $500,000 Vampire Queen," last modified March 23, 2021, accessed June 16, 2021, https://news.artnet.com/market/most-expensive-nfts-1952597.

23 Cascone, "Here Are the 10 Most," Artnet.

24 Hope Mutie, "What's with the Trend of Turning Old Tweets into NFTs?," CryptoVantage, last modified March 3, 2021, accessed June 16, 2021, www.cryptovantage.com/news/whats-with-the-trend-of-turning-old-tweets-into-nfts/.

25 Amy S. Osatinski, "Ghosts in the Machine: Digital Technology and Screen-to-Stage Musicals," in *iBroaadway: Musical Theatre in the Digital Age*, ed. Jessica Hillman-Mccord (Cham, Switzerland: Palgrave, 2017), 74.

26 Nicole Rosky, "Broadway by Design: Scott Pask, Finn Ross, Adam Young and Gregg Barnes Bring *Mean Girls* from Page to Stage," *Broadwayworld.com*, last modified June 2, 2018, accessed June 18, 2021, www.broadwayworld.com/article/Broadway-By-Design-Scott-Pask-Finn-Ross-Adam-Young-Gregg-Barnes-Bring-MEAN-GIRLS-from-Page-to-Stage-20180602.

27 Quoted in Rosky, "Broadway by Design," *Broadwayworld.com*.

28 *Morning Edition*, "'King Kong' on Broadway Is the 2,400-Pound Gorilla in the Room," hosted by Jeff Lunden, aired November 7, 2018, on NPR.

29 *Morning Edition*, "'King Kong.'"

30 Quoted in *Morning Edition*, "'King Kong.'"

31 Quoted in *Morning Edition*, "'King Kong.'"

32 *Morning Edition*, "'King Kong.'"

33 *Broadway: The American Musical*, directed by Michael Kantor, PBS, 2004.

34 Bikini Bottom is the name of the underwater town where SpongeBob and his friends reside in the cartoon and it's spinoffs.

35 Plankton and Karen are often the villains in episodes of the original cartoon and in several of the films.

Screen-to-Stage Musicals 111

36 The Chumbucket is the restaurant that belongs to Plankton and is a competitor of the restaurant, The Krusty Krab where SpongeBob works.

37 "How SpongeBob BROKE Broadway," video, YouTube, posted by Wait in the Wings, September 16, 2019, accessed May 19, 2022, www.youtube. com/watch?v=IuzcyO9xewQ.

38 Jeremy Dick, "SpongeBob SquarePants Renewed for Season 14 as Franchise Continues to Expand," *Movieweb*, last modified March 25, 2022, accessed May 19, 2022, https://movieweb.com/spongebob-squarepants-season-14-renewed/.

39 "How SpongeBob."

40 "How SpongeBob," video.

41 "How SpongeBob," video.

42 Tina Landau, "An Interview with Tina Landau," by Victoria Myers, *The Interval*, last modified January 30, 2018, accessed May 20, 2022, www. theintervalny.com/interviews/2018/01/an-interview-with-tina-landau/.

43 Landau, "An Interview," interview, *The Interval*.

44 Landau, "An Interview," interview, *The Interval*.

45 Tina Landau, "How Director Tina Landau Found the Broadway Musical in SpongeBob SquarePants," interview by Ryan McPhee, *Playbill.com*, last modified November 5, 2017, accessed May 20, 2022, www.playbill.com/article/how-director-tina-landau-found-the-broadway-musical-in-spongebob-squarepants.

46 Landau, "An Interview."

47 Landau, "An Interview," interview, *The Interval*.

48 Landau, "An Interview," interview, *The Interval*.

49 Landau, "An Interview," interview, *The Interval*.

50 Qtd. in "How SpongeBob."

51 Tina Landau, "Stage Directions: Tina Landau Gets Real about Being a Director Who Plays and Explores," interview by Mervyn Rothstein, *Playbill.com*, last modified July 5, 2018, accessed May 20, 2022, https://playbill. com/article/stage-directions-tina-landau-gets-real-about-being-a-director-who-plays-and-explores

52 Barrie Gelles, interview by the author, Virtual, June 13, 2022.

53 "Everything All at Once: A SpongeBobian Approach to Art and Life," video, 16:20, YouTube, posted by Tedx Talks, May 15, 2017, accessed December 8, 2022, https://youtu.be/R3HhaWWHEOE.

54 Gelles, interview by the author.

55 Gelles, interview by the author.

56 Gelles, interview by the author.

57 Gelles, interview by the author.

58 Qtd. in Kyle Jarrow, *The SpongeBob Musical* (n.p.: Concord Theatricals, n.d.).

59 Broadway League, "The Lion King," *Internet Broadway Database*, accessed May 20, 2022, www.ibdb.com/broadway-production/the-lion-king-4761.

60 This only includes film adaptations that were originally produced by Disney. There are other productions produced by Disney Theatrical Productions that came before *Newsies* that were not based on Disney films.

112 Screen-to-Stage Musicals

61 "Newsies (1992)," *Internet Movie Database*, accessed May 23, 2022, www.imdb.com/title/tt0104990/?ref_=fn_al_tt_1.

62 Qtd. in "Alan Menken Interview—Disney—Newsies the Musical," video, 01:55, YouTube, posted by DanceOn, October 14, 2011, accessed May 23, 2022, www.youtube.com/watch?v=1o-C2kAJeDo.

63 Qtd. in Ken Cerniglia, *Newsies: Stories of the Unlikely Broadway Hit* (New York: Disney-Hyperion, 2014), 27.

64 "The Graham Show Ep. 4, Finale: Thomas Schumacher, 'The Lion King, Newsies & Paying It Forward'," video, YouTube, posted by The Graham Show, November 23, 2012, accessed May 23, 2022, www.youtube.com/watch?v=7avMd7v0mL4&t=8s.

65 Amy Sara Osatinski, *Disney Theatrical Productions: Producing Broadway Musicals the Disney Way* (New York: Routledge, 2019), 138.

66 Osatinski, *Disney Theatrical*, 133.

67 Cerniglia, *Newsies: Stories*, 59.

68 Osatinski, *Disney Theatrical*, 144.

69 Sarah Jane Arnegger, "Disney's Newsies Now Available for Amateur Licensing," *Playbill.com*, last modified March 1, 2018, accessed May 23, 2022, https://playbill.com/article/disneys-newsies-now-available-for-amateur-licensing#:~:text=Disney's%20Newsies%20Now%20Available%20for%20Amateur%20Licensing%20%7C%20Playbill&text=Industry%20News%20Disney's%20Newsies%20Now,schools%20and%20community%20theatre%20groups.

70 Qtd. in Cerniglia, *Newsies: Stories*, 120.

71 Osatinski, *Disney Theatrical*, 150.

72 "Chicago Awards," Internet Movie Database, accessed May 24, 2022, www.imdb.com/title/tt0299658/awards/?ref_=tt_awd.

73 Kelly Kessler, *Broadway in the Box: Television's Lasting Love Affair with the Musical* (New York: Oxford University Press, 2020), 226

74 Broadway.com Staff, "Bailey Hanks Wins MTV Legally Blonde Search; Starts as Elle Woods on July 23," last modified July 21, 2008, accessed May 24, 2022, www.broadway.com/buzz/97534/bailey-hanks-wins-mtv-legally-blonde-search-starts-as-elle-woods-on-july-23/#:~:text=The%20Broadway%20Show-,Bailey%20Hanks%20Wins%20MTV%20Legally%20Blonde%20Search%3B%20Starts,Elle%20Woods%20on%20July%2023&text=Bailey%20Hanks%2C%20a%2020%20year,show's%20finale%20on%20July%202021.

75 When *Newsies Live* was first released it was available on Netflix. Once Disney + emerged, the title was moved to the new platform as it was a Disney property.

76 Kessler, *Broadway in the Box*, 230.

77 Kessler, *Broadway in the Box*, 231.

78 Kessler, *Broadway in the Box*, 245.

79 Daniel Frankel, "Disney Plus 'Hamilton' Viewership Exceeds Those Who've Seen It Live, Research Company Says," Next TV, last modified July 20, 2020, accessed May 25, 2022, www.nexttv.com/news/disney-plus-hamilton-

viewership-exceeds-those-whove-seen-it-live-research-company-says#:~:text
=YouTube%20Ad%20Sales-,Disney%20Plus%20'Hamilton'%20Viewership%2
0Exceeds%20Those%20Who've%20Seen,It%20Live%2C%20Research%20Co
mpany%20Says&text=Around%202.7%20million%20households%20streamed,
analytics%20company%20Samba%20TV%20said.

80 Frankel, "Disney Plus."

5

OTHER ORIGINAL MUSICALS

TABLE 5.1 Other original musicals in 20 seasons

Show Title	Season	Run	Category(ies)	Sub-category
Jane Eyre	2000–2001	209	Other original	Book
Seussical	2000–2001	198	Other original	Book
The Adventures of Tom Sawyer	2000–2001	21	Other original	Book
By Jeeves	2001–2002	73	Other original	Book
Thou Shalt Not	2001–2002	85	Other original	Book
Urinetown	2001–2002	965	Other original	Invention
A Year with Frog and Toad	2002–2003	73	Other original	Book
Amour	2002–2003	17	Other original	Book
Assassins	2003–2004	101	Other original	Historical event
Avenue Q	2003–2004	2534	Other original	Invention

DOI: 10.4324/9781003139171-6

Other Original Musicals 115

Show Title	Season	Run	Category(ies)	Sub-category
Bombay Dreams	2003–2004	284	Other original	Invention
Caroline, or Change	2003–2004	136	Other original	Invention
Wicked	2003–2004	7098★	Other original	Book
Brooklyn	2004–2005	284	Other original	Invention
Dracula, The Musical	2004–2005	157	Other original	Book
Little Women	2004–2005	137	Other original	Book
The 25th Annual Putnum County Spelling Bee	2004–2005	1136	Other original	Invention
The Frogs	2004–2005	92	Other original	Play
The Light In the Piazza	2004–2005	504	Other original	Book
In My Life	2005–2006	61	Other original	Invention
Lestat	2005–2006	39	Other original	Book
The Drowsy Chaperone	2005–2006	674	Other original	Invention
The Woman in White	2005–2006	109	Other original	Book
Curtains	2006–2007	511	Other original	Invention
Dr. Seuss How the Grinch Stole Christmas	2006–2007	107	Other original	Book
Martin Short: Fame Becomes Me	2006–2007	165	Other original	Invention
Spring Awakening	2006–2007	859	Other original	Play
The Pirate Queen	2006–2007	85	Other original	Book
Glory Days	2007–2008	1	Other original	Invention
In the Heights	2007–2008	1184	Other original	Invention

116 Other Original Musicals

Show Title	Season	Run	Category(ies)	Sub-category
Passing Strange	2007–2008	165	Other original	Invention
13	2008–2009	105	Other original	Invention
[Title of Show]	2008–2009	102	Other original	Invention
A Tale of Two Cities	2008–2009	60	Other original	Book
Next To Normal	2008–2009	733	Other original	Invention
The Story of My Life	2008–2009	5	Other original	Invention
All About Me	2009–2010	20	Other original	Invention
Memphis	2009–2010	1165	Other original	Historical event
The Addams Family	2009–2010	94	Other original	Invention
Bloody Bloody Andrew Jackson	2009–2010	94	Other original	Invention
The Book of Mormon	2010–2011	3959★	Other original	Invention
The People in the Picture	2010–2011	60	Other original	Historical event
The Scottsboro Boys	2010–2011	49	Other original	Historical event
Wonderland	2010–2011	33	Other original	Book
Bonnie and Clyde	2011–2012	36	Other original	Historical event
Lysistrata Jones	2011–2012	30	Other original	Play
Spiderman: Turn Off the Dark	2011–2012	1066	Other original	Comic book/strip
Chaplin	2012–2013	135	Other original	Historical event
Matilda the Musical	2012–2013	1554	Other original	Book
A Gentleman's Guide to Love and Murder	2013–2014	905	Other original	Book

Other Original Musicals 117

Show Title	Season	Run	Category(ies)	Sub-category
First Date	2013–2014	174	Other original	Invention
Hedwig and the Angry Inch	2013–2014	507	Other original	Invention
If/Then	2013–2014	401	Other original	Invention
Violet	2013–2014	128	Other original	Book
Fun Home	2014–2015	583	Other original	Comic book/strip
It Shoulda Been You	2014–2015	135	Other original	Invention
Something Rotten	2014–2015	708	Other original	Invention
The Last Ship	2014–2015	105	Other original	Invention
The Visit	2014–2015	61	Other original	Play
Allegiance	2015–2016	111	Other original	Historical event
Amazing Grace	2015–2016	116	Other original	Historical event
Bright Star	2015–2016	109	Other original	Invention
Dames at Sea	2015–2016	85	Other original	Invention
Hamilton	2015–2016	2174★	Other original	Historical event
Shuffle Along, or the Making of the Musical Sensation of 1921 and All That Followed	2015–2016	100	Other original /revival	Play
Tuck Everlasting	2015–2016	39	Other original	Book
Bandstand	2016–2017	39	Other original	Invention
Come From Away	2016–2017	1251★	Other original	Historical event
Dear Evan Hansen	2016–2017	1522★	Other original	Invention

118 Other Original Musicals

Show Title	Season	Run	Category(ies)	Sub-category
In Transit	2016–2017	145	Other original	Invention
Natasha, Pierre, and the Great Comet of 1812	2016–2017	336	Other original	Book
War Paint	2016–2017	236	Other original	Historical event
Be More Chill	2018–2019	177	Other original	Book
Getting the Band Back Together	2018–2019	40	Other original	Invention
Hadestown	2018–2019	644★	Other original	Myth
The Prom	2018–2019	309	Other original	Invention
The Lightning Thief: The Percy Jackson Musical	2019–2020	95	Other original	Book

★The totals for these musicals, which were running at the time of this writing, represent the show total through May 8, 2022.

Source Material

During the 20 seasons, there were 77 musicals that opened on Broadway that fall into the "other original musicals" category. Musicals in this category are original, in that they have never before played on Broadway,[1] and they do not fit into the screen-to-stage or jukebox categories. This category is fascinating as the source material for these productions varies widely. Though there is a great deal of variety, these musicals can be broken down into several categories based on their source material: book, play, comic book/strip, myth, historical event (or person), and those that were newly invented (no source material). The numbers break down as follows: 24 were based on a book, five on a play, three on a comic book/strip, one on a myth, 11 on a historical event or person, and 33 were newly invented.

During the 20 seasons, the musicals in the other original category were often viewed more favorably than screen-to-stage or jukebox musicals as they were seen as authentically original whereas musicals with existing music or those based on films were seen as less original.

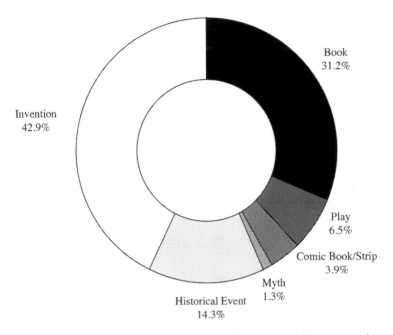

FIGURE 5.1 Percentage of musical in the "other original" category by source material

The argument that a jukebox musical is not original because it does not have an original score does hold some weight and if this book were using different criteria to determine what is original and not original, then jukebox musicals might be categorized differently. However, screen-to-stage musicals (with original scores) are original by all criteria if they have never played on Broadway. This leads to the question, what makes a musical based on a book, play, etc. more original than a musical based on a film? This author has found no valid answer to this question, which again points to the bias against screen-to-stage musicals.

Just as with screen-to-stage musicals, as long as there have been musicals there have been musical adaptations of existing books and plays and musical dramatizations of historical events and important historical figures. In fact, *The Black Crook* (1866), which many scholars

120 Other Original Musicals

point to as the first musical, was based on existing material including Goethe's *Faust* and Weber's *Der Freischütz* among others.[2] Clearly, the source for "original" musicals has varied widely and a musical can be original even if it is an adaptation.

This category also contains many contradictions. It houses both the longest-running musical to open in the 20 seasons, 2005's *Wicked*, which as of May 8, 2022, had run for 7098 performances, and the shortest running, 2008's *Glory Days*, which closed on opening night. Even within its subcategories, there are wildly different musicals. Take for example the Comic book/strip category which houses both *Spiderman: Turn Off the Dark*, a $75 million behemoth of a musical based on one of the most recognizable characters in the world, and *Fun Home* an intimate adaptation of a graphic novel that shares a queer coming of age story. *Fun Home* only cost $5.25 million to mount on Broadway.[3]

Musicals Based on a Book

Books have always been popular source material for musicals. In fact, the longest-running musical in the history of Broadway, which is still running at the time of this writing, is based on a novel. *The Phantom of the Opera*, Andrew Lloyd Webber's 1990 smash hit is based on a novel of the same name from the early 20th century. The same goes for many canonical musicals including *Les Misérables* and *Cabaret*. In the 20 seasons, many familiar literary titles came to the stage. Some of these include *Matilda* (2013), which is based on Roald Dahl's children's classic, and *A Gentleman's Guide to Love and Murder* (2013), which is based on *Israel Rank*, a 1907 novel by Roy Horniman.[4] The longest-running musical to open in the 20 seasons was also based on a book. 2003's *Wicked* is based on Gregory Maguire's 1995 novel of the same name. The novel is a revisionist version of *The Wonderful Wizard of Oz*, L. Frank Baum's 1900 novel that has become a staple of popular culture and spawned many adaptations across multiple mediums including the 1939 film *The Wizard of Oz* and several musical adaptations. Maguire's novel is part of a series of books that revisit the beloved land of Oz through a more contemporary and political lens.

The books chosen for adaptation are often popular or canonical titles. The 20 seasons saw adaptations of Tolstoy's *War and Peace* and

Other Original Musicals **121**

Dickens's *A Tale of Two Cities* as well as two Dr. Seuss-inspired musicals: *Seussical*, which was primarily based on the story *Horton Hears a Who,* and *Dr. Seuss's How the Grinch Stole Christmas*, based on the story of the same name. There were also musicals based on Mark Twain's *The Adventures of Tom Sawyer* and Lewis Caroll's *Alice in Wonderland*, another title that has seen multiple adaptations across many mediums. Young adult novels proved to be popular fodder for musicals in this period with Natalie Babbitt's 1975 novel *Tuck Everlasting* receiving the song and dance treatment in 2016 and 2018 saw *Be More Chill*, based on Ned Vizzini's 2004 book of the same name, unexpectedly land on Broadway because of the viral popularity of its original cast recording on Spotify. Despite the popularity of many of the books adapted, musicals based on popular books did not receive the same backlash as musicals based on popular films. These musicals were judged on their own merits rather than on their source material.

The least successful of these shows was 2002's *Amour*, which was based on *Le Passe-Muraille* a 1941 short story by French writer Marce Aymé. The musical was originally a hit in France and then was translated by Jeremy Sans and directed on Broadway by James Lapine. However, it was not as well received in New York as it was in Paris. The *New York Times*'s Ben Brantley begins his review by stating "Even charming is too weighty a word to describe the [musical's] wispy appeal …" He continues, "Americans for who French means crimes passionels and sinfully rich desserts may be disappointed by the production's exceedingly mild taste."[5] In fact, Brantley was so bored by the production that the title of his review includes the word milquetoast. Audiences agreed with Brantley's assessment and the production closed after a short run of 17 performances.

In contrast, the most successful musical based on a book in this period, *Wicked*, is still running and as of May 8, 2022, is the fifth longest-running musical in the history of Broadway.[6] Though the production has endured and is wildly popular with audiences, originally, the reviews were mixed. The critics at *Time Out New York* and *USA Today* both rated the show highly, Elysa Gardener of *USA Today* even mentioned that it was "the most complete, and completely satisfying, new musical [she's] come across in a long time."[7] But most other critics including Ben Brantley of the *New York Times*, Roma Torre

122 Other Original Musicals

from *NY1*, and Charles Isherwood of *Variety* dismissed it. Isherwood called the show "earnest one minute, self-mocking the next; a fantastical allegory about the perils of fascism in one scene, a Nickelodeon special about the importance of inner beauty in another."[8]

Gardener's assessment, however, was more in line with audiences and Tony nominators as *Wicked* has proven to be one of the most successful musicals ever on Broadway. The production was nominated for ten Tony Awards, including Best Musical, winning three: Best Actress for Idina Menzel, Best Scenic Design for Eugene Lee, and Best Costume Design for Susan Hilferty.[9] *Wicked* has run for twenty years and over seven thousand performances and at the time of this writing, production is underway for a stage to screen adaptation starring Ariana Grande as Galinda and Cynthia Erivo as Elphaba.[10]

In total, 24 musicals based on books opened on Broadway during the 20 seasons, accounting for 31% of the musicals in the "Other Original" category.

Musicals Based on a Comic Book/Strip

This category houses a relatively small number of musicals in the 20 seasons, but it is also one of the most diverse categories as the three shows contained in it are wildly different. Those three shows are *The Addams Family* (2010), *Spiderman: Turn Off the Dark* (2011), and *Fun Home* (2015). All three of these musicals are based on material or characters that first appeared in a comic book, graphic novel, or comic strip.

Though there have been many iterations of *The Addams Family* since the premiere of the television series in the 1960s, the musical is based on the original single-panel comic rather than any of those adaptations.[11] The first comic, drawn by Charles "Chas" Addams, appeared in *The New Yorker* in 1938. The Broadway iteration takes Addams's iconic characters and imagines what would happen if Wednesday, the daughter, fell in love and brought her fiancé and his seemingly "normal" family home to the Addams house for dinner. As one can imagine, hilarity and hijinks ensue and the moral of the musical is that no family is actually "normal."

The production was skewered in the press but still ran for almost two years, likely due to its name recognition and the fact that it starred

Nathan Lane and Bebe Neuwirth, two recognizable stars. However, when the production closed, something interesting happened. Rather than immediately releasing the Broadway version of the production for licensing, the book was reworked prior to it being made available for professional and amateur productions. That decision paid off and in 2020, Steve Spiegel, the president, and CEO of Theatrical Rights Worldwide, the company that licenses productions of the musical, noted "it's our best seller by volume of production … In the last five years [it] was the No. 1-produced high school show four of those years, and the other year it was No. 2."[12] Though the show was less successful in its initial outing on Broadway, it followed a path that became more common in the 20 seasons, it became a hit in regional, community, and educational productions.

The same cannot be said of the second production in this category, *Spiderman: Turn Off the Dark*, which is based on the Marvel comic *The Amazing Spiderman*, which debuted in 1963. The character has gone on to become a staple of popular culture with appearances in multiple movies and comics and all over the clothing and accessories of several generations of children and teens. The musical holds the record for both the money spent to mount it, $75 million, and the amount lost when it closed after over 1000 performances, $60 million. This loss is more remarkable because the production took in over $200 million in ticket sales and when it closed, was the 16th highest-grossing Broadway production of all time.[13] The scale and expense of the production (and possibly the legal battle surrounding the ousting of the show's original director) made it difficult to adapt for licensing and at the time of this writing, the production has not been made available. However, when it closed in 2014, the producers announced that it would be moving to Las Vegas for a resident production.[14] As of the time of this writing, no Las Vegas production has materialized and no further information about a Vegas residency has been released. Producers also toyed with the idea of an area tour, but that too has not come to fruition. *Spiderman: Turn Off the Dark* will be discussed in more detail in a case study later in this chapter.

The last of the musicals in this category is perhaps the polar opposite of the first two. Based on Alison Bechdel's autobiographical graphic novel of the same name, *Fun Home*, chronicles the coming of age of a

124 Other Original Musicals

young queer woman in her family's funeral home, which she and her siblings refer to as the "fun home." Though the musical played for the fewest number of performances in the category, 583 to *Addams Family*'s 722 and *Spiderman*'s 1066, it was also the cheapest and the only one to recoup its investment, which it did within eight months.

Fun Home is intimate and dramatic while not without its lighter moments. Its characters are real people rather than cartoons and though all three shows were nominated for multiple Tony Awards, *Fun Home* was the only one to be nominated for Best Musical, Book, or Score, all of which it won, making Kron and Tesori the first all-female writing team to win the award for best score. *Fun Home*, while certainly contemporary in its subject matter, feels more like a traditional mid-20th-century musical in its storytelling and production and did not rely on well-known source material or stars with name recognition to find success. Though the smallest production and the shortest run, *Fun Home* was the most critically and financially successful of the three productions and has also gone on to have a presence in professional and community theatre productions around the country.

Musicals Based on a Play

As long as there have been musicals, there have been musicals based on plays. Taking a non-musical play and turning it into a musical one is a time-honored practice of the American theatre. Some of the best-known and best-loved musicals came to life this way including the Golden Age classic, *Oklahoma!*, which is based on Lynn Riggs's 1930 play *Green Grow the Lilacs*. Another popular musical from the Golden Age, *Hello Dolly*, was based on Thornton Wilder's play *The Matchmaker*. Despite the long-standing tradition, more recently, fewer Broadway musicals have utilized plays as their source material. In fact, in the 20 seasons, only five musicals based on plays premiered on Broadway. But of those five, one was a huge hit and has become a popular choice for revival and licensing around the United States: 2006's *Spring Awakening*.

Spring Awakening is based on Frank Wedekind's 1891 play of the same name. Both the play and the musical follow a group of teenagers as they come of age at the turn of the 20th century in Victorian society. The play documents the mental and physical damage that the

Other Original Musicals **125**

time's strict morals cause to young people, including the death of two of the characters, one by suicide and the other by a botched back-alley abortion. Though set in the 1890s, the musical's themes resonated in the 21st century and the show saw two Broadway productions (the original and an innovative 2015 revival from Deaf West Theatre). It is not only the themes that allowed the production to capture the attention of 21st-century audiences, it was also the music as the production utilizes rock music to open a window into the minds of the 19th-century teen protagonists. Composed by Duncan Shiek, a one-hit-wonder pop star from the 1990s, with book and lyrics by Stephen Sater, the show was nominated for 11 Tony Awards, winning eight, including Best Musical, Book, and Score.

Musicals Based on a Myth

Though there were several musicals mounted on Broadway during the 20 seasons that were in some way inspired by Greek or Roman mythology,[15] only one, 2019's *Hadestown*, was a direct adaptation of a Greek/Roman myth. Broadway musicals directly based on mythology have been few and far between and many of them were adaptations of other works that were based on those myths rather than direct adaptations of the myth.

Hadestown is an adaptation of two myths, Orpheus and Eurydice and Hades and Persephone. The musical utilizes New Orleans-style jazz to comment on love and climate change, making it timely to the late twenty-teens. Created by folk singer/songwriter Anïas Mitchell and director Rachel Chavkin, the production opened in April 2019 and won eight Tony Awards, including Best Musical, and the Grammy Award for Best Musical Theatre Album. The production also made headlines because of its creative team. Anïas Mitchell is only the fourth woman to ever write the book, music, and lyrics for a Broadway musical[16] and *Hadestown* is one of the rare musicals to be both written and directed by women. In fact, *Hadestown* is only the second musical in Broadway history to win the Tony Award for Best Score with an all-female composing team. The first was in 2015 with Janine Tesori and Lisa Kron's historic win for *Fun Home*. In all, only seven musicals written entirely by women have ever played on Broadway, and five of

126 Other Original Musicals

them opened in the latter half of the 20 seasons.[17] Clearly, as illuminated in the first chapter of this book, Broadway has a problem with the representation of women on its creative teams. Musicals like *Hadestown* prove that women can create excellent work when given the opportunity.

Musicals Based on a Historical Event or Person

Musicals based on real people and events are another common feature of Broadway history. From dramatizations of the founding fathers to portraits of those who tried to assassinate US presidents. From musicals about the personal experiences of historical figures to musicals about some of the most impactful events in history, turning to the past for source material has been a popular choice for musical theatre creators. It was no different during the 20 seasons. In this period there were 11 musicals that opened on Broadway that were based on historical events or people. The subject matter of these musicals encompasses some of the most devastating events in recent history including *Come From Away* (2017) which dramatizes events related to 9/11, *The People in the Picture* (2011) which discusses The Holocaust, and *Allegiance* (2015) which dramatizes the imprisonment of Japanese Americans in incarceration camps[18] during WWII. This category also includes the most visible musical of the 20 seasons, 2015's *Hamilton*, which is about Alexander Hamilton, one of the founding fathers.

Stephen Sondheim's *Assassins*, a musical that played on Broadway twice during the 20 seasons and originally premiered Off-Broadway in 1990, is also in this category. The show has been in rotation at regional and professional theatres since the early 1990s but did not have a production on Broadway until 2004.[19] As any musical that has never had a production on Broadway is considered original by the criteria used for this book, *Assassins* is considered an original musical. The 2004 production doubled down on the history utilizing the film of the JFK assassination captured by Abraham Zapruder with his home-movie camera, presenting actual images of history alongside a musical interpretation of that history. In the musical, the Zapruder film was projected onto Lee Harvey Oswald's white T-shirt when the assassination is dramatized in the show.

Other Original Musicals **127**

This category also includes both *Memphis*, about Memphis Tennessee disc jockey Dewey Phillips, who was one of the first white DJs to play Black music in the 1950s, and *The Scottsboro Boys*, the musical discussed in the introduction that told the story of the nine Black teenagers who were falsely convicted of raping two white women in Alabama in the 1930s. Both musicals raised questions about authorship and who gets to tell what story. As previously mentioned, *The Scottsboro Boys* had an all-white creative team and utilized the framework of a minstrel show to tell its story, leading to protests outside the theatre and a justified backlash. *Memphis* elicited critique for the ways in which it centered whiteness and a "white savior" as its main character while trying to tell a story about Black characters and Black music. *Memphis* also had a mostly white creative team and no Black artists in top positions on the writing/directing teams. These two musicals, among others in this period, raise questions about the way that history is depicted on stage. Questions of authorship and who gets to tell what story as well as conversations about access and gatekeeping became more and more common toward the end of the 20 seasons. As the statistics presented in the introduction to this book show, Broadway has a long way to go when it comes to representation and one can only hope that the conversations that began at the end of the 20 seasons will continue and Broadway will see fewer productions like *Memphis* and *The Scottsboro Boys* in which white artists exploit Black history.

Musical Inventions

It could be argued that this category is the only category in which the musicals are entirely original as titles in this category have no formal source material. Though many are inspired by other things, including all the above types of source material, the musicals in this category do not move past inspiration to adaptation. Additionally, some of these musicals are new inventions that sprang forth from their creators' imaginations. As there is no unifying factor for these shows other than their spontaneous invention, they vary widely.

This category contains some of the biggest hits of the 20 seasons and some of the period's biggest flops. The latter column includes the only musical to close on opening night in the 20 seasons, 2008's *Glory Days*.

128 Other Original Musicals

Prior to 2008, a Broadway musical had not closed on opening night since 1985. *Glory Days* tells the story of four high school friends who reunite a year after they graduate to reconnect but discover just how much they have changed. The production had a successful run in Washington D.C. and received mostly favorable reviews, but not without criticism. The show's small cast of four and small orchestra made it an inexpensive (by Broadway standards) venture and Broadway's smallest and most intimate theatre, Circle in the Square, happened to be available. So, Eric Schaeffer the co-founder and artistic director of the Signature Theatre, a theatre known for excellent musicals, backed a Broadway production. The show's creators, Nick Blaemire and James Gardiner were young and new to the world of commercial musical theatre and jumped at the chance even though the show was not yet ready for a Broadway outing.[20] The team was also not given enough time to adjust and rehearse the production between the D.C. iteration and the Broadway opening. In his book *Flop Musicals of the 21st Century*, Stephen Purdy notes, "Two months is hardly enough time … to properly take the show back to the typewriter and workshop rooms to implement changes, the precise kinds of revisions that critics of the show in Washington had stated were needed."[21] The combination of inexperience and not enough time led to a musical that was half-baked. Add in an underwhelming marketing campaign and it was a recipe for disaster. By the time opening night arrived, ticket sales were dismal. In fact, there were so few tickets sold that producers had to "paper the house," or give away tickets to fill the seats, hoping for positive word of mouth. Once the opening night reviews dropped and they were not positive, producers knew that running the show was a losing proposition and it was immediately shuttered.[22]

In addition to *Glory Days*, this category holds several other short-running musicals including 2009's *The Story of My Life*, which ran for five performances, 2010s *All About Me*, which ran for 20, and 2018's *Getting the Band Back Together,* which closed after 40 performances. These short runs point to the risk associated with producing unknown material. While all Broadway openings are risky, betting on a title that has no name recognition is especially risky. If tourists are only going to pick one show, you want it to be yours. Apart from *All About Me*, which featured Dame Edna Everage, a television personality and the

Other Original Musicals **129**

alter ego of Australian actor Barry Humphries, none of the productions had name recognition or big stars. One can see why producers are often hesitant to back unknown properties on Broadway when even the smallest show, *Glory Days*, cost \$2.5 million to mount on Broadway, likely losing it all when it closed.[23]

On the other end of this category is the 4th longest-running musical of the 20 seasons, *The Book of Mormon*. The production opened in 2011 and is still running at the time of this writing. As of May 8, 2022, it had performed 3959 times and launched several national tours. The show is named after the religious text of the Church of Jesus Christ of Latter-day Saints but is not affiliated with (or sanctioned by) the church. Rather it is the creation of Trey Parker and Matt Stone, who are best known for creating the adult cartoon *South Park* which premiered on Comedy Central in 1997 and became a cultural juggernaut. At the time of this writing, *South Park* is in its 25th season with no sign of slowing down. The musical *The Book of Mormon* tells the story of two Mormon missionaries, one bright young man, Elder Price, and one hapless fool, Elder Cunningham. A classic shlemiel and schlimazel setup. The pair are sent to Uganda where they encounter resistance from the people and a scheming warlord, and it is Cunningham who is finally able to convert the locals by recognizing that bending the doctrine to the people is the only way to win. He creates an entirely new book, *The Book of Arnold (Cunningham)*, and a new religion in the process.

Parker and Stone partnered with Composer Robert Lopez, who at the time was best known for his Tony Award-winning work on *Avenue Q*. The team created a show that was raunchy and irreverent but also had a heart and paid dutiful homage to the form of the American musical, and it worked. This is evidenced in the *New York Times* review from the notoriously fickle Ben Brantley. After comparing the musical to those of Rodgers and Hammerstein, calling it "a newborn, old-fashioned, pleasure-giving musical," he infers that the show itself is a religious experience.[24] He muses:

> all the forms of mythology and ritual that allow us to walk through the shadows of daily life and death are, on some level, absurd; that's what makes them so valiant and glorious. And by the way,

130 Other Original Musicals

that includes the religion of the musical, which lends ecstatic shape and symmetry to a world that often feels overwhelmingly formless.[25]

Brantley was not the only critic enamored with the production, the reviews were overwhelmingly positive. And combined with the celebrity of the show's creators and its success at the Tony Awards, the production took off and didn't stop until the 2020 shutdown.

However, despite the success of the production, it was not without issues. The reaction from the Mormon Church was mixed. When the show opened, the Church released the following statement, "The production may attempt to entertain audiences for an evening, but the Book of Mormon as a volume of scripture will change people's lives forever by bringing them closer to Christ."[26] The LDS Church also launched an ad campaign that read "You've seen the play … now read the book," which appeared in the *New York Times* and in show programs around the country as the production toured. On the other hand, the production was not without its detractors in the Church, and many Mormons spoke out against it in response.

In addition to the Church's response, the production also has a problem with racism. In the wake of the 2020 Black Lives Matter uprising, twenty current cast members from the production wrote a letter to the show's creators asking them to make changes to the production. They explained that the United States was in the midst of a reckoning about "the systemic racism and racial inequality" that exists in all facets of society and that the theatre industry was no exception.[27] After the letter was sent, Stephi Wild of *Broadwayworld.com* reported that, "the group of creatives consulted producers Anne Garefino, Scott Rudin, and Sonia Friedman, and [decided] to invite principal actors from productions around the world to attend a workshop. During the reading, they will read through the show line-by-line and sort out any problematic parts."[28] The production is one of many where Black stories are being told without Black representation on the creative team. Prior to reopening in 2021, Michael Paulson of the *New York Times* reported that the creators "wound up making a series of alterations that elevate the main Black female character and clarify the satire."[29] *The Book of Mormon* is one of several musicals that retooled

Other Original Musicals **131**

their narrative based on feedback from BIPOC cast and creatives during the shutdown.

Case Studies

Spider-Man: Turn Off the Dark

- **Opened: June 14, 2011**
- **Closed: January 4, 2014**
- **Performances: 1066**

By the time *Spider-Man: Turn Off the Dark* closed in January 2014, it had broken many records. Yes, it cost more than any other Broadway production ever mounted, $75 million, but it also reached a million audience members faster than any other production in Broadway history.[30] According to Glen Berger, the co-book writer of the musical, *Spider-Man* also "shattered the record for the highest single-week gross of any show in Broadway history, taking in over $2,900,000."[31] The musical also holds the record for the highest number of previews at 182.[32] In fact, the number of *Spider-Man* previews is higher than the number of performances for 133 of the musicals that opened in the 20 seasons, that's almost half of all musicals original and revival combined. The production was the 27th longest-running musical in the 20 seasons having played 1066 performances.[33] Additionally, Berger observes:

> Since 1857, thousands of shows have opened on Broadway, yet only ninety-seven have had a longer run than *Spider-Man: Turn Off the Dark*. And if you include the show's unprecedented number of previews in the tally, *Turn Off the Dark*'s 1,268[34] total performances vaults the show to 74th place, racking up more performances than the original productions of *Guys and Dolls, Annie Get Your Gun*, or *Kiss Me Kate*.[35]

It was no matter that the production grossed almost $250 million dollars or that over two million people bought tickets, it still lost $60 million when it closed, making it the "biggest flop in the history of Broadway."[36]

132 Other Original Musicals

But why did the production fail? One might conjecture the obvious, a *Spider-Man* musical was just a bad idea. However, despite all its troubles, the production was running at a profit for a good portion of its 2.5-year run. Though no one can say for sure, there are several factors that may have contributed to the demise of the production. The first, and perhaps the most obvious, is the mismanagement of the production's finances. While this may not have been the main reason for the musical's artistic failure, it certainly contributed to the show's exorbitant price tag. The production was ambitious from the beginning, not only because it would be a large-cast spectacle, but also because it would contain never-before-seen on Broadway technology and high-flying stunts. Much of the technology used in the production was new to the stage. In the theatre, new often equals expensive as more time is needed to make it work.

On May 2, 2007, in the first article written about the production, Michael Riedel reported in the *New York Post* that "the show, which is getting a staged reading this summer, could cost almost $30 million to bring to Broadway."[37] In *Song of Spider-Man*, Berger shares that in response to the article, producer David Garfinkle estimated that the production would cost "more like twenty-three … twenty-four [million]."[38] Throughout the early days of the process as the price tag was rising daily. Garfinkle told the team, "if there is one thing we don't have to worry about, it's money."[39] However, Marvel, who owns the *Spider-Man* IP and had granted the producers the rights to create the musical, asked the team for big changes partway through the development process, changes that would cost money and Marvel was not contributing to the production financially. Additionally, despite Director Julie Taymor's desire for the show not to be on Broadway, she envisioned a stadium/circus spectacle that would have perhaps better suited the material, the Hilton Theatre, one of the only Broadway houses big enough for the behemoth production, became available. Millions of dollars were needed to renovate the theatre to meet the technical and storytelling needs of the show. Berger shares, "The renovations weren't merely intended to accommodate the aerial stunts. From installing a new proscenium to altering the angle and arrangement of every row of seats, a sincere attempt had been underway to address some of the long-standing complaints about the barn-like auditorium."[40]

The producers also began the renovation before raising all the money necessary to cover the show's capitalization, which at that point was $37.5 million. Though Marvel owns *Spider-Man* and had given their blessing, and at one time had even indicated they might put up the money needed to keep things on track, the company never invested money in the production.[41] The producers were responsible for raising all the capital on their own. This was unlike other expensive musicals based on a massive IP like *Shrek*, which was funded by DreamWorks, and all the Disney musicals, which rely on a nearly endless supply of money from the Walt Disney Corporation. At one point in the development process, the financial situation was so bad that all the actors were released from their contracts and all work stopped on the renovations in the theatre. During that time, none of the creatives were paid as the production was $20 million in the hole.[42] Eventually, Hello Entertainment, the original producer, was let go and a new company, Goodbye Entertainment was brought in to get the production back on track. But, by that point, it was too late. Not only had the production costs already spiraled out of control (and the show would continue to hemorrhage money for years) but they calculated that "with forty stagehands needed to operate the backstage rigging, operating costs were going to be $1.1 million per week (a good $300,000 more than any other musical currently in town). This number meant that even with every single performance sold out, it could still take over four years to break even."[43] Given these numbers and the fact that the capitalization of the show would only go up, *Spider-Man: Turn Off the Dark* never even had a chance at financial success.

While the production's finances may have been doomed from the start, the production might still have been artistically successful. After all the show had director Julie Taymor who had already done the seemingly impossible on Broadway by turning Disney's *The Lion King* into one of the most successful stage musicals of all time. Unfortunately, lightning did not strike twice, and Taymor became one of the production's greatest liabilities. Julie Taymor is regarded as a genius, an uncompromising genius, and an auteur. It is these qualities that led to success for Disney's *The Lion King* but also led to the demise of *Spider-Man*. The fundamental difference between the process for *The Lion*

134 Other Original Musicals

King and the process for *Spider-Man* is that in the case of the former, the powers that be at Disney gave Taymor carte blanche to do whatever she thought best to bring the film to the stage. Yes, there were concerns early on about the direction that she was envisioning for the show, Disney didn't understand her concept that didn't put actors in full costumes and makeup to make them look like their cartoon counterparts. But Disney allowed Taymor to workshop some scenes for them in both styles, the truer to the film version the executives thought they wanted, and a more expressionistic version that was evocative rather than literal that Taymor wanted. The executives saw where Taymor was going and said yes, go there. They got out of the artist's way and what they ended up with was Taymor's singular vision, which translated into a highly successful and highly lucrative production.[44]

In the case of *Spider-Man: Turn Off the Dark* Julie Taymor was not allowed a singular vision. From the beginning, there were multiple stakeholders who were undermining and criticizing her choices. After receiving the initial outline and concept for the production, executives at Marvel rejected it out of hand. Avi Arad, the then chief creative officer at Marvel Entertainment responded, noting that the "concept is entirely wrong and the tone of the treatment, which is quite dark, is not what Marvel anticipated receiving at all."[45] At this point, perhaps the wise choice would have been for Taymor and Spidey to part ways, as her dark, mythic vision did not align with what Marvel wanted. In fact, Marvel would not be completely happy with the musical until after Taymor's departure and after the entire show had been reworked into a cartoonish theme-park production. Taymor had no interest in staging a theme park, but Marvel only wanted a theme park.

Throughout the process, Marvel and the producers chipped away at Taymor's singular vision and what ended up on stage as the first iteration of *Spider-Man: Turn Off the Dark* just didn't work. That's not to say that Taymor was blameless. In Glen Berger's book, *Song of Spiderman*, he reports many times when Taymor was uncollaborative, uncooperative, stubborn, or just plain cruel. Clearly, there was a mismatch between the artist and the material that served neither the artist nor the material. However, Julie Taymor would stay at the helm of the production through millions of dollars and dozens of previews. In early

Other Original Musicals **135**

March 2011, Taymor delivered a TED Talk titled: *Spider-Man, The Lion King*, and *Life on the Creative Edge*. After discussing her process, and inspiration, and sharing an often-cited story about witnessing a ritual in Indonesia in which the performers' only audience was God, she remarked:

> I'm in the crucible right now. It's my trial by fire. It's my company's trial by fire. We survive because our theme song is "Rise Above." Boy falls from the sky, rise above. It's right there in the palm of both of our hands, of all of my company's hands. I have beautiful collaborators, and we as creators only get there all together. I know you understand that. And you just stay going forward, and then you see this extraordinary thing in front of your eyes.[46]

Shortly after delivering the TED Talk, Taymor was fired from the production. Eventually, this led her to sue the producers and several of her co-writers. She would win that suit and as a result, her name was added back to the show's record as its director, and she received royalties for her work on the production. The litigation kept the musical in the papers even after the new version opened and gave reporters more fuel to add to the fire with which they were consistently burning the production.

With Taymor out, producers brought in a new director, Phil McKinley, who was known for directing the Ringling Brothers, Barnum and Bailey Circus, and several large-scale spectaculars. They also brought in writer and comic-book aficionado Roberto Aguirre-Sacasa. The hope was that with a new leader and some fresh eyes on the book, the musical could be salvaged. Under McKinley's direction, the show was gutted, re-written, and re-arranged and what came out the other end, while very pleasing to Marvel, would have been more at home at Disneyland than on Broadway. This new version, referred to by the company as *Spider-Man* 2.0, did receive much better reviews than version 1.0, while still taking a beating. Berger shares:

> So were the reviews good? Bad? Well, true to form, every critic put forth an opinion so unequivocal, so unassailable, that they all

136 Other Original Musicals

must be right. So the show *must* be "a spectacular for the ages" with "the best Act Two on Broadway," while also finding a way to be "an imbecilic entertainment for nap-loving preschoolers." It's a "fun family show" that was "*definitely*" worth the wait, and also "a bloated monster with bad music." The show had somehow managed to be "just a bore," while at the same time "never boring."[47]

Many of the reviews invoked the theme park comparison and Elizabeth Vincintelli of the *New York Post* declared the production was "ready to join Madame Tussauds and Shake Shack on a tourist's Times Square Itinerary."[48] As has been discussed previously, a show being "for the tourists" can be a good thing for producers as long as the tourists keep coming and the money keeps flowing. Unfortunately for the producers of *Spider-Man: Turn Off the Dark*, ticket sales began to decline and by the end of 2013, the weekly grosses were not nearly covering the enormous cost of running the show. So, it closed, losing $60 million dollars despite running for several years and selling over 2 million tickets.

Shuffle Along, Or The Making of the Musical Sensation of 1921 and All That Followed

- **Opened: April 28, 2016**
- **Closed: July 24, 2016**
- **Performances: 100**

Shuffle Along, Or The Making of the Musical Sensation of 1921 and All That Followed is an interesting case study as it is part original musical and part revival. However, the production was eventually deemed Tony Award-eligible in the category of new musical and classified by the Broadway League as a new musical, which means it is relevant as a case study in this chapter. This musical might also be categorized as a Jukebox musical as much of the music in it also appeared in the original version of *Shuffle Along* or other early-20th-century musicals, but the production's connection to the play that serves as its source material is more important to and more impactful on its creation than just its

Other Original Musicals **137**

preexisting music. Therefore, it has been included in this chapter rather than categorized as a Jukebox musical.

The 1921 musical *Shuffle Along* was noteworthy not only for its popularity but also for its status as the first Broadway musical to feature an entirely black cast and creative team. The production also marked the first time that black patrons were seated at the same level as white patrons in a Broadway theatre and its success led to an influx of all-black musicals throughout the 1920s, though none would reach the same heights as *Shuffle Along*. [49] The original was also the first musical on Broadway to feature a serious love song sung by two black performers. Additionally, the show is pointed to as the inciting incident for the Harlem Renaissance. In his 1940 book, *The Big Sea*, Langston Hughes commented:

> The 1920s were the years of Manhattan's black renaissance. It began with *Shuffle Along* (1921), *Running Wild* (1923), and the Charleston. But it was the musical revue *Shuffle Along* that gave a scintillating send-off to that Negro vogue in Manhattan ... [it] gave just the proper push—a pre-Charleston kick—to that Negro vogue of the 1920s that spread to books, African sculpture, music, and dancing.[50]

In addition to its cultural importance, the success of the original *Shuffle Along* proved to producers that the "Black" musical was a formula that would sell even to white audiences, and a string of imitators followed. In fact, nine musicals written by and starring Black performers premiered on Broadway within three years of *Shuffle Along*. [51]

Shuffle Along first opened on Broadway in May 1921 and ran for over a year. However, the show did not find success in subsequent productions. There were two unsuccessful revivals, the first in December 1932, which ran for 17 performances, and the second in May 1952, which ran for only four performances.[52] After the disastrous 1952 iteration, the musical was mostly forgotten until 2016 when a production featuring a who's who of Black Broadway led by George C. Wolfe titled, *Shuffle Along, Or The Making of the Musical Sensation of 1921 and All That Followed*, opened on Broadway at the Music Box Theatre. The production featured the music of the original with a new book[53] that told the story of how the original *Shuffle Along* made it to

138 Other Original Musicals

Broadway in 1921. The entirely new book is the reason that the production landed in the "New Musical" category for the Tony Awards rather than the "Revival" category despite lobbying by the show's producers for it to be considered a revival. One must remember that *Hamilton* was also under consideration in the "New Musical" category for the 2015–2016 season and any production pitted against it had little chance of winning.

The 2016 production had a remarkable cast including Brandon Victor Dixon, Joshua Henry, Brian Stokes Mitchell, Billy Porter, and Audra McDonald, and was choreographed by tap legend Savion Glover. However, despite the depth of star power, producers anticipated that multiple Tony Award winner McDonald would be the biggest draw. And here, is where things get interesting. Because of the producers' assertion that the show would fail without McDonald, they took out a $14 million dollar insurance policy that would pay out in the event that she was unable to perform due to illness or an accident, or injury.[54] Then, in June 2016, the producers announced that the show would close on July 24th, when McDonald, who had unexpectedly become pregnant, would be leaving the show on maternity leave.[55] They had determined that without McDonald, the show would not be a big enough draw and could not weather the financial strain of her absence. In a statement issued with the closing notice, they shared that it had "become clear that the need for Audra to take a prolonged and unexpected hiatus from the show has determined the unfortunate inevitability of our show running at a loss for significantly longer than the show can responsibly absorb."[56]

Though the production was selling well, there was a sharp drop in ticket sales for show dates after McDonald's scheduled departure. She originally planned to take a short leave from the production in June 2016 to perform *Lady Day at Emerson's Bar & Grill* in London, and ticket sales for performances during that absence were noticeably less robust than for performances where McDonald was scheduled to perform. Though *Shuffle Along* would close at a loss, the producers believed that it would sustain an even greater loss by continuing to run without McDonald. One must remember that Broadway productions are expensive and commercial producers are first and foremost responsible to their investors.[57]

Other Original Musicals **139**

While the show's closure was a loss for Broadway, not only because of the show's quality but also because of the historic nature of its run and subject matter, another controversy was brewing. In November 2016, Michael Paulson of the *New York Times* reported that the producers of *Shuffle Along* were suing their insurance company, Lloyd's of London, for payment on the policy they had purchased to cover McDonald's absence due to illness or injury.[58] Kirk A. Pasich, one of the show's lawyers explained, "from our perspective, *Shuffle Along* bought an insurance policy to cover it in the event that Ms. McDonald was unable to perform, and she was unable to perform."[59] 46-year-old McDonald's pregnancy was unplanned and took both her and the show by surprise. The lawsuit stated, "given her age and medical history, the news of her viable pregnancy came as a surprise to her and, consequently, to *Shuffle Along*."[60] Now in addition to its historic importance to musical theatre, the 2016 production of *Shuffle Along* was poised to have an impact on labor regulations.

The lawsuit left it up to a court to decide if the pregnancy could be classified as an accident or an illness under the terms of the insurance policy. The producers asked for $12 million in damages, but the impact of a verdict decided in their favor could have wide implications outside of the theatre industry. If pregnancy is grounds for a production to cash in an insurance policy taken out for an accident or illness, then the ruling could have far-reaching consequences and fundamentally change the ways that American companies handle pregnant employees and maternity leave. However, the issue of pregnancy as an illness had been litigated before. In his article for *Forbes.com*, "Audra McDonald Stars in New Lawsuit," Marc Hershberg points out that the New York courts decided "decades ago" that pregnancy is "a normal biological function and is not an illness."[61]

The insurance company, Lloyd's of London, argued that the lawsuit was not justified because, to receive a payout, the show had to close because of an incident (death, accident, illness) beyond the control of the person who was insured.[62] Though the pregnancy was not planned, it was certainly within McDonald's control as she and her husband had contributed to it. Lloyd's of London also argued that "*Shuffle Along* didn't need to be shut down. The show was nominated for 10 Tony Awards, and the talented cast featured several other award-winning performers."[63]

140 Other Original Musicals

Additionally, in December 2016, Ruthie Fierberg of *Playbill.com* reported that Lloyd's of London put forward the claim that McDonald knew about her pregnancy in February 2016 and failed to disclose it when filling out the paperwork for the insurance policy in March 2016.[64]

The lawsuit soon fell out of the headlines as it worked its way through the courts and ended up being quietly dropped by both the producers and the insurance company in October 2020.[65] Though in the end, the lawsuit came to nothing, it did raise many questions about the ways in which producers of Broadway productions place value on star performers over the production as a whole. *Shuffle Along* was a highly artistically successful and historically important production, one that may have been able to weather the departure of Audra McDonald, particularly because she was not the show's only star. It must also be noted that it was a white producer, Scott Rudin, who shuttered an important Black production. This mirrors the problematic dynamics at play in many musicals produced on Broadway in the 20 seasons. Rudin ignored the show's importance and its potential, and instead closed the show at a loss and filed a frivolous lawsuit to try and recoup some of the production's shortfall. Representation matters at the top of a production just as it matters on the stage, and *Shuffle Along* was perhaps a casualty of not giving the people whose story was being told a seat at the table.

Reading Questions

1. What are the categories for the "other original" musicals and what is in each of those categories?
2. Why are these musicals seen as more "original" than jukebox or screen-to-stage musicals? Do you agree? Disagree? Why?
3. What lessons do you take away from the story of *Spider-Man: Turn Off the Dark* and *Shuffle Along*?

Notes

1. This does not mean that they were originally created for Broadway as there are several that played off Broadway or elsewhere prior to coming to Broadway but are still original to Broadway.
2. John Kenrick, *Musical Theatre: A History*, 2nd ed. (London: Bloomsbury Methuen Drama, 2018), 46.

Other Original Musicals **141**

3 Michael Paulson, "'Fun Home' Recoups on Broadway," *New York Times*, December 13, 2015, sec. C, 3, accessed June 6, 2022, www.nytimes.com/2015/12/14/theater/fun-home-recoups-on-broadway.html#:~:text=First%2C%20the%20producers%20kept%20costs,cost%20more%20than%20%2415%20million.

4 David Rooney, "A Gentleman's Gide to Love & Murder: Theater Review," review of *A Gentleman's Guide to Love & Murder*, New York, NY, *Hollywood Reporter*, last modified November 17, 2013, accessed June 7, 2022, www.hollywoodreporter.com/news/general-news/a-gentlemans-guide-love-murder-656830/.

5 Ben Brantley, "Theater Review; A French Milquetoast's Talent Lights the Fuse of Mischief," review of *Amour*, *New York Times*, last modified October 21, 2002, accessed June 7, 2022, www.nytimes.com/2002/10/21/theater/theater-review-a-french-milquetoast-s-talent-lights-the-fuse-of-mischief.html.

6 By the time you are reading this, it is likely that it will be the fourth longest-running as it will soon overtake the original production of *Cats* which is not still running. Numbers 1–4 are all currently still running.

7 Qtd. in "WICKED Broadway Reviews," Broadwayworld.com, accessed June 7, 2022, www.broadwayworld.com/reviews/Wicked.

8 Qtd. in "WICKED Broadway," Broadwayworld.com.

9 "Wicked," *Internet Broadway Database*, accessed June 7, 2022, www.ibdb.com/broadway-production/wicked-13485#Awards.

10 In the book and the musical Glinda the Good Witch is named Galinda until she changes her name and the Wicked Witch of the West is named Elphaba.

11 There is an argument to be made that the musical is based on the television show as well because the characters in the original comic strip did not have names. They were named for the 1964 show.

12 Qtd. in Laura Collins-Hughes, "'The Addams Family' Musical Was Panned. Then It Became a Hit.," *New York Times*, April 7, 2020, accessed June 8, 2022, www.nytimes.com/2020/04/07/theater/addams-family-musical-history.html.

13 Michael Gioia, "Broadway's Spider-Man Turn Off the Dark Sets Closing Date; Las Vegas Production Planned," *Playbill.com*, last modified November 19, 2013, accessed June 8, 2022, www.playbill.com/article/broadways-spider-man-turn-off-the-dark-sets-closing-date-las-vegas-production-planned-com-211951#:~:text=News%20Broadway's%20Spider%2DMan%20Turn,Harris%20announced%20Nov.

14 Gioia, "Broadway's Spider-Man."

15 This includes productions like *The Frogs*, which was based on a Greek play that featured mythological characters, *Xanadu* that was based on a film that featured mythological characters, and *The Lightening Thief* that was based on a young adult novel that featured mythological characters.

16 Leah Marilla Thomas, "How Anaïs Mitchell's Musical 'Hadestown' Is Making Broadway History For Women," *Bustle*, last modified May 6,

142 Other Original Musicals

2019, accessed June 9, 2022, www.bustle.com/p/anais-mitchells-hades
town-is-making-broadway-history-for-women-but-she-wants-it-to-be-nor
mal-for-the-next-generation-17130069.

17 Thomas, "How Anaïs," *Bustle*.

18 These camps are most often referred to as "internment camps" but the
team at *Allegiance* asked that they be referred to as incarceration or con-
centration camps in the educational materials for the production. Therefore, that is the language used here.

19 The 2004 production of *Assassins* was scheduled to open in 2001 shortly
after 9/11. The producers postponed the production as they felt that a
musical about presidential assassinations was not appropriate in the wake of
a national tragedy.

20 Stephen Purdy, *Flop Musicals of the Twenty First Century: How They Happened, When They Happened (and What We've Learned)* (London: Routledge,
2020), 80–82.

21 Purdy, *Flop Musicals*, 83.

22 Purdy, *Flop Musicals*, 83–84.

23 Campbell Robertson, "Fleeting Stage Glory, Savored and Survived," *The
New York Times*, May 19, 2008, accessed June 9, 2022, www.nytimes.com/
2008/05/19/theater/19glory.html#:~:text=But%20after%2017%20preview
s%2C%20a,its%20entire%20%242.5%20million%20investment.

24 Ben Brantley, "Missionary Men with Confidence in Sunshine," review of
The Book of Mormon, New York Times, March 24, 2011, sec. C, 1, accessed
June 9, 2022, www.nytimes.com/2011/03/25/theater/reviews/the-boo
k-of-mormon-at-eugene-oneill-theater-review.html.

25 Brantley, "Missionary Men With," review, sec. C, 1.

26 Morgan Jones, "How the LDS Church's Response to 'The Book of
Mormon' Musical Is Actually Working," Deseret News, last modified
November 16, 2016, accessed June 9, 2022, www.deseret.com/2016/11/
16/20600593/how-the-lds-church-s-response-to-the-book-of-mormon-m
usical-is-actually-working.

27 Qtd. in Stephi Wild, "*The Book of Mormon* Creatives Will Convene to
Address Concerns From Black Cast Members," Broadwayworld.com, last
modified March 12, 2021, accessed June 9, 2022, www.broadwayworld.
com/article/THE-BOOK-OF-MORMON-Creatives-Will-Convene-to-
Address-Concerns-From-Black-Cast-Members-20210312.

28 Wild, "*The Book*," Broadwayworld.com.

29 Michael Paulson, "As Broadway Returns, Shows Rethink and Restage
Depictions of Race," *New York Times* (New York, NY), October 24,
2021, sec. A, 1, accessed June 9, 2022, www.nytimes.com/2021/10/23/
theater/broadway-race-depictions.html.

30 Glen Berger, *Song of Spider-Man: The inside Story of the Most Controversial
Musical in Broadway History* (New York: Simon & Schuster, 2014), 345.

31 Berger, *Song of Spider-Man*, 345.

32 Broadway League, *Internet Broadway Database*, accessed June 20, 2022,
www.ibdb.com.

Other Original Musicals **143**

33 Broadway League, *Internet Broadway Database*.
34 Here Berger's tally differs from what is reported by the Broadway league. The Broadway league has the total number at 1,248 which is reflected in the numbers reported above
35 Berger, *Song of Spider-Man*, 354.
36 Berger, *Song of Spider-Man*, 355.
37 Michael Riedel, "Spinning A $30M Show," *New York Post* (New York, NY), May 2, 2007, accessed July 1, 2022, https://nypost.com/2007/05/02/spinning-a-30m-show/.
38 Berger, *Song of Spider-Man*, 48.
39 Qtd. in Berger, *Song of Spider-Man*, 78.
40 Berger, *Song of Spider-Man*, 106.
41 In *Song of Spider-Man* Berger conjectures that the fact that Disney was buying Marvel at the time that the discussions about Marvel bailing the show out occurred kept the company from investing in the production.
42 Berger, *Song of Spider-Man*, 107–112.
43 Berger, *Song of Spider-Man*, 177–118.
44 Amy Sara Osatinski, *Disney Theatrical Productions: Producing Broadway Musicals the Disney Way* (New York: Routledge, 2019), 74–90.
45 Qtd. in Berger, *Song of Spider-Man*, 25.
46 "Spider-Man, The Lion King, and Life on the Creative Edge," video, 18:16, *Ted.com*, posted March 2011, accessed June 30, 2022, www.ted.com/talks/julie_taymor_spider_man_the_lion_king_and_life_on_the_creative_edge/transcript?language=en.
47 Berger, *Song of Spider-Man*, 342–343.
48 Elizabeth Vincentelli, "Spidey's Back," review of *Spiderman: Turn Off The Dark*, New York, NY, *New York Post*, last modified June 15, 2011, accessed June 30, 2022, https://nypost.com/2011/06/15/spideys-back/.
49 Elizabeth L. Wollman, *A Critical Companion to the American Stage Musical* (London: Bloomsbury Methuen Drama, 2020), 69.
50 Langston Hughes, *The Big Sea* (New York: Alfred A. Knopf, 1940), 224.
51 Allen Woll, *Black Musical Theatre: From Coontown to Dreamgirls* (New York: Da Capo, 1989), 70–74.
52 Broadway League, *Internet Broadway Database*, accessed June 20, 2022, www.ibdb.com.
53 The original *Shuffle Along* had a very thin plot about a mayoral election in a fictional Southern town called "Jimtown." Only a few small sections of that original book were used in the 2016 production.
54 Michael Paulson, "Pregnancy Prompted Closing of 'Shuffle Along.' Should Insurance Pay?," *New York Times*, November 16, 2016, sec. C, 3, accessed June 20, 2022, www.nytimes.com/2016/11/16/theater/pregnancy-prompted-closing-of-shuffle-along-should-insurance-pay.html.
55 Michael Paulson, "Decision to Close 'Shuffle Along' Is Debated Along Broadway," *New York Times*, June 25, 2016, sec. C, 3, accessed June 20, 2022, www.nytimes.com/2016/06/25/theater/decision-to-close-shuffle-along-is-debated-along-broadway.html.

144 Other Original Musicals

56 Qtd. in David Gordon, "Shuffle Along to Close Abruptly on Broadway," *Theatremania*, accessed June 20, 2022, www.theatermania.com/broadway/news/shuffle-along-closing-date_76939.html.
57 Paulson, "Decision to Close," sec. C, 3.
58 Paulson, "Pregnancy Prompted," sec. C, 3.
59 Qtd. in Paulson, "Pregnancy Prompted," sec. C, 3.
60 Paulson, "Pregnancy Prompted," sec. C, 3.
61 Marc Hershberg, "Audra McDonald Stars in New Lawsuit," *Forbes.com*, last modified November 14, 2016, accessed June 20, 2022, www.forbes.com/sites/marchershberg/2016/11/14/audra-mcdonald-stars-in-new-lawsuit/?sh=1fb430f754c2.
62 Hershberg, "Audra McDonald," *Forbes.com*.
63 Hershberg, "Audra McDonald," *Forbes.com*.
64 Ruthie Fierberg, "New Development in Shuffle Along Lawsuit," *Playbill.com*, last modified December 24, 2016, accessed June 20, 2022, www.playbill.com/article/new-development-in-shuffle-along-lawsuit.
65 Michael Paulson, "'Shuffle Along' and Insurer Drop Pregnancy-Prompted Lawsuit," *New York Times*, October 27, 2020, sec. C, 4, accessed June 20, 2022, www.nytimes.com/2020/10/21/theater/shuffle-along-audra-mcdonald-insurer-pregnancy-lawsuit.html#:~:text=Scott%20Rudin%2C%20the%20lead%20producer,when%20its%20star%20became%20pregnant.&text=As%20a%20subscriber%2C%20you%20have,articles%20to%20give%20each%20month.

6

REVIVALS AND REMOUNTS

TABLE 6.1 Revivals in 20 seasons

Show Title	Season	Run	Category(ies)
Follies	2000–2001	117	Revival
Bells Are Ringing	2000–2001	68	Revival
42nd Street	2000–2001	1524	Revival/screen-to-stage
Oklahoma!	2001–2002	388	Revival
Into the Woods	2001–2002	279	Revival
The Boys from Syracuse	2002–2003	73	Revival
Flower Drum Song	2002–2003	169	Revival
Man of La Mancha	2002–2003	302	Revival/screen-to-stage
Nine	2002–2003	302	Revival
Gypsy	2002–2003	451	Revival
Big River	2003–2004	67	Revival
Little Shop of Horrors	2003–2004	372	Revival
Wonderful Town	2003–2004	497	Revival
Fiddler on the Roof	2003–2004	781	Revival
Pacific Overtures	2004–2005	69	Revival
La Cage Aux Folles	2004–2005	229	Revival/screen-to-stage
Sweet Charity	2004–2005	279	Revival/screen-to-stage

DOI: 10.4324/9781003139171-7

146 Revivals and Remounts

Show Title	Season	Run	Category(ies)
Sweeney Todd	2005–2006	349	Revival
The Pajama Game	2005–2006	129	Revival
The Threepenny Opera	2005–2006	77	Revival/operetta
A Chorus Line	2006–2007	759	Revival
Les Misérables	2006–2007	463	Revival
Company	2006–2007	246	Revival
The Apple Tree	2006–2007	99	Revival
110 In the Shade	2006–2007	94	Revival
Grease	2007–2008	554	Revival
Sunday in the Park with George	2007–2008	149	Revival
Gypsy	2007–2008	332	Revival
South Pacific	2007–2008	996	Revival
Pal Joey	2008–2009	85	Revival
Guys and Dolls	2008–2009	121	Revival
West Side Story	2008–2009	748	Revival
Hair	2008–2009	519	Revival
Bye Bye Birdie	2009–2010	117	Revival
Finian's Rainbow	2009–2010	92	Revival
Ragtime	2009–2010	65	Revival
A Little Night Music	2009–2010	425	Revival
La Cage Aux Folles	2009–2010	433	Revival/screen-to-stage
Promises, Promises	2009–2010	289	Revival/screen-to-stage
How to Succeed in Business Without Really Trying	2010–2011	473	Revival
Anything Goes	2010–2011	521	Revival
Follies	2011–2012	152	Revival
Godspell	2011–2012	264	Revival
On A Clear Day You Can See Forever	2011–2012	57	Revival
The Gershwin's Porgy and Bess	2011–2012	293	Revival/opera
Jesus Christ Superstar	2011–2012	116	Revival
Evita	2011–2012	337	Revival
Annie	2012–2013	487	Revival
The Mystery of Edwin Drood	2012–2013	136	Revival
Jekyll and Hyde	2012–2013	30	Revival
Pippin	2012–2013	709	Revival
Les Misérables	2013–2014	1024	Revival

Revivals and Remounts **147**

Show Title	Season	Run	Category(ies)
Cabaret	2013–2014	388	Revival
On the Town	2014–2015	368	Revival
Sideshow	2014–2015	56	Revival
On the 20th Century	2014–2015	144	Revival/screen-to-stage
Gigi	2014–2015	86	Revival/screen-to-stage
The King and I	2014–2015	499	Revival
Spring Awakening	2015–2016	135	Revival
The Color Purple	2015–2016	450	Revival/screen-to-stage
Fiddler on the Roof	2015–2016	431	Revival
She Loves Me	2015–2016	132	Revival
Cats	2016–2017	593	Revival
Falsettos	2016–2017	84	Revival
Sunset Boulevard	2016–2017	138	Revival/screen-to-stage
Sunday in the Park with George	2016–2017	61	Revival
Miss Saigon	2016–2017	340	Revival
Hello, Dolly	2016–2017	550	Revival
Once on This Island	2017–2018	457	Revival
Carousel	2017–2018	181	Revival
My Fair Lady	2017–2018	509	Revival
Kiss Me Kate	2018–2019	125	Revival
Oklahoma!	2018–2019	328	Revival

TABLE 6.2 Remounts in 20 seasons

Show Title	Season	Run	Category(ies)	Original Production Year
Dr. Seuss' How the Grinch Stole Christmas	2007–2008	96	Remount/screen-to-stage	2006
Irving Berlin's White Christmas	2009–2010	51	Remount/jukebox/screen-to-stage	2008
Hair	2011–2012	67	Remount	2009
Fela!	2012–2013	28	Remount/jukebox	2009
Elf	2012–2013	74	Remount/screen-to-stage	2010
Motown: The Musical	2016–2017	24	Remount/jukebox	2013

148 Revivals and Remounts

This chapter shifts its focus away from original musicals toward revivals. In its most basic definition, a revival is a play or musical that has already had a production on Broadway. In the 20 seasons, 74 musical revivals opened on Broadway. Each of the 20 seasons had at least one revival. There were also six remounts. A remount is a re-opening of a production that recently played on Broadway. All these remounts were re-opened within only a few years of the original production closing and while some of these productions were reworked while closed, they were not significantly altered, and not changed enough to be considered a new production.

History of the Revival

If the 1866 musical *The Black Crook* is the first musical, as pointed to by some scholars, then the revival is almost as old as the musical itself because, in 1870, just four years after the first production opened, *The Black Crook* had its first revival. However, if one looks to the Broadway League, the revival is even older. *The Internet Broadway Database* names *The Agreeable Surprise* as the first revival. This one-act comic opera by John O'Keefe and Samuel Arnold played for one performance in November 1793 and was revived for four performances in 1794.[1] In all, *The Internet Broadway Database* cites 65 musical revivals that opened prior to the 1870 production of *The Black Crook*. Either way, the practice of creating a new production of works that have previously played on Broadway has a long history.

Though the revival dates to the beginning of the musical, its popularity rose sharply in the middle of the twentieth century. In his 2013 book, *Anything Goes: A History of American Musical Theatre*, Ethan Mordden observes:

> The obsession with revivals is relatively new. In the First Age [pre-1900], there were few revivals. Rather, productions would tour interminably, so that each New York stand was no more than a reappearance. A few very famous titles got rebooted from time to time, mainly *The Black Crook*, whose notoriety alone sold tickets. However, the habilitation of sharper writing in the Second Age [1910s–1940s], and the arrival of the great songwriters in the Third Age [1950s–1960s], made reviving old shows largely unnecessary.[2]

This is not to say that there were no revivals in the first half of the 20th century. Prior to 1940, there were over 200 productions that were revivals of previous works, the majority of which were revivals of Gilbert and Sullivan operettas. However, in 1932 the first revival of *Show Boat* opened. Jerome Kern and Oscar Hammerstein's 1927 musical marked the transition between the more frivolous form of musical comedy and the more serious form of musical theatre as the production tackled weighty themes in addition to its song and dance. Therefore, it might be said that the 1932 production of *Show Boat* was the first musical theatre revival. In the 1940s and early 1950s, the majority of the revivals were still of operas or operettas, with *Porgy and Bess* receiving five productions between 1942 and 1953 alone.[3] Musical theatre revivals began to appear on Broadway more regularly in the 1950s and 1960s as popular titles from the Golden Age began to be revived: *Carousel* (1949, 1954, 1957), *Brigadoon* (1950, 1957, 1963), *Oklahoma!* (1951, 1953), etc. Many of the big-name revivals in this period were produced by the New York City Center in its "annual spring season of authentic restaging of classics."[4] While these revivals often found success, none of them were runaway hits with most playing under 100 performances. Several did move into the triple digits, for example, the 1952 production of *Pal Joey* was an anomaly with 540 performances and the 1960 production of *West Side Story* played for 249 performances.[5]

In 1971 that would all change when the 1925 musical, *No, No, Nanette* was revived on Broadway. The production marked the return of Busby Berkley, who was famous for his elaborate showgirl choreography in the musicals of the 1920s and who had spent the past several decades in Hollywood choreographing dreamy, kaleidoscopic production numbers and eventually turning to directing. Berkeley was credited with supervising the production of *Nanette* and Burt Shevlove, who was known for his collaboration on the book for Stephen Sondheim's *A Funny Thing Happened on the Way to the Forum*, adapted and directed the production. The new version of *Nanette* was a hit running for two years and 861 performances far outpacing the original production's 321 performances.[6] The success of *No, No, Nanette* also impacted the landscape of the Broadway musical in the 1970s. Musical theatre scholar Bryan Vandevender observes, "musical theatre historians credit

150 Revivals and Remounts

[*No, No, Nanette's*] success with re-igniting the Broadway producing community's interest in revivals, thereby creating something of a revival craze on Broadway throughout the 1970s ..."[7] In fact, the practice of revival became so prevalent that in 1977 a "Revival" category was added to the annual Tony Awards with that year's revival of *Porgy and Bess* taking home the prize.[8] From 1977–1993 this category would recognize one production of either a play or a musical as the best revival. In 1994 the category was split into two categories and one revival of a play and one revival of a musical has been recognized each year since.

The new categories point to the rise of revivals in the 1990s. In his 2010 book, *Showtime: A History of the Broadway Musical Theatre*, Larry Stempel asserts:

> The investment of major talent and resources in reinterpreting old musicals through new productions of all kinds became a fact of life in the 1990s ... and when [these revivals] became long-running Broadway hits in their own right, the re-production of such pieces took on a level of importance comparable to the production of new ones.[9]

Vandevender points out that the mid-1990s saw a string of popular revivals including the 1992 revival of *Guys and Dolls*, the 1994 production of *Show Boat* and the 1994 production of *Grease*. [10] Stempel remarks that in 1994, due to the sheer number of revivals playing on Broadway, "if only on economic grounds, the Broadway community could no longer ignore the new reality."[11] Whereas prior to the expanding popularity of the revival in the 1970s, most musicals that opened on Broadway were new, from the late 1980s into the 1990s, the revival was king. Vandevender notes, "Between 1989 and 1994, only thirty-five original book musicals opened on Broadway–seven of which were imports from Europe."[12] In 1994, the year the Best Revival of a Musical Tony Award category began, there were seven revivals, which outnumbered the six new musicals. 1994 was also the year that New York City Center began its "Great American Musicals in Concert" series which presented "forgotten" musicals in concert. While these productions are not considered "Broadway," they do share a local audience with Broadway and add to the growing number of revivals playing in the city at any given time. Additionally, Vandevender argues that the existence of a Tony Award category specific to the revival of musicals has ensured that "revivals remain a mainstay of the Broadway season."[13] This is evidenced in the fact that there was at least one revival that opened on Broadway in each of the 20 seasons, including the shortened 2019–2020 season.

While the quest for a Tony Award is certainly a driving factor, it is not the only one. As has been mentioned several times in previous chapters, musicals are expensive and two-thirds of musicals that open on Broadway never recoup their initial investment while playing on Broadway. Just as producers look to familiar titles when backing a screen-to-stage musical in order to mitigate the risk, they also look to familiar titles that have already played on Broadway. Furthermore, producers of revivals can take comfort in the fact that unlike many other forms of media where the announcement of a "remake" is often met with scorn or incredulity, in the theatre, a revival is often celebrated in its inception. Unlike screen-to-stage adaptations, revivals have already proven that they are worthy of production because they've previously played on Broadway. Even revivals that were unsuccessful often receive a warmer reception from the Broadway establishment than their cross-medium counterparts. Whether or not the celebration continues, however, depends on the production, and just like screen-to-stage musicals, revivals face scrutiny for their fidelity to and/or their deviation from the original version.

Types of Revivals

Revivals most often fall into one of several categories: traditional, revisionist, and revisal.[14] These categories indicate the relationship between the revival and the original production of the musical. Traditional revivals are those that stay true to the original source material as much as possible. The category contains both revivals that maintain the original book and score with some minor revisions and new staging and revivals that have complete fidelity to the original. Some of these revivals, like the 2006 production of *A Chorus Line,* even attempt to restage the original production. For this revival a member of the original cast, Baayork

152 Revivals and Remounts

Lee, restaged the choreography from the first production for the new production, literally reproducing the original. While some shows like *A Chorus Line* stand the test of time and resonate without major revision decades later, other shows do not. Traditional revivals often sound great on paper but can be far less successful when staged, particularly for musicals of the Golden Age and earlier. The farther from the original production a revival premieres, the more revision is most often needed for it to "work" for a contemporary audience.

The next category is the revisionist revival. These revivals maintain most of the book and score from the original production but make revisions that alter major plot points or character traits and trajectories. These changes are most often made to make the musical more palatable for contemporary audiences. For example, in the 2018 revival of *My Fair Lady*, director Bartlett Sher made a significant change to the musical's ending. Sher informs that George Bernard Shaw, the author of *Pygmalion* which serves as the source material for the musical, was trying to "write the opposite of a romantic comedy" as a means of social critique.[15] However, the ending of the original musical adaptation (and its subsequent film) reads as a romantic comedy. In the end, the heroine, Eliza Doolittle, bends her own will to that of the man she loves, Henry Higgins, for the sake of that love. She stays with him and submits to him even though the predominant message of the musical prior to the ending is that women are not objects to be owned. *My Fair Lady* has not aged well and to a contemporary audience it can feel anti-feminist and out of date. At the end of the play, Professor Higgins shouts "where the devil are my slippers." In the original, Eliza responds by bringing him those slippers, a sign that she has submitted to his will and to the traditional position society expects her as a woman to occupy. For the 2018 production, Sher changed that ending and instead of bringing him the slippers, Eliza walks out. This change shifts the narrative, revising not only the text of the play but its meaning. This type of revival was very popular during the 20 seasons as to revive many older musicals, such revisions are necessary. Some other productions that utilized this model to varying degrees of success are *On the Town* (2014), *Once on This Island* (2018), and the problematic 2018 production of *Carousel*, which will be discussed in detail later in this chapter.

The final category is the revisal. Revisals are new productions of musicals that have had significant changes made to their book and/or score. Like their revisionist counterparts, revisals are most often undertaken to make an out-of-date property "work" in the current moment. To be in need of a revisal, however, these productions are often so unpalatable to modern tastes as to need major surgery. In the 20 seasons, there were several revisals that attempted to "fix" the problems of older musicals like 2011's *On a Clear Day You Can See Forever*, a musical that in its original form now comes off as misogynist and dated. To update it, the gender of one of the main characters was swapped leading to a queer love triangle, an attempt to bring the 1965 musical into the 21st century.

Another musical that received a revisal was the radioactive 1958 Rodgers and Hammerstein musical *Flower Drum Song*. The musical wears its racism and misogyny on its sleeve and is impossible to successfully revive in the 21st century without a major overhaul. In 2002, playwright David Henry Hwang attempted to "fix" it by writing an entirely new book. Hwang was asked to "take the songs, keep the spirit, keep the themes, and in essence do [his] best to try and write the book that Oscar Hammerstein would have written had he been Asian-American."[16] Hwang tried to update the property by focusing on its themes of culture clash and assimilation and attempting to get rid of its racism and stereotypes. However, the latter were so ingrained in the musical that not even Hwang, one of the greatest American playwrights of his generation, could salvage it. The musical's songs, while excellent and tuneful as is expected of Rodgers and Hammerstein, are the location of many of its problems. There is simply no way for "I Enjoy Being a Girl" to not be cringeworthy in the 21st century, despite its catchy tune. Audiences agreed and the production closed after only 169 performances.

Another revival that fits into the revisal category is the 2009 revival of *West Side Story*. For this production, Arthur Laurents, the book writer for the original production, decided to not only revive and revise the musical but to also direct it. In an article in the *New York Times*, Laurents share that he doesn't see a point to a revival unless there is a "fresh approach" and his approach includes a shift in language and a renewed focus on the story, which he thought was shortchanged

154 Revivals and Remounts

in the original. In Laurents's new version, the Puerto Rican characters speak Spanish.[17] While simply casting Latinx/Latine actors to play the Sharks would have been a welcome update (something that is shockingly still not done in all productions of the musical), Laurents "liked the idea of a production in which both gangs were perceived equally as villains; [it was] suggested that a bilingual version was the way to do it."[18] Laurents explains that incorporating Spanish "gives the Sharks infinitely more weight than they've ever had …"[19]

To make Laurent's vision a reality, the producers brought in then-up-and-coming writer Lin-Manuel Miranda to work on the translations. Miranda had recently found success with his first Broadway production, *In the Heights* but was not yet a superstar, as he would become with 2015's *Hamilton*. Miranda was tasked with "the hardest bilingual crossword puzzle" he had ever tackled. He had to not only translate the words but also make sure that they evoked the right tone and location while adhering to Stephen Sondheim's wish that he "observes the rhyme schemes."[20] When the production was reviewed in its out-of-town tryout in Washington D.C., it seemed as if the bilingual libretto was working. Peter Marks of the *Washington Post* shared that the new version provided "a truer sense of the cultural misunderstandings at the heart of *West Side Story* as expressed in the characters' disparate languages."[21] However, in the same review Marks points out that in the moments where the lyrics are critical to understanding the plot, "non-Spanish speakers and those new to the musical will be frustratingly at sea …"[22] This is doubly true because a decision was made to not include supertitles for the production, meaning those who were not fluent in Spanish or did not already know every word of the musical would miss crucial information. Prior to opening on Broadway sections of the musical were translated back to English to try and mitigate the issue, weakening the concept and the production in the process. The revival was still popular despite its issues and played for 748 performances.

A third, fascinating and important revisal in this period is the 2018 production of *Oklahoma!*. Though the revisions to the actual text were fewer than many other productions that are considered revisals, the staging of the production was so radically different from the original that the production can be considered a revisal. This production will be explored in detail later in this chapter.

To Revive or Not to Revive

When a work of art is created, it is influenced by and a part of the cultural moment of its birth. In other mediums like film and television, works are immutably recorded, unable to be easily altered. When revisited decades later, many works no longer meet the cultural moment and become museum pieces of the time in which they were created. The cultural norms and expectations of one decade are not the same as the cultural norms and expectations of the next decade, often rendering older works obsolete or even offensive. The same is true of live theatre except that the only part of the work that is recorded and fully reproduced is the text. Each new production has the opportunity to take the text and through the process of restaging it, create a new work of art. It is no wonder then that many productions of older works end up starting conversations (or even arguments) about the appropriateness of that particular text in a new cultural moment. Viewing an old film or television show that does not meet the current moment may be met with a response to the effect of "well, it was a different time back then and things have changed." Conversely, revivals of musicals create a new version of a text from that "different time" and by deciding to revive the text, producers make a statement that they subscribe to the values contained in that text. This leads to an interesting question, is it appropriate to revive a "classic" or "important" work of theatre even when its values no longer meet the cultural moment?

However, the decision to revive is not just about appropriateness. Musicals, like any cultural product, have the power to make profound statements about the present, statements that are not always true. Musical Theatre scholar Donatella Galella observes, "When old musicals have newly revised books and lyrics, they can elide past and present material inequalities. By obscuring structural oppression or relegating oppression to the past, revivals can allay anxieties as if United States society has already dismantled structural oppression."[23] By reviving musicals that align with outdated values and that even uphold racism and colonialism (as many "classic" musicals do), these new productions serve as propaganda that feeds into the incorrect assertion that the United States as a society has moved past structural inequality. That is why interrogating whether a property should be revived is so

156 Revivals and Remounts

important. Unfortunately, there were many times during the 20 seasons when that question was not asked, or it was asked and answered by the wrong person. One of the major lessons of this period in musical theatre history is that the people whose stories are being told need a seat at the table. This author would take that one step further and say that a variety of marginalized voices are needed at every table and need to be empowered to point out blind spots to ensure that the work of art created meets the current moment and puts forth the intended values.

During the 20 seasons, there were many revivals that led producers, audiences, and critics to ask if a musical should be revived, and if so, how, and what adjustments needed to be made to make the musical acceptable for a contemporary audience. For example, as discussed above, the team that produced the 2018 production of *My Fair Lady* decided to update the classic text to make it more palatable to a contemporary audience and was successful enough for the musical to have a long run.[24] In contrast, as will be discussed in detail later in the chapter, the 2018 revival of *Carousel* made several decisions that undercut the production's ability to appropriately speak to that moment and even created new problems with its casting.

In another example, against better judgment, in 2015 a revival of the 1973 Lerner and Lowe musical *Gigi* opened. The musical, based on the 1958 hit film, tells the love story of a young girl, Gigi, and a much older man who first met her when she was a girl and who thought of her as his little sister. When she returns as a teenager (in the original she is 15), he falls in love with her, she agrees to be his mistress, and eventually, he realizes he wants to marry her instead. It is a love story that to a contemporary audience is at best inappropriate and at worst, horrifying. Though the production did make some updates, including raising the age of the leading lady to 18 when she returns, the material at its core was completely out of step with the culture of 2018. Though there were a few positive reviews, which mainly focused on the production values and performances, most critics pointed out how uncomfortable and anti-feminist the story was despite the updates. Additionally, many thought that the musical wasn't very good and didn't understand the choice to revive it at all. For example, Matt Windman of amNY quipped, "*Gigi* is a good example of what the late composer Mary Rodgers called a 'why musical'—a tolerable but ultimately pointless adaptation that adds little to, and is inferior than, the source upon which it is based …"[25] The production left many wondering what producers were thinking when they decided to mount an expensive revival of such an outdated property.

Another production from the 20 seasons that raised questions about whether it should be revived at all was 2017's *Miss Saigon*. *Miss Saigon* is a spectacular, long-running mega-musical that opened on Broadway in 1991[26] that was written by the French team of Boublil and Schönberg who are best known as the creators of another late 20th century mega-musical, *Les Misérables*. The original production of *Miss Saigon* was not without controversy. A white actor, Jonathan Pryce, was cast to play a half-Asian character, The Engineer. The casting of a white man in an Asian role is in itself problematic and inappropriate, however, this original London production doubled down and had Pryce wear makeup that changed the color of his skin and facial prosthetics that changed the shape of his eyes to make him look more "Asian." When it was announced that the production would be opening on Broadway, the assumption was that yellowface casting[27] would not happen on Broadway as the Asian-American acting community had worked tirelessly for years to prove why it was inappropriate for white actors to play Asian roles on stage or screen. When it was announced that Pryce would be transferring with the production, letters were written to Actors' Equity, the stage actors' union, in protest of the decision. Equity had to approve Pryce's visa to work in the United States and therefore had the power to deny him the opportunity to perform the role on Broadway. At first, Equity denied the visa, but later, due to pressure from the show's producer Cameron Mackintosh, who threatened to cancel the production if not allowed the freedom to cast the production as thought best, Pryce's casting was approved with the stipulation that he would not wear any racial prosthetics.[28] Though the production opened and quickly became a hit, the problem was not solved.

Yellowface casting is not the only issue with the production. By 2017 when the property had its first revival, the producers followed through with the commitment to cast the show with Asian actors in all Asian roles. Additionally, the gibberish that was passed off as the

158 Revivals and Remounts

Vietnamese language in the original version was replaced with actual Vietnamese. However, even with these changes, the story told in the musical is deeply rooted in colonialism and white supremacy. *Miss Saigon* does not represent the Vietnamese people in Vietnam or in the Vietnamese diaspora. In her 2017 article for *American Theatre*, Theatre Critic Diep Tran explains,

> If the show was trying to tell the story of Vietnamese people, we did not recognize ourselves or our parents in any of the faces we were seeing on that stage. Instead, all we could see were desperate, pathetic victims—people who were completely different from the resilient, courageous, multifaceted men and women of Little Saigon. And if I needed a sign that *Miss Saigon* was not for me, it was in the lobby. They were selling a baseball shirt featuring Ho Chi Minh and the communist flag, the very symbols my family fled from.[29]

The musical perpetuates the tired trope of the subservient Asian woman who needs to be rescued by the strong American hero. It asserts the idea that America is superior and that life in a place like Vietnam is not worth living. *Miss Saigon* upholds colonialism because it declares that white, Western (US) culture is superior to Eastern (Vietnamese) culture and that it is better to die (as Kim does by her own hand at the end of the musical) than to remain without Western culture. Tran explains:

> In *Miss Saigon*, Vietnam is a place not worth saving, and America is a holy grail worth killing and dying for. We hate ourselves because we are not white (the Engineer), and we will even shoot ourselves in the name of America (Kim). Why would you want to be with a Vietnamese man when you can be with a white man? Why would you want to be Vietnamese when you can be American instead?[30]

While conversations about the values of the production were far more common during the revival than the original production, there were some within the Asian acting community who were glad to see the show revived despite its problems because *Miss Saigon* provided many jobs for Asian actors, jobs that are few and far between, particularly on Broadway. In the ten-year edition of the *Ethnic Representation on New York Stages* report, The Asian American Performers Action Coalition reports that in ten seasons (2005–2006 to 2015–2016) only 4% of the roles on the stages of New York (in both plays and musicals) were filled with Asian actors.[31] Though that number jumped to 7.3% the next season (the season in which *Miss Saigon* opened), the numbers are still startlingly low.[32] With so few opportunities, a production like *Miss Saigon* that offered roles to many Asian actors could be considered a win, and many in the Asian theatre community were hesitant to completely dismiss the revival for that reason. However, Tran responds to that hesitation by noting that roles like those in *Miss Saigon* do more harm than good:

> Many actors have defended *Miss Saigon* for the jobs it's provided for generations of Asian-American actors. But what kinds of jobs are these? Playing stereotypes, people who hate their skin and idolize whiteness to the point of suicide? Almost 30 years after *Miss Saigon* first premiered … Asian Americans are still fighting an industry that would rather cast white actors to play us and would rather we play sidekicks and prostitutes—stereotypes that narratives like *Miss Saigon* have only helped perpetuate. Properties like *Miss Saigon* offer a way for white producers to feed us stereotypical scraps while continuing to starve us. They profit off of our bodies while silencing our voices.[33]

Clearly, there is more at stake than just money when a producer decides to revive a musical. And while these concerns are not new, the fact that conversations about them are happening more openly and that some of the people in power (certainly not all) are beginning to listen, is new. As was discussed in the introduction to this book, the end of this period saw discourse about equity and representation gain traction in ways that it had not before and the question of not whether a show "can" be revived, but rather whether a show "should" be revived became more common.

160 Revivals and Remounts

Case Studies

Revisal—Oklahoma!

- **Opened: April 7, 2019**
- **Closed: January 19, 2020**
- **Performances: 328**

When Rodgers and Hammerstein's *Oklahoma!* premiered on Broadway in March 1943, its form, and content were so novel the show defied categorization. In his 2007 book, *Oklahoma! The Making of an American Musical*, Tim Carter discusses the confusion over the show's genre, pointing to the assertion that it was a "musical play" rather than a musical comedy, opera, or operetta.[34] Carter notes that since its premiere, "no one seems to have tired of the claim that in *Oklahoma!* ... [Rodgers and Hammerstein] had consciously and consistently escaped the typical conventions of Broadway musical comedies to produce a much worthier art form, the 'musical play.'" Regardless of its genre, *Oklahoma!* was a watershed moment for the American musical and is often labeled the first musical of the Golden Age.

From the moment of its premiere, the show's setting, sound, and themes resonated as deeply American.[35] In his 1943 article in the *New York Times*, Olin Downs informs, "there is something special of the nation and its earlier adventure in [*Oklahoma!*]. Under the comedic mask ... we recognize an ancestral memory, echo of an experience that went deep, a part of the adventure that has made ourselves."[36] The original production presented a vision of the United States that met the cultural moment. In 1943, the United States was at war. Thousands of young men were fighting on a foreign front and back home the patriotic propaganda machine was working on overdrive. On December 7, 1941, the attack on Pearl Harbor plunged the United States even deeper into the conflict and by the end of 1942, just months before *Oklahoma!* Opened, all men aged 18–64 were required to register for the draft. *Oklahoma!* Provided both an escape from the realities of wartime and reinforced the patriotic idea that one "belongs to the land," supporting the notion that one must fight for that land.

Revivals and Remounts **161**

However, the America that was on display in the 1943 production and in many productions since was one of exclusion and erasure. The musical is set in the Oklahoma Territory in 1906, the year before Oklahoma became a state. 1906 is only 50 years after the Trail of Tears, the brutal forced migration of indigenous peoples to the Oklahoma territory, and less than twenty years after the 1899 land run in which settlers literally ran to claim the unassigned lands that were stolen from the indigenous people of the area. Yet, the musical presents an idyllic, white version of the American frontier that erases the complicated and violent history of the "grand" land on which the story takes place. The musical offers an easy version of the nation's history and also connects the pioneering spirit that allowed Oklahoma to become a "great" state to its contemporary moment by centering the women in the narrative, showing that just like in wartime when the women had to take up the roles most often inhabited by men, Laurey and Aunt Eller could run the farm and take care of the land. Men and women alike made the land that many were now dying for on foreign shores grand, and it was the duty of those at home to stay strong and "run the farm."

The 2019 Broadway revival of *Oklahoma!* also taps into the "ancestral memory" of the American frontier but in a very different way. The 2019 Broadway iteration of *Oklahoma! Is* an indictment of the American practice of exclusion. The dark production reveals the consequences for those who are outsiders and the lack of accountability for those who are insiders. Its message is haunting, contemporary, and timely to 2019, tapping into the darkness that musical theatre scholars have recognized in the libretto for years. The production sought to re-invent *Oklahoma!* and was successful in that reinvention in some aspects and less successful in others.

Director Daniel Fish's 2019 *Oklahoma!* was referred to by many as "Woke-lahoma" for the way that it revised the original to embody ideas about contemporary American culture that move away from the patriotic ideas in the original. For the production, *Oklahoma!* was deconstructed and reassembled in a new shape, making it a revisal. The production's score was reorchestrated, taking it from a full orchestra to a small combo. That reorchestration was one of the production's most successful changes as the new instrumentation included traditional country western instruments lending a more authentically "American"

162 Revivals and Remounts

sound to the musical. The casting of the musical also contributed to the revision, both in the fact that it was paired down from a large cast with a full ensemble and converted into a chamber musical,[37] and in its intentional diversity of race and ability in its performers.[38]

In this production, the stage, the walls, and the floor on stage and beneath the audience are covered in light-colored wood, reminiscent of a barn. The walls are adorned with dozens of gun racks and the ceiling is festively decorated with mylar streamers. The stage is set with rows of tables that served as both set and audience seating. Atop the tables rest red, steaming crock pots full of chili that bubble away throughout the first act. As the production begins, the house lights stay up, invoking the feeling of a communal picnic rather than a Broadway show. As the cast casually enters a few at a time, they sit in chairs to the inside of the on-stage audience and converse as Aunt Eller pours Jiffy mix into an enormous bowl, preparing cornbread. Gone is the traditional butter-churning old Aunt Eller, this Eller belongs to now.

There were also adjustments made to the structure of the show, most notably, the Dream Ballet, in which Laurie sleep-dances her way to a decision about the men in her life. Most revivals have utilized Agnes de Mille's choreography for the dream ballet, but this production reimagined it. The ballet was moved from the end of the first act to the beginning of the second and rather than the ballet-driven original, choreographer John Higgenbotham created a modern dance-driven piece that he refers to as an "Expressionist Explosion."[39] Gia Kourlas of the *New York Times* observed that the new piece was revised "for the modern world, making a dance about outsiders that brings to mind issues of race, inequality and the treatment of women."[40]

Another important change to the production is the communal experience of intermission in which the crock pots full of chili and the cornbread that Aunt Eller made during the action of the first act are served to the audience family style. The audience in this production is attending the community cookout, the audience in this production is a part of the community. The stripped-down nature of the show, the setting, the new orchestrations, and the chili serve a specific purpose. These elements make the production feel like a communal event, an event in which audience members are not merely spectators, but rather participants. As the characters exclude and harass Jud throughout the

Revivals and Remounts **163**

musical, the audience is also excluding and harassing Jud. Then, as the second act hurtles toward its inevitable conclusion, the experience becomes more and more uncomfortable. Watching the characters frantically help Curly beat Jud in a bidding war for Laurie's cooler (in the production the "hampers" are coolers) there is an urgency and a menace that is palpable in the room and audience members are in that room, not watching from another room.

In this *Oklahoma!* The final climactic confrontation between Jud and Curley becomes an indictment of the American criminal justice system and how it protects those with privilege and power at the expense of justice. In the original, the show peaks at the wedding of Laurey and Curley when Jud appears and a fistfight ensues between him and Curley. Jud pulls a knife and, in the struggle, Curley dodges the knife, causing Jud to fall on that knife and inflict a fatal wound on himself. The community then comes together for a quick trial and acquits Curley of any wrongdoing so he and Laurey can start their lives together. In the 2019 version, Curley, without provocation, shoots and kills Jud, and is then acquitted of any wrongdoing by a quick sham trial. As he stands trial, his and Laurie's white wedding attire is spattered with Jud's blood, but even though the evidence of his cold-blooded crime lingers on his suit, he is quickly found innocent of any wrongdoing. The revision of the manner of Jud's death makes the hasty trial and "not guilty" verdict feel like a shocking miscarriage of justice, a miscarriage of justice that might have been ripped out of 2019 headlines. The production ends with an extreme and visually arresting finale that substitutes the usually cheerful reprise of the title song with a version shouted by the cast led by an angry Curly and a distraught Laurey.

The 2019 production of *Oklahoma!* had big ideas and a big message but there were moments in the production where Fish's directorial concept felt gimmicky and overtook the story as the focus, lessening the impact of the sharp and uncomfortable re-interpretation. The reinvention of the musical was sometimes stymied by bold directorial choices that felt as if they existed only to be bold, not to shed new light on the narrative. For example, on several occasions the production dropped the audience into complete blackness for minutes at a time, having the actors speak through handheld microphones. The confrontation between Curly and Jud in the smokehouse in Act 1 happens

164 Revivals and Remounts

in complete darkness. The scene is brought out of that darkness using a live-feed camera that projects a night-vision image of Jud's face onto the back wall. While startling, the purpose of the choice is unclear. The same can be said of the handheld microphones, which actors use during several moments in the show. Other than the times that the microphones are used for a performance within the performance or for the hamper auction, the microphones feel random and gimmicky rather than purposeful and connected to the narrative.

There are also moments within the show that are anti-feminist and racist in an insidious way. In her article "Sympathy for the Incel? On *Oklahoma!* And Jud Fry in the #MeToo Era," musical theatre scholar Catherine M. Young points out that in this production, "The stakes of interpretation are high when it comes to Laurey's agency and Jud's culpability, particularly because this production shows two white men vying for a black woman."[41] The production fails to fully explore the power dynamics at play and even makes the mistake in the second act of having Laurey seem to seduce Jud in another sudden blackout. Just prior to the picnic the lights again went out and Laurey and Jud breathe heavily in the handheld microphones which also pick up the sound of Jud's belt unbuckling. When the lights come back up as the moment is interrupted, it is unclear who unbuckled the pants, Laurey or Jud. The implication that Laurey was the one to unbuckle Jud's pants is problematic as it paints her as promiscuous and reinforces racist ideas about the sexuality of Black women that can be traced back centuries. The idea that Laurey is a tease and is playing with Jud also implicates her in his death in a way that upholds misogynistic stereotypes. This moment was not fully thought through and felt disconnected from much of the rest of the production.

These and other choices seem to only exist in the production to shock or to provide an edge and distract from the production's central message. The reimagining of the setting and emphasis on the darkness in this revised version of a canonical musical stand on their own. Though the revisions made to the source text for the 2019 production of *Oklahoma!* were not as extensive as many other revisals, the ways in which these changes and the adjustments to the staging and casting of the musical altered the focus and message of the show to such a high degree make this production an excellent example of a revisal.

Revisionist Revival—Carousel

- **Opened: April 12, 2018**
- **Closed: September 16, 2018**
- **Performances: 181**

Rodgers and Hammerstein's 1945 musical is often pointed to as one of the greatest scores in the history of musical theatre. It is hard to deny that the musical is masterfully crafted and that it contains some of the greatest songs of the Golden Age. But the merits of the score can't erase the problem at the center of the story. *Carousel* tells the story of Julie Jordan and Billy Bigelow. Jordan, a traditional ingenue, falls in love with ne'er-do-well anti-hero Billy Bigelow. Their love is big but so is Billy's anger. Billy beats Julie and when he dies, he must redeem himself to get into heaven, which he eventually does. But the message of the show is not that you shouldn't beat your spouse, the message is that sometimes your spouse might hit you because they love you. In one scene after Billy's death, Julie tells her daughter "it is possible, dear, for someone to hit you—hit you hard—and not hurt at all."[42] This moment in the show might have been ignored in 1945 and even in revivals in the 1950s and 1960s, but in the latter part of the 20th century and certainly in the 21st century, the characterization of Julie as a pathetic, lovestruck puppy who accepts her husband's abuse is out of line with contemporary sensibilities and makes the production difficult to revive. However, many producers and directors still want to try.

The 2018 Broadway revival of *Carousel* falls into the revisionist category not for any changes to its libretto, but for its new choreography and its casting. Rather than utilizing Agnes de Mille's original choreography for the show, as had been common practice for revivals of the property, choreographer Justin Peck reimagined the dance in the musical and won a Tony Award for his efforts. The production also engaged in "colorblind" casting, which will be discussed shortly. In his article "The Problem with Broadway Revivals: They Revive Gender Stereotypes, Too," Michael Paulson of the *New York Times* reported that producer Scott Rudin didn't plan to change any of the text. So, a major and expensive Broadway revival of a work that is over eighty years old opened on Broadway, and one of its main characters declared

166 Revivals and Remounts

that her husband beat her because he loved her. In her review for *Vulture*, Sara Holdren notes, "if *Carousel* were a person, he (definitely *he*) would be an incredible singer, a splendid dancer, and would often look very, very pretty—all while sidestepping the question of exactly what he's doing right here right now by putting his fingers in his ears and going 'La, la, la, la, la.'"[43] The revival may have been beautiful, but the production had no answer to the all-important question, "why this play now?"

The revival could not have been more out of touch with the culture in 2018. Just one year earlier in response to the accusations of sexual harassment against Hollywood producer Harvey Weinstein, the #MeToo movement[44] exploded on social media, starting a national conversation and empowering many women to speak out about their experiences of harassment and violence. And yet, Julie Jordan appeared on Broadway the next year explaining away violence against women. In an interview with Mervyn Rothstein of *Playbill.com*, director Jack O'Brien shared, "I did not want to focus on the domestic violence aspect of it any more than I wished to in a sense make a point by nontraditional casting. And both of those things in a rather remarkable way blended, by being cautious about overdoing or ignoring certain aspects of it."[45] Rather than interrogating the message that *Carousel* would send in 2018, he decided to ignore the message, a choice that is deeply rooted in his privilege as an established white, male director. Like *My Fair Lady*, the team for *Carousel* was composed of white men (other than a white female costume designer). So the production stands as another example of how a homogeneous production team can lead to an out-of-touch production.

Additionally, the fact that a notorious male producer, Scott Rudin, who himself would come under fire several years later for harassment and violence against his employees, would make the decision not to revise the libretto speaks to the need for more diverse voices at the table when decisions about what to produce and how to produce it are being made. Mounting a high-profile production on Broadway gives voice to the values of the property being revived and in 2018 a pro-domestic-violence musical was not acceptable on a Broadway stage. Frankly, an unedited *Carousel* is not acceptable on any stage in the 21st century. About the revival, Carol Rothman, the Artistic Director of the Broadway non-profit theatre company Second Stage remarked, "So the music is beautiful, does that mean you want to spend $20 million producing it?"[46] In the 21st century, the answer should be no.

However, it is not only the musical's support of domestic violence that made the 2018 production problematic. The casting team engaged in the outdated practice of "colorblind" casting. "Colorblind" casting refers to the casting of any actor in any role without regard to the color of their skin. This practice came to prominence in the 1990s and continued to be accepted as a best practice into the beginning of the 21st century. While at first glance, this might seem like a progressive and equitable way to cast a production, on further examination, it is not. Bodies on stage have meaning and extratextual narratives are conveyed by the bodies cast in a role. In the case of 2018's *Carousel*, the decision to cast a Black actor, Joshua Henry, as Billy Bigelow and a very slight white woman, Jessie Muller, as Julie Jordan, led to several problematic extratextual narratives. This is not to say that Henry was not well equipped to play the role as his Tony Award nomination attests. However, the casting reinforced a harmful stereotype that Black men are violent and prey on white women. It also made an Act Two reference to Billy having to enter heaven by the "back door" extremely uncomfortable. In addition, there were very few other actors of color in the cast and one of the only other visible BIPOC men was Amar Ramasar,[47] who is of Indo-Trinidadian and Puerto Rican descent.[48] Ramasar played the character of Jigger, who is painted as the true villain in the story as he is the one that encourages Billy to commit the criminal acts that lead to his death. These casting choices meant that the two "bad" men in the play were the only two male actors of color in prominent roles in the production. The production therefore contained an extratextual narrative telling an insidious story about BIPOC men. As mentioned above, director Jack O'Brien chose to ignore the implications of his casting choices, rather than interrogating the story that those choices would tell on stage. One must wonder if more care would have been taken in the casting if there were people of color on the creative team.

The casting in *Carousel* was woefully behind the times. Beginning in the second decade of the 20 seasons, the conversation about casting was updated and the term "color-conscious" casting came into use and

168 Revivals and Remounts

practice. "Color-conscious" casting recognizes that bodies on stage have meaning and that the race of an actor can't be ignored. Extratextual narratives must be considered when making casting decisions, not only about individual actors but about the entire company and the relationships between characters within the production. In 2020 Lavinia Jadhwani and Victor Vazquez published an article for *The Howlround Theatre Commons* entitled "Identity Conscious Casting: Moving Beyond Color-Blind and Color-Conscious Casting." In it, they introduce the idea of "Identity Conscious Casting" in which all of the identities, not just the race, of an actor, are taken into consideration when casting the production and assembling a creative team.[49] This new way of thinking about who is on the team for the production, both on and off stage, and how that impacts the story being told was just beginning to enter the world of Broadway musicals at the very end of the 20 seasons.

The creative team for the 2018 revival of *Carousel* was woefully behind the times and their attempt at inclusive casting was unsuccessful and created more issues than it solved. Overall, the production proved two things. First, *Carousel* and other musicals like it have to be handled with great care if they are revived and perhaps they should not be revived at all. Next, it is the responsibility of creative leaders to make decisions that are in line with contemporary values and norms. To do that, there need to be more voices at the table.

The Remount

As mentioned at the beginning of this chapter, during the 20 seasons there were six productions that were remounted on Broadway within a short time of their closing. These productions are not considered revivals because they are re-openings of recent Broadway productions, not new productions of a musical that had previously played on Broadway. Of the six remounts, three are holiday musicals: the 2007 remount of 2006's *Dr. Seuss' How the Grinch Stole Christmas*, the 2009 remount of 2008's *Irving Berlin's White Christmas*, and the 2012 remount of 2011's *Elf.* These remounts are a part of a long tradition of holiday offerings on Broadway. Two of the other productions were remounted to capture media attention ahead of a tour of the original production. 2011's *Hair* revival and 2009's *Fela!* Were both remounted to kick off a national tour. *Hair* played a short run in the summer of 2011 and *Fela!* Played a short run in the summer of 2012.[50] The 2016 remount of 2013's *Motown: The Musical* took the opposite strategy and scheduled a Broadway return for the end of the first national tour. The production landed in NYC in July 2016 and was originally scheduled for an 18-week run that would end in November, but a lack of ticket sales forced it to close at the end of July after only 24 performances.[51]

Though it is certainly interesting that there were half a dozen remounts on Broadway in the 20 seasons, this author does not ascribe any specific significance to these productions. Half of them took advantage of an available theatre to begin or end a tour and half of them had holiday-specific content and therefore made a smart decision to close after one holiday season and reopen for the next holiday season.

Reading Questions

1. What is a revival and how is that different from a remount?
2. How are revivals similar to screen-to-stage musicals?
3. Name and describe the three types of revivals
4. What kinds of questions should producers be asking before reviving a musical?
5. What musicals can you think of that you think should not be revived? Why?

Notes

1 Broadway League, *Internet Broadway Database*, accessed June 20, 2022, www.ibdb.com.
2 Ethan Mordden, *Anything Goes: A History of American Musical Theatre* (Oxford: Oxford University Press, 2015), 247.
3 *Porgy and Bess* has had more revivals to date than any other production in Broadway history.
4 Mordden, *Anything Goes*, 248.
5 Broadway League, *Internet Broadway Database*.
6 Broadway League, *Internet Broadway Database*.
7 Bryan M. Vandevender, "'Kiss Today Goodbye, and Point Me Toward Tomorrow'. Reviving the Time-Bound Musical, 1968–1975" (PhD diss., University of Missouri, 2014), 2.
8 *Tony Awards*, accessed July 5, 2022, www.tonyawards.com.

170 Revivals and Remounts

9 Larry Stempel, *Showtime: A History of the Broadway Musical Theater* (New York: W.W. Norton, 2011), 653.

10 Vandevender, "Kiss Today," 2.

11 Stempel, *Showtime: A History*, 653.

12 Vandevender, "Kiss Today," 2–3.

13 Vandevender, "'Kiss Today," 4.

14 These categories have been adapted from Pamyla Stiehl and Bud Coleman, *Backstage Pass: A Survey of American Musical Theatre* (Dubuque, IA: Kendall Hunt, 2013).

15 Diep Tran, "S.F. Theatre Director Bartlett Sher Shifts 'My Fair Lady' from Frothy Romance to Social Critique," *Datebook*, last modified November 1, 2021, accessed July 6, 2022, https://datebook.sfchronicle.com/theater/s-f-theater-director-bartlett-sher-shifts-my-fair-lady-from-frothy-romance-to-social-critique.

16 "The Flowering of Drum Song: A Sneak Peek at the R&H Musical," *Playbill.com*, last modified September 4, 2002, accessed July 6, 2022, https://playbill.com/article/the-flowering-of-drum-song-a-sneak-peek-at-the-r-h-musical-com-108044.

17 Patricia Cohen, "Same City, New Story," *New York Times*, March 11, 2009, accessed July 6, 2022, www.nytimes.com/2009/03/15/theater/15cohe.html.

18 Cohen, "Same City."

19 Qtd. in Cohen, "Same City."

20 Cohen, "Same City."

21 Peter Marks, "'West Side Story' at the National Theatre," *Washington Post* (Washington, DC), January 9, 2009, accessed July 6, 2022, www.washingtonpost.com/wp-dyn/content/article/2009/01/08/AR2009010803931.html.

22 Marks, "'West Side."

23 Donatella Galella, "Feeling Yellow: Responding to Contemporary Yellowface in Musical Performance," *Journal of Dramatic Theory and Criticism* 32, no. 2 (2018): 10, https://doi.org/10.1353/dtc.2018.0005.

24 It should be noted that other than a female costume designer, the entire creative team for this production were men.

25 Qtd in "Gigi Broadway Reviews," Broadwayworld.com, accessed July 8, 2022, www.broadwayworld.com/reviews/Gigi#:~:text=The%20musical%2C%20based%20on%20a,by%20leading%20lady%20Vanessa%20Hudgens.

26 The musical originally opened in London in 1989 and then transferred to Broadway in 1991.

27 Yellowface refers to the practice of white actors playing Asian roles. While the term derives from the practice of putting on makeup that makes the actor appear more "yellow," the term is used whether or not makeup is used.

28 Michael Paulson, "The Battle of 'Miss Saigon,'" *New York Times*, March 19, 2017, sec. AR, 1.

29 Diep Tran, "I Am Miss Saigon, and I Hate It," editorial, *American Theatre*, April 13, 2017, accessed July 8, 2022, www.americantheatre.org/2017/04/13/i-am-miss-saigon-and-i-hate-it/

Revivals and Remounts **171**

30 Tran, "I Am Miss," editorial.
31 AAPAC, *Ethnic Representation on New York City Stages: Special 10-Year Edition* (n.p., 2016), 6.
32 AAPAC, *Ethnic Representation on New York City Stages: 2016–2017* (n.p., 2017), 2.
33 Tran, "I Am Miss," editorial.
34 Tim Carter, *Oklahoma! The Making of an American Musical* (New Haven, CT: Yale University Press, 2007), digital file.
35 In this context, American in referring to the culture of the United States of America as it is commonly used. The author would like to acknowledge the limitations of this term as there are multiple Americas.
36 Olin Downs, "Broadway's Gift to Opera: 'Oklahoma' Shows One of the Ways to an Integrated and Indigenous Form of American Lyric Theatre," *New York Times* (New York, NY), June 6, 1943, sec. X, ProQuest Historical Newspapers.
37 A chamber musical is a musical that employs a small cast, usually fewer than 10, and has no ensemble. They are often small in scale and designed to play in smaller spaces and with smaller orchestras.
38 On tour the production was also diverse in the actor's gender identity.
39 Gia Kourlas, "A Dark 'Oklahoma!' Brings Barefoot Modern Dance to Broadway," *The New York Times* (New York, NY), April 21, 2019, sec. AR, 16, accessed July 26, 2022, www.nytimes.com/2019/04/16/arts/dance/oklahoma-dream-ballet.html#:~:text=For%20the%20show's%20choreographer%2C%20John,take%20this%20time%20to%20dream.%E2%80%9D.
40 Kourlas, "A Dark," sec. AR, 16.
41 Catherine M. Young, "Sympathy for the Incel? On 'Oklahoma!' and Jud Fry in the #MeToo Era," *Howlround.com*, last modified June 26, 2019, accessed July 19, 2022, https://howlround.com/sympathy-incel.
42 Qtd in Michael Paulson, "The Problem with Broadway Revivals: They Revive Gender Stereotypes, Too," *The New York Times*, February 25, 2018, sec. AR, 18, accessed July 26, 2022, www.nytimes.com/2018/02/22/theater/gender-stereotypes-carousel-my-fair-lady-pretty-woman.html.
43 Sara Holdren, "Theater Review: Can Carousel Be Brought Around?," review of *Carousel, Vulture.com*, last modified April 12, 2018, accessed December 27, 2022, www.vulture.com/2018/04/theater-review-can-carousel-be-brought-around.html.
44 It should be noted that the #MeToo was originally created in 2006 by New York based women's advocate Turana Burke.
45 Mervyn Rothstein, "Stage Directions: Why a Decades-Long Connection to Carousel Led Jack O'Brien to Direct the 2018 Broadway Revival," *Playbill.com*, last modified May 29, 2018, accessed December 27, 2022, www.playbill.com/article/stage-directions-why-a-decades-long-connection-to-carousel-led-jack-obrien-to-direct-the-2018-broadway-revival.
46 Qtd in Paulson, "The Problem," sec. AR, 18.
47 This is the same Amar Ramasar that was discussed in connection to the *West Side Story* controversy earlier in this book.

48 Kristan M. Hanson, "Amar Ramasar," in *Encyclopaedia Britannica*, accessed July 26, 2022, www.britannica.com/biography/Amar-Ramasar.
49 Lavinia Jahdwani and Victor Vazquez, "Identity Conscious Casting: Moving Beyond Color-Blind and Color-Conscious Casting," *Howlround Theatre Commons*, last modified February 2, 2021, accessed July 26, 2022, https://howlround.com/identity-conscious-casting.
50 Patrick Healy, "Search ArtsBeat SEARCH 'Fela!' Will Return to Broadway for a Summer Run," *Artsbeat*, last modified June 11, 2012, accessed July 26, 2022, https://archive.nytimes.com/artsbeat.blogs.nytimes.com/2012/06/11/fela-will-return-to-broadway-for-summer-run/.
51 Paul Resnikoff, "'Motown: The Musical' Forced to Close after Two Weeks…," *Digital Music News*, last modified July 24, 2016, accessed July 26, 2022, www.digitalmusicnews.com/2016/07/24/motown-musical-closes-two-weeks/.

7

BEYOND 20 SEASONS

On the afternoon of March 12, 2020, New York Governor Andrew Cuomo announced a ban on large gatherings in the state due to the rising threat of a novel coronavirus strain, COVID-19. The ruling forced the closure of Broadway theatres at 5 p.m. that night. Shortly after, the Broadway League announced that all Broadway shows would be closed for one month, reopening on April 12.[1] Across town, director Lucy Moss was in a cab headed to get her hair done for the opening of *Six: The Musical*, which she directed and co-wrote with Toby Marlow. Moss recalls, "I heard the announcement on the radio as it was happening. I went on my phone to check if that was a thing, and then I just got out of my taxi and back in a different one. I don't know why I didn't just go, 'Can we turn around this taxi?'"[2] In an interview with Patrick Ryan of *USA Today*, Moss shared that in the leadup to opening night, she was "so in the headspace of tech" that she didn't really pay attention to the news about COVID-19. She remembers thinking, "'That's weird. Everyone is so interested in this thing that's happening far away.' And then a few days leading up (to opening), it was like, 'Oh, this is actually right on your doorstep.'"[3] *Six* producer Kevin McCallum shares:

DOI: 10.4324/9781003139171-8

174 Beyond 20 Seasons

> There were starting to be rumblings, but it hadn't been declared that this is anything more than a surface virus, so we were operating on "Keep everything clean" … We even cleaned the entire outside of the theatre. It was pretty clear leading up to the (opening) that we might have to take a pause, but it was also something that hadn't happened (before), so it was hard to imagine.[4]

Co-creator Toby Marlow remembers thinking, "Oh, that isn't a thing that affects us, it's happening elsewhere. We'll be fine—things like that don't happen here."[5] But it did happen in New York and across the United States as an unprecedented viral emergency shut down the entire nation and closed Broadway theatres for over a year.

The COVID-19 Shutdown

The first case of COVID-19 was detected in New York State on March 1, 2020, and the governor declared a state of emergency six days later, on March 7. By March 8, New York City authorities issued guidelines urging citizens to avoid tightly packed public transit, and on March 12, all events with 500 or more people were canceled. This included the shutdown of Broadway theatres. On March 13, President Donald Trump declared a national emergency and on March 14 the first two deaths in New York State were reported. On March 16, New York City Public Schools shut down, and on March 17 all bars and restaurants closed for in-person dining. By March 27, the United States reported more COVID-19 cases than anywhere else in the world, and by March 31, New York City surpassed 1,000 deaths due to COVID-19. By the end of May, that number would top 100,000.[6]

On March 22, 2020, at his home in Manhattan, Broadway performer Danny Burstein, fell to his knees in his shower and asked himself, "Is this it? Is it time to go to the emergency room?"[7] Burstein, along with many other performers in Broadway's *Moulin Rouge* had been exhibiting symptoms of COVID-19. Burstein had been tested, but after five days, had still not received his results. However, as he had been coughing up blood, he knew, that test would be positive. Burstein recalls that as he stood up, he "couldn't stop coughing up blood. It felt like there was an 80-pound boy standing straight up on [his] chest."[8]

Beyond 20 Seasons **175**

He remembers declaring, "Guys, I need to go to the hospital."[9] So Burstein, accompanied by his son Zach, walked to St. Luke's Hospital on the Upper West Side of Manhattan. They walked because walking was faster than waiting for the ambulance.[10]

In a chilling essay published in *The Hollywood Reporter* on April 13, 2020, Burstein shares his harrowing experience of hospitalization and a long recovery from COVID-19. Burstein would spend six days in the hospital where he would watch the chaos of the early days of the pandemic unfold with countless patients in need of ventilators and others being rushed to the ICU. Burstein was lucky, he survived, but the recovery was long and arduous. In the essay, he shares, "As I type this I haven't taken Tylenol in four days – and that's huge. My lungs will probably take a couple of weeks to fully recover."[11] Though Burstein did recover, and eventually he and the rest of the company of *Moulin Rouge* would reopen the production on Broadway, his story is one of many Broadway artists who battled the virus. Stories like Burstein's also showed the world (and producers) just how serious COVID-19 was and how quickly it could spread through a company.

As Burstein and the company of *Moulin Rouge* recovered, theatres remained closed, and Times Square became a ghost town. On April 21, 2020, *The New York Times* published an article by Michael Paulson and Photographer David S. Allee titled, "Showtime on Broadway, Suspended." In the article, Paulson recounts his walks through the theatre district a month after the shutdown began:

> The first thing I noticed, after weeks away, was absence. Gone are the buskers promoting shows, the panhandling costumed characters, the Naked Cowboy and the fake monks, and the school groups and the selfie sticks. Gone are the actors and the stagehands and the ushers and the fans. Then I saw presence. The shows are still there—or at least their shells are. The district is a sort of theatrical petrified forest, fossilized on March 12.[12]

Paulson and Allee captured the eerie sights of a silent theatre district where the marquees still blazed with light, but the streets and the theatres were dark and empty. They captured the digital sign on the TKTS booth in Times Square promising an April 13 reopening long

176 Beyond 20 Seasons

after April 13 had come and gone. They snapped photos of many theatres advertising opening dates that wouldn't happen, at least not in 2020. The musicals *Six* and *MJ the Musical* (the Michael Jackson musical) were among them. Paulson ends the article by sharing:

> I've long loved the view down West 45th Street, with its row of vertical signs naming the theatres and the dizzying variety of shows they house. And yet, I can't help but wonder: Which long-running hits will never return? And which new shows will never even open? As with so much these days, there are only questions, not answers.[13]

As it became clear that the pandemic would not be over in a few weeks, or even a few months. Productions and theatre companies began to find creative ways to share their art and put artists to work. In the early days, many theatres released recordings of their productions (often taken at dress rehearsals) streaming on the internet. These productions were sometimes shared for free and sometimes audiences were asked to purchase tickets. The major streaming platforms also got involved with proshots[14] of several titles becoming available: *Hamilton* on Disney+, *Come From Away* on Apple TV+, and the ill-fated *Diana: The Musical* premiering before its Broadway run on Netflix.

Streaming productions not only included recorded versions of live shows but also included performances, often in the form of readings, on the video conferencing platform Zoom. This led to a need for new technologies for collaboration as syncing musicians and singers on Zoom led to challenges. Broadway even "reopened" briefly with a virtual benefit production on New Year's Eve 2020. The Actor's Fund organized a performance of *Ratatouille: The TikTok Musical*, a crowd-sourced musical version of the 2007 Disney Pixar film. The performance featured a roster of Broadway stars and raised $2 million dollars making it the highest-grossing event in the fund's history. Though not a musical, one of these digi-native productions was even nominated for the Pulitzer Prize in Drama. In 2021, Michael Breslin and Patrick Foley of the Brooklyn-based theatre and media company *Fake Friends* were nominated for their groundbreaking virtual live performance *Circle Jerk*. Though they did not win the prize, the inclusion of theatre built for streaming is significant.

Beyond 20 Seasons **177**

These new avenues for commercial theatre led to the need for new union contracts and negotiations between Actors' Equity and SAG-AFTRA, the unions for stage and screen actors. They had to wrestle with questions about who had jurisdiction over these new streaming productions. When the industry shut down in March 2020, producers had to scramble to figure out if they would be able to continue to create and disseminate work and then figure out how. As productions began to stream, there were no clear answers about which union covered actors in these productions.[15] On October 19, 2020, Diep Tran reported in *Backstage*:

> Equity has claimed that these works, which are created by theater producers, fall under its union contracts, while SAG-AFTRA maintains that anything that is recorded for a screen is under its purview. The unions had been in conversation privately over the summer to iron out an agreement. Traditionally, any live theater productions that have been recorded for the screen, such as "Hamilton" on Disney+ or the upcoming "Diana" on Netflix, have been covered by SAG-AFTRA and Equity contracts. During the pandemic, Equity has approved 249 remote theater productions that were presented to audiences via screen.[16]

A month later, the two unions reached a deal that allowed Equity to have jurisdiction over the streaming productions until December 2021 as long as certain stipulations were met. These included provisions that the performance itself had to be similar to live performances represented by Equity and limiting ticketing and length of availability. SAG-AFTRA also demanded that Equity acknowledge their jurisdiction over filmed media as a part of the contract.[17] This agreement was set to expire after one year, but as the pandemic continued, it was extended, expiring in June 2022.

Despite the creative solutions to dark theatres and the reopening of theatres in other parts of the country with safety protocols like social distancing, masking, and mandatory vaccination, Broadway theatres remained closed. Though New York would begin the slow process of reopening in June 2020, the lights of Broadway would stay dim for another year. Multiple reopening dates were announced as the

178 Beyond 20 Seasons

pandemic dragged on, as was mentioned in Chapter 1, but it would take 15 months and 471 days for paying audiences to sit in a Broadway theatre once again. During the shutdown, many Broadway productions, both plays, and musicals announced that they would not reopen. In June 2020, Disney's *Frozen* was the first major Broadway musical to make that decision. Though Disney cited economic concerns and the fear that three Disney productions on Broadway would be too many in a post-pandemic landscape, the closure came as a surprise to many. In 2020, *Frozen* had been doing relatively well prior to the shutdown, running at an average of 89% of its gross potential through January and February,[18] a time of the year that typically sees fewer tourists and ticket sales. The show was also based on the highest-grossing animated feature of all time, making it a prime title to capture post-pandemic tourist dollars. In January 2021, with theatres having been closed for almost 10 months, *Mean Girls*, also announced it would close. In addition, several highly anticipated productions were postponed, including *MJ the Musical* and the revival of *The Music Man* with Sutton Foster and Hugh Jackman. Though the shutdown was devastating to Broadway at all levels, the forced pause presented an opportunity. With the shows closed and much of the nation on lockdown, the theatre industry finally had time to listen and to reinvent.

On May 25, 2020, George Floyd, an unarmed Black man, was killed by a white Minneapolis police officer, Derek Chauvin. The incident was recorded on a cell phone. Chauvin kneeled on Floyd's neck for over nine minutes despite Floyd's pleas that he couldn't breathe and the urging of bystanders that he let Floyd up. After a few minutes, Floyd stopped breathing, making the incident one in a long line of Black citizens unjustly killed by police officers. The murder set off a national firestorm and the summer of 2020 became a summer of protest unlike anything seen since the Civil Rights Movement in the mid-20th century. Protestors across the country, and across the internet, raised their voices in a cry of "Black lives matter." Though the shutdown and the focused attention of a locked-down nation led to protests on a scale not seen in recent memory, the Black Lives Matter movement did not start with the murder of George Floyd. The movement was started in 2013 by three Black women, Alicia Garza, Patrisse Cullors, and Opal Tometi with a social media hashtag, #BlackLivesMatter, in response to the killing of another unarmed Black man, Trayvon Martin, in Florida. The movement came to prominence after the police killings of Michael Brown in Missouri and Eric Garner in New York in 2014.[19] Sadly, Floyd's killing was not unique and the conversation about police killing Black citizens had been ongoing. But this time was different. Not because the situation was different, but because the entire country had stopped, and white citizens and politicians were finally forced to see what was happening and forced to listen.

In the summer of 2020, the conversation about race in the United States and the experience of Black Americans rose to the surface and couldn't be ignored. The protests sparked conversations about equity across many industries and theatre was no exception. As mentioned in Chapter 1, this led to "We See You White American Theatre" and their list of demands for the American Theatre. There were also several Broadway-specific organizations that spoke up. Including the Broadway Advocacy Coalition. Like Black Lives Matter, the BAC was not new. It began in 2016 with the mission to "[Build] the capacity of individuals, organizations, and communities to dismantle the systems that perpetuate racism through the power of storytelling and the leadership of people directly affected."[20] In the summer of 2020, the BAC organized Broadway for Black Lives Matter (#BwayforBLM) and hosted a string of virtual forums for the theatre community as a place for healing and action. The first, which was held on June 10, 2020, was specifically for Black industry members and was titled "A Day of Healing." This was followed on June 11 by "A Day of Listening," which centered the experiences of Black professionals and challenged white allies to step up in support, and then "A Day of Accountability" on June 12, which sought to "collectively manifest an anti-racist theatrical landscape …"[21] An additional forum, "The Miseducation" was held on June 27th and featured the experiences of Black students and faculty members of colleges and universities in order to illuminate the needs for systemic change in theatre training programs at predominantly white institutions.

These conversations combined with the work that was already being done by individual scholars and advocacy groups, like the Asian American Performers Action Coalition (AAPAC), which had been compiling data about representation on Broadway stages for over a decade, led to a reckoning about representation on and off the stage. At first, it seemed like the industry was listening. For example, The Broadway Advocacy Coalition won a special Tony Award for their work at the postponed 2020 Tony Awards and the AAPAC won the same award in 2022. As discussed earlier in this book, some shows like *The Book of Mormon* reexamined the representation of people of color in their shows. Additionally, when theatres finally reopened, seven plays by Black playwrights opened on Broadway. However, the same was not true for musicals. The musicals that opened in the first post-COVID season looked a lot like the musicals that opened before COVID, with the notable exception of Michael R. Jackson's *A Strange Loop*, which was entirely written by Jackson, a Black man, and featured an all-Black cast. It should also be noted that *MJ the Musical*, the Michael Jackson bio-musical, had a libretto written by Lynn Nottage and the arrangements were done by Jason Michael Webb, both of whom are Black. The musical *Paradise Square* also added BIPOC artists to its team prior to opening on Broadway, likely in response to the conversations of 2020. At the time of this writing, the 2022–2023 musical season is also much of the same with BIPOC artists scarce on the creative teams for new musicals.

Unfortunately, the explosion of Black plays on Broadway came in a season plagued by intermittent closures due to COVID-19 outbreaks within companies and in a season with low attendance due to the pandemic and its impact on tourism in New York City. Many plays and musicals closed early or were not able to find financial and/or critical success, leading to concerns that producers might see the closures as a reason not to program work by Black playwrights in the future. It is also possible that there will be an influx of diverse musicals on Broadway in a few seasons. It takes a great deal more time to develop a musical than a play, so there may be more in the pipeline that will lead to more diverse productions in future seasons. Possible, but sadly, unlikely. Though Broadway musicals have not yet caught up to the conversation, there have been some small steps forward as now these conversations about equity and representation are happening within the industry and falling on more receptive ears. There are also many musicals being created Off-Broadway and in other venues that are by artists of color, but the economic realities of Broadway have

Beyond 20 Seasons **181**

kept many of them, despite their quality and success, from transferring. Hopefully, there will be change, perhaps in another 20 seasons.

Broadway Reopening

On April 29, 2021, Mayor Bill de Blasio announced that New York City would fully reopen on July 1. Despite the threat of new variants, de Blasio cheerfully stated:

> This is going to be the summer of New York City … You're going to see amazing activities, cultural activities coming back. I think people are going to flock to New York City, because they want to live again.[22]

On July 1, 2021, New York City did reopen, but Broadway didn't. Though, as mentioned in Chapter 1, Bruce Springsteen played to a paying audience on June 26, 2021, Broadway was not yet back. The first play would eventually open in August, but no musicals opened until September 2021. On May 5, 2021, Michael Paulson reported in the *New York Times* that most shows were not planning to reopen until September despite being allowed to do so. He shares, "With as many as eight shows a week to fill, and the tourists who make up an important part of their customer base yet to return, producers need time to advertise and market. They need to reassemble and rehearse casts who have been out of work for more than a year. And they need to sort out and negotiate safety protocols."[23] Though some productions trickled open through August and the first weeks of September, Broadway's official opening night was September 14, 2021. That night, many shows opened, including *Hamilton, The Lion King*, and *Wicked*. The night included celebration and visits from past stars and Broadway royalty. It also included mandatory masking and proof of vaccination. In order to attend a production, audience members were required to wear a mask and show proof that their COVID-19 vaccinations were up to date.

From the early days of the reopening, it was clear that the 2021–2022 season would not be a return to normal. As shows reopened, performances began to be cancelled because of COVID-19 outbreaks

182 Beyond 20 Seasons

within companies. As a contingency, producers stacked productions with understudies, standbys, and swings to try and prevent cancellation. The 2021–2022 season became the season of the understudy as productions got creative to keep the lights on. In addition to hiring extra coverage, performers playing roles on national tours were sometimes flown into New York to cover for sick actors. Despite the creativity and ingenuity, as the fall progressed, so did the closures. The more stable shows, those that had been hits before the pandemic, closed for days or weeks and then reopened, but many of the newer shows and those without name recognition ended up ending their runs early, often because of illness combined with dire financial situations. December 2021 was particularly rough. On December 23, 2021, Michael Paulson reported that "only 16 shows had performances, down from the 33 that would have performed without the surge in cases."[24] Broadway may have been able to reopen, but that didn't mean that all productions would successfully stay open.

As 2021 became 2022, it was clear that the record attendance and revenue that Broadway had seen before the pandemic would not quickly return. At the time of this writing, Broadway grosses, though steadily rising, are still trending lower than they were before the pandemic.[25] For example, the grosses in the first week of February 2022, were lower than they had been for that week since 2011 even without adjusting for inflation.[26]

Though many productions closed during and after the pandemic, one closure above all best represents the state of the Broadway musical post-COVID. On September 16, 2022, producers announced that Broadway mainstay and longest-running musical in history *The Phantom of the Opera* would close on February 18, 2023, shortly after commemorating its 35th year on Broadway.[27] The landscape of the Broadway musical after the COVID-19 shutdown was going to be very different.

What's Next

On October 11, 2022, it was announced that Pulitzer Prize and Best Musical Tony Award Winner *A Strange Loop* would close on January 15, 2023. Marc J. Franklin of *Deadline* reported the closure, noting that the show "has seen steadily declining box office and attendance in recent months. For the week ending Oct. 4, the production filled only 79% of available seats, grossing \$579,354, compared to a high point of \$860,496 last June."[28] *A Strange Loop*, which bills itself as "the big, Black and queer-ass Great American Musical," is groundbreaking in many ways including in its representation of fat, Black, queer artists, but at 314 performances, it is also the shortest-running Best Musical Tony Award winner in the 21st century. Though the musical's closure is likely due to the circumstances brought about by the pandemic, it is also due to the challenging material that while brilliant, innovative, and important, wasn't able to capture a wide audience.

The challenges presented by the pandemic, growing inflation, rising interest rates, and the threat of recession as well as changes in travel habits by tourists in the United States and abroad have all converged to create a new paradigm for commercial musicals on Broadway. While the later part of the 20 seasons began to sow the seeds of innovation and better representation, it is possible that the uncertainty and instability of the early 2020s will derail those efforts, leading to less innovation, less representation, and less movement forward on many of the concerns that were finally acknowledged during the shutdown. Will the Broadway musical finally be less white? Will attendance and revenue ever return to pre-pandemic levels? Will Broadway musicals continue to occupy a place in popular culture? Will innovation stagnate or will it find new ways to creep into commercial musical theatre? These are questions that can't be answered now, but perhaps will be illuminated in another 20 seasons.

Notes

1 Alexa Lardieri, "New York Bans Large Gatherings, Closes Broadway as Coronavirus Spreads," *US News & World Report*, last modified March 12, 2020, accessed October 14, 2022, www.usnews.com/news/health-news/a rticles/2020-03-12/new-york-bans-large-gatherings-closes-broadway-as-co ronavirus-spreads.
2 Qtd in Patrick Ryan, "They Closed on Opening Night Due to COVID; Here's How 'Six' Bounced Back to Rule Broadway", *USA Today*, www. usatoday.com/story/entertainment/music/2021/10/10/six-musical-broad way-interview-covid-pandemic-shutdown-reopening/5921224001/.
3 Qtd in Ryan, "They Closed on Opening Night," *USA Today*.

184 Beyond 20 Seasons

4 Qtd in Ryan, "They Closed on Opening Night," *USA Today*.

5 Qtd in Ryan, "They Closed on Opening Night," *USA Today*.

6 Alexandra Kerr, "A Historical Timeline of COVID-19 in New York City," *Investopedia*, last modified April 5, 2021, accessed October 14, 2022, www.investopedia.com/historical-tim
eline-of-covid-19-in-new-york-city-5071986.

7 Danny Burstein and David Rooney, "Broadway Star Danny Burstein on Harrowing Coronavirus Experience: 'Strength Through Stillness' (Guest Column)," *The Hollywood Reporter*, April 13, 2020, accessed October 14, 2022, www.holly
woodreporter.com/lifestyle/arts/broadway-star-danny-burstein-his-harrowing-c
oronavirus-experience-strength-stillness-guest-column-1289839/.

8 Burstein and Rooney, "Broadway Star."

9 Burstein and Rooney, "Broadway Star."

10 Burstein and Rooney, "Broadway Star."

11 Burstein and Rooney, "Broadway Star."

12 Michael Paulson, "Showtime on Broadway, Suspended," *New York Times*, April 21, 2020, sec. C, 1, accessed October 14, 2022, www.nytimes.com/
2020/04/20/theater/broadway-closed-coronavirus.html.

13 Paulson, "Showtime on Broadway," sec. C, 1.

14 This is the term for a professionally produced recording of a Broadway production.

15 The contracts for SAG-AFTRA and Actor's Equity are very different, so which contract performers would work under was very important.

16 Diep Tran, "SAG-AFTRA and Actors' Equity Feud over Streaming Rights for Theater Productions," *Backstage.com*, last modified October 19, 2020, accessed October 28, 2022, www.backstage.com/magazine/article/sa
g-aftra-actors-equity-theater-streaming-rights-jurisdiction-71925/.

17 Dan Meyer, "Actors' Equity and SAG-AFTRA Reach Agreement on Streamed Theatre," *Playbill.com*, last modified November 20, 2020, accessed October 28, 2022, https://playbill.com/article/actors-equity-and-sag-a
ftra-reach-agreement-on-streamed-theatre.

18 Broadway League, "Frozen," Grosses—Broadway in New York City, accessed December 13, 2022, www.broadwayleague.com/research/gros
ses-broadway-nyc/515657/48668/.

19 Howard University School of Law, "Black Lives Matter Movement," Law Library, last modified 2018, accessed October 21, 2022, https://library.law.
howard.edu/civilrightshistory/BLM.

20 "About," Broadway Advocacy Coalition, accessed October 21, 2022, www.bwayadvocacycoalition.org/about.

21 Broadway for Black Lives Matter, accessed October 21, 2022, www.bwa
yforblm.com.

22 Qtd. in Bill Chappell, "New York City, Former COVID-19 Epicenter, To 'Fully Reopen' On July 1," *npr.com*, last modified April 29, 2021, accessed October 21, 2022, www.npr.org/sections/coronavirus-live-upda
tes/2021/04/29/991949214/new-york-city-former-covid-19-epicenter-to
-fully-reopen-on-july-1.

Beyond 20 Seasons **185**

23 Michael Paulson, "Broadway, Baby? Curtains Go up in September, and the Box Offices Open Soon," *New York Times*, May 6, 2021, sec. A, 1, accessed October 21, 2022, www.nytimes.com/2021/05/05/theater/broadway-reopening-new-york.html?searchResultPosition=8.

24 Michael Paulson, "Two More Broadway Shows Close as Omicron Takes a Toll on Theater," *New York Times*, December 23, 2021, accessed October 21, 2022, www.nytimes.com/2021/12/23/theater/broadway-shows-close-omicron-waitress-thoughts.html.

25 For details on grosses by week both pre- and post-pandemic, see www.broadwayworld.com/grosses.cfm

26 "Broadway Grosses—Week 5," Broadwayworld.com, accessed October 21, 2022, www.broadwayworld.com/grossesbyweek.cfm?week=5.

27 Michael Paulson, "*Phantom of the Opera*, Broadway's Longest-Running Show, to Close," *New York Times*, September 16, 2022, accessed October 21, 2022, www.nytimes.com/2022/09/16/theater/phantom-of-the-opera-broadway-closing.html.

28 Marc J. Franklin, "Tony-Winning 'A Strange Loop' Announces Broadway Closing," *Deadline.com*, last modified October 11, 2022, accessed October 21, 2022, https://deadline.com/2022/10/strange-loop-broadway-closing-1235141259/.

APPENDIX A

TABLE A.1 Shows by opening date

Title	Season	Opening	Number of Performances	Category
The Full Monty	2000–2001	10/26/2000	770	Screen-to-stage
The Rocky Horror Show	2000–2001	11/15/2000	437	Screen-to-stage
Seussical	2000–2001	11/30/2000	198	Original/book
Jane Eyre	2000–2001	12/10/2000	209	Original/book
A Class Act	2000–2001	3/11/2001	105	Jukebox
Follies	2000–2001	4/5/2001	117	Revival
Bells Are Ringing	2000–2001	4/12/2001	68	Revival
The Producers	2000–2001	4/19/2001	2502	Screen-to-stage
The Adventures of Tom Sawyer	2000–2001	4/26/2001	21	Original/book
42nd Street	2000–2001	05/02/2001	1524	Revival/ Screen-to-stage
Urinetown	2001–2002	09/20/2001	965	Original/invention
Mamma Mia	2001–2002	10/18/2001	5758	Jukebox
Thou Shalt Not	2001–2002	10/25/2001	85	Original/book
By Jeeves	2001–2002	10/28/2001	73	Original/book
One Mo' Time	2001–2002	03/06/2002	21	Revue
Sweet Smell of Success	2001–2002	3/14/2002	109	Screen-to-stage
Oklahoma	2001–2002	3/21/2002	388	Revival
Thoroughly Modern Millie	2001–2002	4/18/2002	903	Screen-to-stage
Into the Woods	2001–2002	4/30/2002	279	Revival
Hairspray	2002–2003	8/15/2002	2642	Screen-to-stage
The Boys from Syracuse	2002–2003	8/18/2002	73	Revival
Flower Drum Song	2002–2003	10/17/2002	169	Revival
Amour	2002–2003	10/20/2002	17	Original/book

Appendix A 187

Title	Season	Opening	Number of Performances	Category
Movin' Out	2002–2003	10/24/2002	1303	Jukebox/dansical
Man of La Mancha	2002–2003	12/5/2002	302	Revival/screen-to-stage
La Bohème	2002–2003	12/8/2002	228	Opera
Dance of the Vampires	2002–2003	12/9/2002	56	Screen-to-stage
Urban Cowboy	2002–2003	3/27/2003	60	Screen-to-stage
Nine	2002–2003	4/10/2003	283	Revival
A Year with Frog and Toad	2002–2003	4/13/2003	73	Original/book
Gypsy	2002–2003	5/1/2003	451	Revival
The Look of Love	2002–2003	05/04/2003	49	Revue
Big River (Deaf West)	2003–2004	07/24/2003	67	Revival
Avenue Q	2003–2004	07/31/2003	2534	Original/invention
Little Shop of Horrors	2003–2004	10/02/2003	372	Revival
The Boy from Oz	2003–2004	10/16/2003	364	Jukebox
Wicked	2003–2004	10/30/2003	7098★	Original/book
Taboo	2003–2004	11/13/2003	100	Jukebox
Wonderful Town	2003–2004	11/23/2003	497	Revival
Never Gonna Dance	2003–2004	12/4/2003	84	Jukebox/screen-to-stage
Fiddler on the Roof	2003–2004	2/26/2004	781	Revival
Assassins	2003–2004	4/22/2004	101	Original/historical event
Bombay Dreams	2003–2004	4/29/2004	284	Original/invention
Caroline, or Change	2003–2004	5/2/2004	136	Original/invention
The Frogs	2004–2005	7/22/2004	92	Original/play
Dracula, The Musical	2004–2005	8/19/2004	157	Original/book
Brooklyn	2004–2005	10/21/2004	284	Original/invention
Pacific Overtures	2004–2005	12/02/2004	69	Revival
La Cage Aux Folles	2004–2005	12/09/2004	229	Revival/screen-to-stage
Little Women	2004–2005	01/23/2005	137	Original/book
Good Vibrations	2004–2005	02/02/2005	94	Jukebox
Dirty Rotten Scoundrels	2004–2005	03/03/2005	627	Screen-to-stage
Spamalot	2004–2005	03/17/2005	1575	Screen-to-stage
All Shook Up	2004–2005	03/24/2005	213	Jukebox
The Light in the Piazza	2004–2005	04/18/2005	504	Original/book
Chitty Chitty Bang Bang	2004–2005	04/28/2005	285	Screen-to-stage/jukebox
The 25th Annual Putnam County Spelling Bee	2004–2005	05/02/2005	1136	Original/invention
Sweet Charity	2004–2005	05/04/2005	279	Revival
Lennon	2005–2006	08/14/2005	49	Jukebox
In My Life	2005–2006	10/20/2005	61	Original/invention
Sweeney Todd	2005–2006	11/03/2005	349	Revival
Jersey Boys	2005–2006	11/06/2005	4642	Jukebox
The Woman in White	2005–2006	11/17/2005	109	Original/book
The Color Purple	2005–2006	12/01/2005	910	Screen-to-stage
Chita Rivera: The Dancer's Life	2005–2006	12/11/2005	72	Revue
The Pajama Game	2005–2006	2/23/2006	129	Revival
Ring of Fire	2005–2006	3/12/2006	57	Jukebox
The Threepenny Opera	2005–2006	4/20/2006	77	Revival
Lestat	2005–2006	04/25/2006	39	Original/book
The Wedding Singer	2005–2006	04/27/2006	285	Screen-to-stage

188 Appendix A

Title	Season	Opening	Number of Performances	Category
Hot Feet	2005–2006	04/30/2006	97	Jukebox
The Drowsy Chaperone	2005–2006	05/01/2006	674	Original/invention
Tarzan	2005–2006	05/10/2006	486	Screen-to-stage/jukebox
Martin Short: Fame Becomes Me	2006–2007	8/17/2006	165	Original/invention
A Chorus Line	2006–2007	10/05/2006	759	Revival
The Times They Are a-Changin'	2006–2007	10/26/2006	28	Dansical/jukebox
Grey Gardens	2006–2007	11/02/2006	307	Screen-to-stage
Dr. Seuss How the Grinch Stole Christmas	2006–2007	11/08/2006	107	Original/book
Les Misérables	2006–2007	11/09/2006	463	Revival
Mary Poppins	2006–2007	11/16/2006	2619	Screen-to-stage/jukebox
Company	2006–2007	11/29/2006	246	Revival
High Fidelity	2006–2007	12/07/2006	14	Screen-to-stage
Spring Awakening	2006–2007	12/10/2006	859	Original/play
The Apple Tree	2006–2007	12/14/2006	99	Revival
The Pirate Queen	2006–2007	04/05/2007	85	Original/book
Curtains	2006–2007	04/22/2007	511	Original/invention
Legally Blonde	2006–2007	04/29/2007	595	Screen-to-stage
Lovemusik	2006–2007	05/03/2007	60	Jukebox
110 In the Shade	2006–2007	05/09/2007	94	Revival
Xanadu	2007–2008	07/10/2007	512	Screen-to-stage/jukebox
Grease	2007–2008	08/19/2007	554	Revival
Young Frankenstein	2007–2008	11/08/2007	485	Screen-to-stage
Dr. Seuss How the Grinch Stole Christmas	2007–2008	11/9/2007	96	Remount
The Little Mermaid	2007–2008	01/10/2008	685	Screen-to-stage/jukebox
Sunday in the Park with George	2007–2008	02/21/2008	149	Revival
Passing Strange	2007–2008	02/28/2008	165	Original/invention
In the Heights	2007–2008	03/09/2008	1184	Original/invention
Gypsy	2007–2008	03/27/2008	332	Revival
South Pacific	2007–2008	04/03/2008	996	Revival
A Catered Affair	2007–2008	04/17/2008	116	Screen-to-stage
Cry-Baby	2007–2008	04/24/2008	68	Screen-to-stage
Glory Days	2007–2008	05/06/2008	1	Original/invention
[Title of Show]	2008–2009	07/17/2008	102	Original/invention
A Tale of Two Cities	2008–2009	09/18/2008	60	Original/book
13	2008–2009	10/05/2008	105	Original/invention
Billy Elliot	2008–2009	11/13/2008	1312	Screen-to-stage
Irving Berlin's White Christmas	2008–2009	11/23/2008	53	Screen-to-stage/jukebox
Shrek the Musical	2008–2009	12/14/2008	441	Screen-to-stage
Pal Joey	2008–2009	12/18/2008	85	Revival
The Story of My Life	2008–2009	02/19/2009	5	Original/invention
Guys and Dolls	2008–2009	03/01/2009	121	Revival
West Side Story	2008–2009	03/19/2009	748	Revival
Hair	2008–2009	03/31/2009	519	Revival
Rock of Ages	2008–2009	04/07/2009	2328	Jukebox

Appendix A 189

Title	Season	Opening	Number of Performances	Category
Next to Normal	2008–2009	04/15/2009	733	Original/invention
9 to 5	2008–2009	04/30/2009	148	Screen-to-stage
Bye Bye Birdie	2009–2010	10/15/2009	117	Revival
Memphis	2009–2010	10/19/2009	1165	Original/historical event
Finian's Rainbow	2009–2010	10/29/2009	92	Revival
Ragtime	2009–2010	11/15/2009	65	Revival
Irving Berlin's White Christmas	2009–2010	11/22/2009	51	Remount
Fela!	2009–2010	11/23/2009	463	Jukebox
A Little Night Music	2009–2010	12/13/2009	425	Revival/screen-to-stage
All About Me	2009–2010	03/18/2010	20	Original/invention
Come Fly Away	2009–2010	03/25/2010	188	Dansical
The Addams Family	2009–2010	04/08/2010	722	Original/comic book/strip
Million Dollar Quartet	2009–2010	04/11/2010	489	Jukebox
La Cage Aux Folles	2009–2010	04/18/2010	433	Revival/screen-to-stage
American Idiot	2009–2010	04/20/2010	422	Jukebox
Sondheim on Sondheim	2009–2010	04/22/2010	76	Revue
Promises, Promises	2009–2010	04/25/2010	289	Revival/screen-to-stage
Everyday Rapture	2009–2010	04/29/2010	85	Jukebox
Bloody Bloody Andrew Jackson	2010–2011	10/13/2010	94	Original/invention
The Scottsboro Boys	2010–2011	10/31/2010	49	Original/historical event
Women on the Verge of a Nervous Breakdown	2010–2011	11/04/2010	69	Screen-to-stage
Elf	2010–2011	11/14/2010	57	Screen-to-stage
Priscilla Queen of the Desert	2010–2011	3/20/2011	526	Screen-to-stage/jukebox
The Book of Mormon	2010–2011	3/24/2011	3959*	Original/invention
How to Succeed in Business Without Really Trying	2010–2011	03/27/2011	473	Revival
Anything Goes	2010–2011	04/07/2011	521	Revival
Catch Me If You Can	2010–2011	04/10/2011	166	Screen-to-stage
Wonderland	2010–2011	04/17/2011	33	Original/book
Sister Act	2010–2011	04/20/2011	561	Screen-to-stage
Baby It's You	2010–2011	04/27/2011	148	Jukebox
The People in the Picture	2010–2011	04/28/2011	60	Original/historical event
Spider Man: Turn Off the Dark	2011–2012	05/14/2011	1066	Original/comic book/strip
Hair	2011–2012	07/13/2011	67	Remount
Follies	2011–2012	09/12/2011	152	Revival
Godspell	2011–2012	11/07/2011	264	Revival
Bonnie and Clyde	2011–2012	12/01/2011	36	Original/historical event
On A Clear Day You Can See Forever	2011–2012	12/11/2011	57	Revival
Lysistrata Jones	2011–2012	12/14/2011	30	Original/Play
The Gershwins' Porgy and Bess	2011–2012	01/12/2012	293	Revival
Once	2011–2012	03/18/2012	1168	Screen-to-stage/jukebox
Jesus Christ Superstar	2011–2012	03/22/2012	116	Revival
Newsies	2011–2012	03/29/2012	1004	Screen-to-stage/jukebox
Evita	2011–2012	04/05/2012	337	Revival

190 Appendix A

Title	Season	Opening	Number of Performances	Category
Ghost: The Musical	2011–2012	04/23/2012	136	Screen-to-stage
Nice Work if You Can Get It	2011–2012	04/24/2012	478	Jukebox
Leap of Faith	2011–2012	04/26/2012	19	Screen-to-stage
Fela!	2012–2013	07/12/2012	28	Remount
Bring It On!	2012–2013	08/01/2012	171	Screen-to-stage
Chaplin	2012–2013	09/10/2012	135	Original/historical event
Annie	2012–2013	11/08/2012	487	Revival
Elf	2012–2013	11/09/2012	74	Remount
The Mystery of Edwin Drood	2012–2013	11/13/2012	136	Revival
A Christmas Story the Musical	2012–2013	11/19/2012	51	Screen-to-stage
Rodgers + Hammerstein's Cinderella	2012–2013	03/03/2013	769	Screen-to-stage/jukebox
Hands on a Hardbody	2012–2013	03/21/2013	28	Screen-to-stage
Kinky Boots	2012–2013	04/04/2013	2505	Screen-to-stage
Matilda the Musical	2012–2013	04/11/2013	1554	Original/book
Motown the Musical	2012–2013	04/14/2013	738	Jukebox
Jekyll and Hyde	2012–2013	04/18/2013	30	Revival
Pippin	2012–2013	04/25/2013	709	Revival
First Date	2013–2014	08/08/2013	174	Original/invention
Soul Doctor	2013–2014	08/15/2013	66	Jukebox
Big Fish	2013–2014	10/06/2013	98	Screen-to-stage
A Night With Janis Joplin	2013–2014	10/10/2013	140	Jukebox
After Midnight	2013–2014	11/03/2013	273	Revue
A Gentleman's Guide to Love and Murder	2013–2014	11/17/2013	905	Original/book
Beautiful the Carole King Musical	2013–2014	01/12/2014	2416	Jukebox
The Bridges of Madison County	2013–4014	02/20/2014	100	Screen-to-stage
Rocky	2013–2014	03/13/2014	180	Screen-to-stage
Aladdin	2013–2014	03/20/2014	2732★	Screen-to-stage/jukebox
Les Misérables	2013–2014	03/23/2014	1024	Revival
If/Then	2013–2014	03/30/2014	401	Original/invention
Bullets Over Broadway	2013–2014	04/10/2014	156	Screen-to-stage
Violet	2013–2014	04/20/2014	128	Original/book
Hedwig and the Angry Inch	2013–2014	04/22/2014	507	Original/invention
Cabaret	2013–2014	04/24/2014	388	Revival
On the Town	2014–2015	10/16/2014	368	Revival
The Last Ship	2014–2015	10/26/2014	105	Original/invention
Sideshow	2014–2015	11/17/2014	56	Revival
Honeymoon in Vegas	2014–2015	01/15/2015	93	Screen-to-stage
Holler If Ya Hear Me	2014–2015	06/19/2014	38	Jukebox
On the 20th Century	2014–2015	03/15/2015	144	Revival/screen-to-stage
Gigi	2014–2015	04/08/2015	86	Revival/screen-to-stage
An American In Paris	2014–2015	04/12/2015	623	Screen-to-stage/jukebox
It Shoulda Been You	2014–2015	04/14/2015	135	Original/invention
Finding Neverland	2014–2015	04/15/2015	565	Screen-to-stage
The King and I	2014–2015	04/16/2015	499	Revival

Appendix A   191

Title	Season	Opening	Number of Performances	Category
Fun Home	2014–2015	04/19/2015	583	Original/comic book/strip
Doctor Zhivago	2014–2015	04/21/2015	23	Screen-to-stage
Something Rotten	2014–2015	04/22/2015	708	Original/invention
The Visit	2014–2015	04/23/2015	61	Original/play
Amazing Grace	2015–2016	07/16/2015	116	Original/historical event
Hamilton	2015–2016	08/06/2015	2174*	Original/historical event
Spring Awakening	2015–2016	09/27/2015	135	Revival
Dames at Sea	2015–2016	10/22/2015	85	Original/invention
On Your Feet	2015–2016	11/05/2015	746	Jukebox
Allegiance	2015–2016	11/08/2015	111	Original/historical event
School of Rock The Musical	2015–2016	12/06/2015	1309	Screen-to-stage
The Color Purple	2015–2016	12/10/2015	450	Revival/Screen-to-stage
Fiddler on the Roof	2015–2016	12/20/2015	431	Revival
She Loves Me	2015–2016	03/17/2016	132	Revival
Bright Star	2015–2016	03/24/2016	109	Original/invention
Disaster!	2015–2016	04/08/2016	72	Jukebox
American Psycho	2015–2016	04/21/2016	54	Screen-to-stage
Waitress	2015–2016	04/24/2016	1544	Screen-to-stage
Tuck Everlasting	2015–2016	04/26/2016	39	Original/book
Shuffle Along, Or The Making of the Musical Sensation of 1921 and All That Followed	2015–2016	04/28/2016	100	Original/play
Motown the Musical	2016–2017	07/12/2016	24	Remount
Cats	2016–2017	07/31/2016	593	Revival
Holiday Inn, The New Irving Berlin Musical	2016–2017	10/06/2016	117	Screen-to-stage/jukebox
Falsettos	2016–2107	10/27/2016	84	Revival
A Bronx Tale the Musical	2016–2017	11/03/2016	700	Screen-to-stage
Natasha, Pierre, and the Great Comet of 1812	2016–2017	11/14/2016	336	Original/book
Dear Evan Hansen	2016–2017	12/04/2016	1522*	Original/invention
In Transit	2016–2017	12/11/2016	145	Original/invention
Sunset Boulevard	2016–2017	02/09/2017	138	Revival/Screen-to-stage
Sunday in the Park with George	2016–2017	02/23/2017	61	Revival
Come From Away	2016–2017	03/12/2017	1251*	Original/historical event
Miss Saigon	2016–2017	03/23/2017	340	Revival
Amelie, A New Musical	2016–2017	04/03/2017	56	Screen-to-stage
War Paint	2016–2017	04/06/2017	236	Original/historical event
Groundhog Day	2016–2017	04/17/2017	176	Screen-to-stage
Hello, Dolly	2016–2017	04/20/2017	550	Revival
Charlie and the Chocolate Factory	2016–2017	04/23/2017	305	Screen-to-stage/jukebox
Anastasia	2016–2017	04/24/2017	808	Screen-to-stage/jukebox
Bandstand	2016–2017	04/26/2017	166	Original/invention
Prince of Broadway	2017–2018	08/24/2017	76	Revue
The Band's Visit	2017–2018	11/09/2017	588	Screen-to-stage
Once on This Island	2017–2018	12/03/2017	457	Revival
SpongeBob SquarePants	2017–2018	12/04/2017	327	Screen-to-stage

192 Appendix A

Title	Season	Opening	Number of Performances	Category
Escape to Margaritaville	2017–2018	03/15/2018	124	Jukebox
Frozen	2017–2018	03/22/2018	825	Screen-to-stage
Mean Girls	2017–2018	04/08/2018	804	Screen-to-stage
Carousel	2017–2018	04/12/2018	181	Revival
My Fair Lady	2017–2018	04/19/2018	509	Revival
Summer: The Donna Summer Musical	2017–2018	04/23/2018	288	Jukebox
Head Over Heels	2018–2019	07/26/2018	188	Jukebox
Getting the Band Back Together	2018–2019	08/13/2018	40	Original/invention
Pretty Woman the Musical	2018–2019	08/16/2018	420	Screen-to-stage
King Kong	2018–2019	11/08/2018	322	Screen-to-stage
The Prom	2018–2019	11/15/2018	309	Original/invention
The Cher Show	2018–2019	12/03/2018	295	Jukebox
Be More Chill	2018–2019	03/10/2019	177	Original/book
Kiss Me Kate	2018–2019	03/14/2019	125	Revival
Ain't Too Proud	2018–2019	03/21/2019	488	Jukebox
Oklahoma!	2018–2019	04/07/2019	328	Revival
Hadestown	2018–2019	04/17/2019	644★	Original/myth
Tootsie	2018–2019	04/23/2019	293	Screen-to-stage
Beetlejuice	2018–2019	04/25/2019	366★	Screen-to-stage
Moulin Rouge	2019–2020	07/25/2019	501★	Screen-to-stage/jukebox
The Lightning Thief: The Percy Jackson Musical	2019–2020	10/16/2019	95	Original/book
Tina: The Tina Turner Musical	2019–2020	11/07/2019	370★	Jukebox
Jagged Little Pill	2019–2020	12/05/2019	171	Jukebox
West Side Story	2019–2020	02/20/2020	24	Revival
Girl From the North Country	2019–2020	03/05/2020	117	Jukebox

★Productions that were still running at the time of writing. These numbers reflect the performance total as of May 8, 2022

APPENDIX B

TABLE B.1 Shows by number of performances

Title	Season	Number of Performances	Category
Wicked	2003–2004	7098★	Original/book
Mamma Mia	2001–2002	5758	Jukebox
Jersey Boys	2005–2006	4642	Jukebox
The Book of Mormon	2010–2011	3959★	Original/invention
Aladdin	2013–2014	2732★	Screen-to-stage/jukebox
Hairspray	2002–2003	2642	Screen to stage
Mary Poppins	2006–2007	2619	Screen-to-stage/jukebox
Avenue Q	2003–2004	2534	Original/invention
Kinky Boots	2012–2013	2505	Screen-to-stage
The Producers	2000–2001	2502	Screen-to-stage
Beautiful: The Carole King Musical	2013–2014	2416	Jukebox
Rock of Ages	2008–2009	2328	Jukebox
Hamilton	2015–2016	2174★	Original/historical event
Spamalot	2004–2005	1575	Screen-to-stage
Matilda the Musical	2012–2013	1554	Original/book
Waitress	2015–2016	1544	Screen-to-stage
42nd Street	2000–2001	1524	Revival/screen-to-stage
Dear Evan Hansen	2016–2017	1522★	Original/invention
Billy Elliot	2008–2009	1312	Screen-to-stage
School of Rock The Musical	2015–2016	1309	Screen-to-stage
Movin' Out	2002–2003	1303	Jukebox/dansical
Come From Away	2016–2017	1251★	Original/historical event
In the Heights	2007–2008	1184	Original/invention

194 Appendix B

Title	Season	Number of Performances	Category
Once	2011–2012	1168	Screen-to-stage/jukebox
Memphis	2009–2010	1165	Original/historical event
The 25th Annual Putnam County Spelling Bee	2004–2005	1136	Original/invention
Spider Man Turn Off The Dark	2011–2012	1066	Original/comic book/strip
Les Misérables	2013–2014	1024	Revival
Newsies	2011–2012	1004	Screen-to-stage/jukebox
South Pacific	2007–2008	996	Revival
Urinetown	2001–2002	965	Original/invention
The Color Purple	2005–2006	910	Screen-to-stage
A Gentleman's Guide to Love and Murder	2013–2014	905	Original/book
Thoroughly Modern Millie	2001–2002	903	Screen to stage
Spring Awakening	2006–2007	859	Original/play
Frozen	2017–2018	825	Screen-to-stage
Anastasia	2016–2017	808	Screen-to-stage/jukebox
Mean Girls	2017–2018	804	Screen-to-stage
Fiddler on the Roof	2003–2004	781	Revival
The Full Monty	2000–2001	770	Screen-to-stage
Rodgers + Hammerstein's Cinderella	2012–2013	769	Screen-to-stage/jukebox
A Chorus Line	2006–2007	759	Revival
West Side Story	2008–2009	748	Revival
On Your Feet	2015–2016	746	Jukebox
Motown the Musical	2012–2013	738	Jukebox
Next to Normal	2008–2009	733	Original/invention
The Addams Family	2009–2010	722	Original/comic book/strip
Pippin	2012–2013	709	Revival
Something Rotten	2014–2015	708	Original/invention
A Bronx Tale the Musical	2016–2017	700	Screen-to-stage
The Little Mermaid	2007–2008	685	Screen-to-stage/jukebox
The Drowsy Chaperone	2005–2006	674	Original/invention
Hadestown	2018–2019	644*	Original/Myth
Dirty Rotten Scoundrels	2004–2005	627	Screen-to-stage
An American In Paris	2014–2015	623	Screen-to-stage/jukebox
Legally Blonde	2006–2007	595	Screen-to-stage
Cats	2016–2017	593	Revival
The Band's Visit	2017–2018	588	Screen-to-stage
Fun Home	2014–2015	583	Original/comic book/strip
Finding Neverland	2014–2015	565	Screen-to-stage
Sister Act	2010–2011	561	Screen-to-stage
Grease	2007–2008	554	Revival
Hello, Dolly	2016–2017	550	Revival
Priscilla Queen of the Desert	2010–2011	526	Screen-to-stage/jukebox
Anything Goes	2010–2011	521	Revival
Hair	2008–2009	519	Revival
Xanadu	2007–2008	512	Screen-to-stage/jukebox
Curtains	2006–2007	511	Original/invention
My Fair Lady	2017–2018	509	Revival
Hedwig and the Angry Inch	2013–2014	507	Original/invention
The Light in the Piazza	2004–2005	504	Original/book

Appendix B 195

Title	Season	Number of Performances	Category
Moulin Rouge	2019–2020	501★	Screen-to-stage/jukebox
The King and I	2014–2015	499	Revival
Wonderful Town	2003–2004	497	Revival
Million Dollar Quartet	2009–2010	489	Jukebox
Ain't Too Proud	2018–2019	488	Jukebox
Annie	2012–2013	487	Revival
Tarzan	2005–2006	486	Screen-to-stage/jukebox
Young Frankenstein	2007–2008	485	Screen-to-stage
Nice Work if You Can Get It	2011–2012	478	Jukebox
How to Succeed in Business Without Really Trying	2010–2011	473	Revival
Les Misérables	2006–2007	463	Revival
Fela!	2009–2010	463	Jukebox
Once on This Island	2017–2018	457	Revival
Gypsy	2002–2003	451	Revival
The Color Purple	2015–2016	450	Revival/screen-to-stage
Shrek the Musical	2008–2009	441	Screen-to-stage
The Rocky Horror Show	2000–2001	437	Screen-to-stage
La Cage Aux Folles	2009–2010	433	Revival/screen-to-stage
Fiddler on the Roof	2015–2016	431	Revival
A Little Night Music	2009–2010	425	Revival/screen-to-stage
American Idiot	2009–2010	422	Jukebox
Pretty Woman the Musical	2018–2019	420	Screen-to-stage
If/Then	2013–2014	401	Original/invention
Oklahoma	2001–2002	388	Revival
Cabaret	2013–2014	388	Revival
Little Shop of Horrors	2003–2004	372	Revival
Tina: The Tina Turner Musical	2019–2020	370★	Jukebox
On the Town	2014–2015	368	Revival
Beetlejuice	2018–2019	366★	Screen-to-stage
The Boy from Oz	2003–2004	364	Jukebox
Sweeney Todd	2005–2006	349	Revival
Miss Saigon	2016–2017	340	Revival
Evita	2011–2012	337	Revival
Natasha, Pierre, and the Great Comet of 1812	2016–2017	336	Original/book
Gypsy	2007–2008	332	Revival
Oklahoma!	2018–2019	328	Revival
SpongeBob SquarePants	2017–2018	327	Screen-to-stage
King Kong	2018–2019	322	Screen-to-stage
The Prom	2018–2019	309	Original/invention
Grey Gardens	2006–2007	307	Screen-to-stage
Charlie and the Chocolate Factory	2016–2017	305	Screen-to-stage/jukebox
Man of La Mancha	2002–2003	302	Revival/screen-to-stage
The Cher Show	2018–2019	295	Jukebox
The Gershwin's Porgy and Bess	2011–2012	293	Revival
Tootsie	2018–2019	293	Screen-to-stage
Promises, Promises	2009–2010	289	Revival/screen-to-stage
Summer: The Donna Summer Musical	2017–2018	288	Jukebox

196 Appendix B

Title	Season	Number of Performances	Category
Chitty Chitty Bang Bang	2004–2005	285	Screen-to-stage/jukebox
The Wedding Singer	2005–2006	285	Screen-to-stage
Bombay Dreams	2003–2004	284	Original/invention
Brooklyn	2004–2005	284	Original/invention
Nine	2002–2003	283	Revival
Into the Woods	2001–2002	279	Revival
Sweet Charity	2004–2005	279	Revival
After Midnight	2013–2014	273	Revue
Godspell	2011–2012	264	Revival
Company	2006–2007	246	Revival
War Paint	2016–2017	236	Original/historical event
La Cage Aux Folles	2004–2005	229	Revival/screen-to-stage
La Bohème	2002–2003	228	Opera
All Shook Up	2004–2005	213	Jukebox
Jane Eyre	2000–2001	209	Original/book
Seussical	2000–2001	198	Original/book
Come Fly Away	2009–2010	188	Dansical
Head Over Heels	2018–2019	188	Jukebox
Carousel	2017–2018	181	Revival
Rocky	2013–2014	180	Screen-to-stage
Be More Chill	2018–2019	177	Original/book
Groundhog Day	2016–2017	176	Screen-to-stage
First Date	2013–2014	174	Original/invention
Bring It On!	2012–2013	171	Screen-to-stage
Jagged Little Pill	2019–2020	171	Jukebox
Flower Drum Song	2002–2003	169	Revival
Catch Me If You Can	2010–2011	166	Screen-to-stage
Bandstand	2016–2017	166	Original/invention
Martin Short: Fame Becomes Me	2006–2007	165	Original/invention
Passing Strange	2007–2008	165	Original/invention
Dracula, The Musical	2004–2005	157	Original/book
Bullets Over Broadway	2013–2014	156	Screen-to-stage
Follies	2011–2012	152	Revival
Sunday in the Park with George	2007–2008	149	Revival
9 to 5	2008–2009	148	Screen-to-stage
Baby It's You	2010–2011	148	Jukebox
In Transit	2016–2017	145	Original/invention
On the 20th Century	2014–2015	144	Revival/screen-to-stage
A Night With Janis Joplin	2013–2014	140	Jukebox
Sunset Boulevard	2016–2017	138	Revival/screen-to-stage
Little Women	2004–2005	137	Original/book
Caroline, or Change	2003–2004	136	Original/invention
Ghost: The Musical	2011–2012	136	Screen-to-stage
The Mystery of Edwin Drood	2012–2013	136	Revival
Chaplin	2012–2013	135	Original/historical event
It Shoulda Been You	2014–2015	135	Original/invention
Spring Awakening	2015–2016	135	Revival
She Loves Me	2015–2016	132	Revival
The Pajama Game	2005–2006	129	Revival

Appendix B 197

Title	Season	Number of Performances	Category
Violet	2013–2014	128	Original/book
Kiss Me Kate	2018–2019	125	Revival
Escape to Margaritaville	2017–2018	124	Jukebox
Guys and Dolls	2008–2009	121	Revival
Follies	2000–2001	117	Revival
Bye Bye Birdie	2009–2010	117	Revival
Holiday Inn, The New Irving Berlin Musical	2016–2017	117	Screen-to-stage/jukebox
Girl From the North Country	2019–2020	117	Jukebox
A Catered Affair	2007–2008	116	Screen-to-stage
Jesus Christ Superstar	2011–2012	116	Revival
Amazing Grace	2015–2016	116	Original/historical event
Allegiance	2015–2016	111	Original/historical event
Sweet Smell of Success	2001–2002	109	Screen to stage
The Woman in White	2005–2006	109	Original/book
Bright Star	2015–2016	109	Original/invention
Dr. Seuss' How the Grinch Stole Christmas	2006–2007	107	Original/book
A Class Act	2000–2001	105	Jukebox
13	2008–2009	105	Original/invention
The Last Ship	2014–2015	105	Original/invention
[Title of Show]	2008–2009	102	Original/invention
Assassins	2003–2004	101	Original/historical event
Taboo	2003–2004	100	Jukebox
The Bridges of Madison County	2013–4014	100	Screen-to-stage
Shuffle Along, Or The Making of the Musical Sensation of 1921 and All That Followed	2015–2016	100	Original/play
The Apple Tree	2006–2007	99	Revival
Big Fish	2013–2014	98	Screen-to-stage
Hot Feet	2005–2006	97	Jukebox
Dr. Seuss' How the Grinch Stole Christmas	2007–2008	96	Remount
The Lightning Thief: The Percy Jackson Musical	2019–2020	95	Original/book
Good Vibrations	2004–2005	94	Jukebox
110 In the Shade	2006–2007	94	Revival
Bloody Bloody Andrew Jackson	2010–2011	94	Original/invention
Honeymoon in Vegas	2014–2015	93	Screen-to-stage
The Frogs	2004–2005	92	Original/play
Finian's Rainbow	2009–2010	92	Revival
Gigi	2014–2015	86	Revival/screen-to-stage
Thou Shalt Not	2001–2002	85	Original/book
The Pirate Queen	2006–2007	85	Original/book
Pal Joey	2008–2009	85	Revival
Everyday Rapture	2009–2010	85	Jukebox
Dames at Sea	2015–2016	85	Original/invention
Never Gonna Dance	2003–2004	84	Jukebox/screen-to-stage
Falsettos	2016–2107	84	Revival
The Threepenny Opera	2005–2006	77	Revival
Sondheim on Sondheim	2009–2010	76	Revue
Prince of Broadway	2017–2018	76	Revue

198 Appendix B

Title	Season	Number of Performances	Category
Elf	2012–2013	74	Remount
By Jeeves	2001–2002	73	Original/book
The Boys from Syracuse	2002–2003	73	Revival
A Year with Frog and Toad	2002–2003	73	Original/book
Chita Rivera: The Dancer's Life	2005–2006	72	Revue
Disaster!	2015–2016	72	Jukebox
Pacific Overtures	2004–2005	69	Revival
Women on the Verge of a Nervous Breakdown	2010–2011	69	Screen-to-stage
Bells Are Ringing	2000–2001	68	Revival
Cry-Baby	2007–2008	68	Screen-to-stage
Big River (Deaf West)	2003–2004	67	Revival
Hair	2011–2012	67	Remount
Soul Doctor	2013–2014	66	Jukebox
Ragtime	2009–2010	65	Revival
In My Life	2005–2006	61	Original/invention
The Visit	2014–2015	61	Original/play
Sunday in the Park with George	2016–2017	61	Revival
Urban Cowboy	2002–2003	60	Screen to stage
Lovemusik	2006–2007	60	Jukebox
A Tale of Two Cities	2008–2009	60	Original/book
The People in the Picture	2010–2011	60	Original/historical event
Ring of Fire	2005–2006	57	Jukebox
Elf	2010–2011	57	Screen-to-stage
On A Clear Day You Can See Forever	2011–2012	57	Revival
Dance of the Vampires	2002–2003	56	Screen to stage
Sideshow	2014–2015	56	Revival
Amelie, A New Musical	2016–2017	56	Screen-to-stage
American Psycho	2015–2016	54	Screen-to-stage
Irving Berlin's White Christmas	2008–2009	53	Screen-to-stage/jukebox
Irving Berlin's White Christmas	2009–2010	51	Remount
A Christmas Story the Musical	2012–2013	51	Screen-to-stage
The Look of Love	2002–2003	49	Revue
Lennon	2005–2006	49	Jukebox
The Scottsboro Boys	2010–2011	49	Original/historical event
Getting the Band Back Together	2018–2019	40	Original/invention
Lestat	2005–2006	39	Original/book
Tuck Everlasting	2015–2016	39	Original/book
Holler If Ya Hear Me	2014–2015	38	Jukebox
Bonnie and Clyde	2011–2012	36	Original/historical event
Wonderland	2010–2011	33	Original/book
Lysistrata Jones	2011–2012	30	Original/play
Jekyll and Hyde	2012–2013	30	Revival
The Times They Are a-Changin'	2006–2007	28	Dansical/jukebox
Fela!	2012–2013	28	Remount
Hands on a Hardbody	2012–2013	28	Screen-to-stage
Motown the Musical	2016–2017	24	Remount
West Side Story	2019–2020	24	Revival
Doctor Zhivago	2014–2015	23	Screen-to-stage

Title	Season	Number of Performances	Category
The Adventures of Tom Sawyer	2000–2001	21	Original/book
One Mo' Time	2001–2002	21	Revue
All About Me	2009–2010	20	Original/invention
Leap of Faith	2011–2012	19	Screen-to-stage
Amour	2002–2003	17	Original/book
High Fidelity	2006–2007	14	Screen-to-stage
The Story of My Life	2008–2009	5	Original/invention
Glory Days	2007–2008	1	Original/invention

*Productions that were still running at the time of writing. These numbers reflect the performance total as of May 8, 2022

BIBLIOGRAPHY

AAPAC. *Ethnic Representation on New York City Stages: Special 10-Year Edition*. N.p., 2016.

AAPAC. *Ethnic Representation on New York City Stages: 2016–2017*. N.p., 2017.

"About." The Asian American Performers Action Coalition. Accessed September 16, 2022. www.aapacnyc.org/.

"About." Broadway Advocacy Coalition. Accessed October 21, 2022. www.bwayadvocacycoalition.org/about.

"About." We See You White American Theatre. Accessed July 31, 2022. www.weseeyouwat.com/about.

Adamson, Charles D. "Defining the Jukebox Musical through a Historical Approach: From The Beggar's Opera to Nice Work if You Can Get It." PhD diss., Texas Tech University, 2013.

"Alan Menken Interview—Disney—Newsies the Musical." Video, 01:55. YouTube.com. Posted by DanceOn, October 14, 2011. Accessed May 23, 2022. www.youtube.com/watch?v=1o-C2kAJeDo.

"American Idiot Broadway Reviews." Broadwayworld.com. Accessed January 16, 2021. www.broadwayworld.com/reviews/American-Idiot.

Arinde, Nayaba. "Protests Shut Down Offensive Scottsboro Boys Play." *Amsterdam News* (New York), April 22, 2013. Accessed September 23, 2022. https://amsterdamnews.com/news/2013/04/22/protests-shut-down-offensive-scottsboro-boys-play/.

Bibliography **201**

Arinde, Nayaba. "'Scottsboro Boys' Fallout Continues." *Amsterdam News* (New York), April 12, 2011. Accessed September 23, 2022. https://amsterdam news.com/news/2011/04/12/scottsboro-boys-fallout-continues/.

Arnegger, Sarah Jane. "Disney's Newsies Now Available for Amateur Licensing." Playbill.com. Last modified March 1, 2018. Accessed May 23, 2022. https://pla ybill.com/article/disneys-newsies-now-available-for-amateur-licensing#:~:text= Disney's%20Newsies%20Now%20Available%20for%20Amateur%20Licensing% 20%7C%20Playbill&text=Industry%20News%20Disney's%20Newsies%20Now, schools%20and%20community%20theatre%20groups.

Bahr, Sarah. "'Beetlejuice' Will Return to Broadway in April." *The New York Times*, September 13, 2021. Accessed August 1, 2022. www.nytimes.com/ 2021/09/13/theater/beetlejuice-broadway-return.html.

Barbour, David. "High School Confidential: Mean Girls Takes Broadway in a Production That Pushes the Technology Envelope." *Lighting&Sound America*, June2018, 64–74.

Berger, Glen. *Song of Spider-Man: The Inside Story of the Most Controversial Musical in Broadway History*. New York: Simon & Schuster, 2014.

Billington, Michael. "Motown the Musical Review—Berry Gordy Show Is a Ball of Confusion." Review of Motown the Musical, London. *The Guardian* (London), March 8, 2016. Accessed December 28, 2022. www.theguardian.com/stage/ 2016/mar/08/motown-the-musical-review-berry-gordy-shaftesbury-theatre.

Brantley, Ben. "From Blue-Collar Boys to Doo-Wop Sensation: A Band's Rise and Fall." Review of Jersey Boys. *New York Times* (New York), November 7, 2005. Accessed January 9, 2021. www.nytimes.com/2005/ 11/07/theater/reviews/from-bluecollar-boys-to-doowop-sensation-a-bands -rise-and-fall.html.

Brantley, Ben. "Missionary Men With Confidence in Sunshine." Review of The Book of Mormon. *New York Times* (New York), March 24, 2011, sec. C, 1. Accessed June 9, 2022. www.nytimes.com/2011/03/25/theater/ reviews/the-book-of-mormon-at-eugene-oneill-theater-review.html.

Brantley, Ben. "Theatre Reiview; A French Milquetoast's Talent Lights the Fuse of Mischief." Review of Amour, New York. *New York Times*. Last modified October 21, 2002. Accessed June 7, 2022. www.nytimes.com/ 2002/10/21/theater/theater-review-a-french-milquetoast-s-talent-lights-the -fuse-of-mischief.html.

Brantley, Ben. "Review: Chasing Shopworn Dreams in 'Pretty Woman: The Musical.'" Review of Pretty Woman: The Musical, New York. *The New York Times* (New York), August 17, 2018, sec. C, 8. Accessed June 9, 2021. www.nytimes.com/2018/08/16/theater/review-pretty-woman-the-musical -broadway.html?rref=collection%2Fdu-guide-theater%2Ftheater-guide&acti on=click&contentCollection=undefined&region=stream&module=stream_ unit&version=latest-stories&contentPlacement=1&pgtype=collection.

202 Bibliography

Brantley, Ben. "Review: 'Finding Neverland,' a Broadway Musical With Matthew Morrison." Review of Finding Neverland, New York. *The New York Times* (New York), April 16, 2015, sec. C, 1. Accessed June 9, 2021. www.nytimes.com/2015/04/16/theater/review-finding-neverland-a-broadway-musical-with-matthew-morrison.html.

Brantley, Ben. "Review: 'Moulin Rouge! The Musical' Offers a Party, and a Playlist, for the Ages." Review of Moulin Rouge: The Musical, New York. *The New York Times*, July 25, 2019. Accessed May 12, 2022. www.nytimes.com/2019/07/25/theater/moulin-rouge-review.html.

Brantley, Ben. "Theatre Review; Tribute to a Jazz Age Lyricist." Review of Swinging on a Star: The Johnny Burke Musical, Music Box Theatre, New York. *New York Times*, October 23, 1995, sec. c, 11. Accessed December 28, 2020. www.nytimes.com/1995/10/23/theater/theater-review-tribute-to-a-jazz-age-lyricist.html.

Broadway.com Staff. "Bailey Hanks Wins MTV Legally Blonde Search; Starts as Elle Woods on July 23." Broadway.com. Last modified July 21, 2008. Accessed May 24, 2022. www.broadway.com/buzz/97534/bailey-hanks-wins-mtv-legally-blonde-search-starts-as-elle-woods-on-july-23/#:~:text=The%20Broadway%20Show-,Bailey%20Hanks%20Wins%20MTV%20Legally%20Blonde%20Search%3B%20Starts,Elle%20Woods%20on%20July%2023&text=Bailey%20Hanks%2C%20a%2020%20year,show's%20finale%20on%20July%2021.

Broadway Idiot. Directed by Doug Hamilton. FilmBuff, 2013.

Broadway for Black Lives Matter. Accessed October 21, 2022. www.bwayforblm.com.

"Broadway Grosses—Week 5." Broadwayworld.com. Accessed October 21, 2022. www.broadwayworld.com/grossesbyweek.cfm?week=5.

Broadway League. Internet Broadway Database. Accessed June 20, 2022. www.ibdb.com.

Broadway League. "Frozen." Grosses—Broadway in New York City. Accessed December 13, 2022. www.broadwayleague.com/research/grosses-broadway-nyc/515657/48668/.

Broadway: The American Musical. Directed by Michael Kantor. PBS, 2004.

Buffone, Trevor. *TikTok Broadway: Musical Theatre Fandom in the Digital Age.* New York: Oxford University Press, 2023.

Burstein, Danny, and David Rooney. "Broadway Star Danny Burstein on Harrowing Coronavirus Experience: 'Strength Through Stillness' (Guest Column)." *The Hollywood Reporter*, April 13, 2020. Accessed October 14, 2022. www.hollywoodreporter.com/lifestyle/arts/broadway-star-danny-burstein-his-harrowing-coronavirus-experience-strength-through-stillness-guest-column-1289839/.

Byrne, Kevin, and Emily Fuchs. *The Jukebox Musical: An Interpretive History.* New York: Routledge, 2022.

Bibliography **203**

Carter, Tim. *Oklahoma! The Making of an American Musical*. New Haven, CT: Yale University Press, 2007. Digital file.

Cascone, Sarah. "Here Are the 10 Most Expensive NFT Artworks, From Beeple's $69 Million Opus to an 18-Year-Old's $500,000 Vampire Queen." Artnet. Last modified March 23, 2021. Accessed June 16, 2021. https://news.artnet.com/market/most-expensive-nfts-1952597.

Cerniglia, Ken. *Newsies: Stories of the Unlikely Broadway Hit*. New York: Disney-Hyperion, 2014.

Chappell, Bill. "New York City, Former COVID-19 Epicenter, To 'Fully Reopen' On July 1." npr.com. Last modified April 29, 2021. Accessed October 21, 2022. www.npr.org/sections/coronavirus-live-updates/2021/04/29/991949214/new-york-city-former-covid-19-epicenter-to-fully-reop en-on-july-1.

"Chart History: Green Day." Billboard. Accessed January 9, 2021. www.bill board.com/music/green-day/chart-history/hot-100/song/458528.

"Chicago Awards." Internet Movie Database. Accessed May 24, 2022. www.imdb.com/title/tt0299658/awards/?ref_=tt_awd.

Citron, Stephen. *Noel and Cole: The Sophisticates*. New York: Oxford University Press, 1993. Accessed December 28, 2020. https://archive.org/deta ils/unset0000unse_a7u7/.

Clement, Olivia. "The Band's Visit Recoups on Broadway." Playbill.com. Last modified September 10, 2018. Accessed June 14, 2021. www.playbill.com/a rticle/the-bands-visit-recoups-on-broadway.

Cohen, Patricia. "Same City, New Story." *New York Times* (New York), March 11, 2009. Accessed July 6, 2022. www.nytimes.com/2009/03/15/theater/15cohe.html.

Cohen, Patricia. "'Scottsboro Boys' Is Focus of Protest." Arts Beat. Accessed September 23, 2022. https://archive.nytimes.com/artsbeat.blogs.nytimes.com/2010/11/07/scottsboro-boys-is-focus-of-protest/.

Collins-Hughes, Laura. "'The Addams Family' Musical Was Panned. Then It Became a Hit." *New York Times* (New York), April 7, 2020. Accessed June 8, 2022. www.nytimes.com/2020/04/07/theater/addams-family-musica l-history.html.

Corasaniti, Nick. "Bruce Springsteen Reopens Broadway, Ushering in Theater's Return." *New York Times* (New York), June 27, 2001, sec. C, 1. Accessed July 30, 2022. www.nytimes.com/2021/06/27/theater/bruce-sp ringsteen-broadway.html?smid=url-share.

Davenport, Ken. "What's the Average Cost of Putting on a Broadway Show? (Updated 2018)." The Producer's Perspective (blog). Entry posted June 7, 2012. Accessed June 14, 2021. www.theproducersperspective.com/my_ weblog/2012/06/whats-the-average-cost-of-putting-on-a-broadway-show. html.

204 Bibliography

Deaville, James. "Play It Again (and Again, and Again): The Superfan and Musical Theatre." In *The Routledge Companion to the Contemporary Musical*, edited by Jessica Sternfeld and Elizabeth L. Wollman. New York: Routledge, 2020.

Diamond, Robert. "Dear Evan Hansen's Ben Platt Tweets Back at Stage Door Complainers." BroadwayWorld.com. Last modified July 3, 2017. Accessed September 2, 2022. www.broadwayworld.com/article/DEAR-EVAN-HANSENs-Ben-Platt-Tw eets-Back-at-Stage-Door-Complainers-20170703.

Dick, Jeremy. "SpongeBob SquarePants Renewed for Season 14 as Franchise Continues to Expand." Movieweb. Last modified March 25, 2022. Accessed May 19, 2022. https://movieweb.com/spongebob-squarepants-season-14-renewed/.

Donahue, Tim, and Jim Patterson. *Stage Money*. Columbia, SC: University of South Caroline Press, 2010.

Downs, Olin. "Broadway's Gift to Opera: 'Oklahoma' Shows One of the Ways to an Integrated and Indigenous Form of American Lyric Theatre." *New York Times* (New York), June 6, 1943, sec. X, 5. ProQuest Historical Newspapers.

Elice, Rick. "As Jersey Boys Prepares for Its New Jersey Premiere, Tony-Nominated Book Writer Rick Elice Shares the Oral History of the Tony-Winning Musical." Interview by Ruthie Fierberg. Playbill.com. Last modified October 11, 2017. Accessed January 7, 2021. www.playbill.com/a rticle/how-the-story-of-frankie-valli-and-the-four-seasons-went-from-jerse y-lore-to-broadway-hit.

Evans, Greg. "Actor Lauren Patten Speaks Out On Broadway's 'Jagged Little Pill' Controversy & Reveals Her Future With The Show As Producers Apologize For Erasing A Nonbinary Character—Update." Deadline. Last modified September 18, 2021. Accessed September 30, 2022. https://dea dline.com/2021/09/jagged-little-pill-broadway-producers-nonbinary-erasur e-lauren-patten-1234839144/.

"Everything All at Once: A SpongeBobian Approach to Art and Life." Video, 16:20. YouTube. Posted by Tedx Talks, May 15, 2017. Accessed December 8, 2022. https://youtu.be/R3HhaWWHEOE.

"Facts and Figures." Judy Cramer. Accessed December 28, 2020. www.judycra ymer.com/press-centre/facts-and-figures.php.

Fierberg, Ruthie. "New Development in Shuffle Along Lawsuit." Playbill. com. Last modified December 24, 2016. Accessed June 20, 2022. www.pla ybill.com/article/new-development-in-shuffle-along-lawsuit.

Fitzpatrick, Felicia. "The Oral History of the Scottsboro Boys." Playbill.com. Last modified October 30, 2020. Accessed September 23, 2022. https://pla ybill.com/article/the-oral-history-of-the-scottsboro-boys.

"The Flowering of Drum Song: A Sneak Peek at the R&H Musical." Playbill. com. Last modified September 4, 2002. Accessed July 6, 2022. https://pla

Bibliography **205**

ybill.com/article/the-flowering-of-drum-song-a-sneak-peek-at-the-r-h-mus
ical-com-108044.

Flynn, Kevin, and Patrick Healy. "How the Numbers Add Up (Way Up) for 'Spider-Man.'" *New York Times*, June 23, 2011, sec. A, 1. Accessed January 7, 2021. www.nytimes.com/2011/06/23/theater/spider-man-by-the-num bers-breaking-down-its-costs.html.

Frankel, Daniel. "Disney Plus 'Hamilton' Viewership Exceeds Those Who've Seen It Live, Research Company Says." Next TV. Last modified July 20, 2020. Accessed May 25, 2022. www.nexttv.com/news/disney-plus-ham ilton-viewership-exceeds-those-whove-seen-it-live-research-company-says# :~:text=YouTube%20Ad%20Sales-,Disney%20Plus%20'Hamilton'%20Viewe rship%20Exceeds%20Those%20Who've%20Seen,It%20Live%2C%20Resear ch%20Company%20Says&text=Around%202.7%20million%20households% 20streamed,analytics%20company%20Samba%20TV%20said.

Franklin, Marc J. "Tony-Winning 'A Strange Loop' Announces Broadway Closing." Deadline.com. Last modified October 11, 2022. Accessed October 21, 2022. https://deadline.com/2022/10/strange-loop-broadway-clos ing-1235141259/.

Frith, Simon. *Performing Rites: On the Value of Popular Music.* Cambridge, MA: Harvard University Press, 1996.

Galella, Donatella. "Being in 'The Room Where It Happens': Hamilton, Obama, and Nationalist Neoliberal Multicultural Inclusion." *Theatre Survey* 59, no. 3 (July 27, 2018): 363–385. https://doi.org/10.1017/S0040557418000303.

Galella, Donatella. "Feeling Yellow: Responding to Contemporary Yellowface in Musical Performance." *Journal of Dramatic Theory and Criticism* 32, no. 2 (2018): 67–77.

Gardner, Eriq. "Judge Overturns Jury's Verdict That 'Jersey Boys' Is a Copyright Infringement." *Hollywood Reporter*, June 14, 2017. Accessed January 9, 2021. www.hollywoodreporter.com/thr-esq/judge-overturns-jurys-verdict-jersey-boy s-is-a-copyright-infringement-1013558.

Gelles, Barrie. Interview by the author. Virtual. June 13, 2022.

"Gigi Broadway Reviews." Broadwayworld.com. Accessed July 8, 2022. www.broadwayworld.com/reviews/Gigi#:~:text=The%20musical%2C%20 based%20on%20a,by%20leading%20lady%20Vanessa%20Hudgens.

Gioia, Michael. "Broadway's Spider-Man Turn Off the Dark Sets Closing Date; Las Vegas Production Planned." Playbill.com. Last modified November 19, 2013. Accessed June 8, 2022. www.playbill.com/article/broadwa ys-spider-man-turn-off-the-dark-sets-closing-date-las-vegas-production-plan ned-com-211951#:~:text=News%20Broadway's%20Spider%2DMan%20Tu rn,Harris%20announced%20Nov.

"The Graham Show Ep. 4, Finale: Thomas Schumacher, 'The Lion King, Newisies & Paying It Forward." Video. YouTube.com. Posted by The

206 Bibliography

Graham Show, November 23, 2012. Accessed May 23, 2022. www.you tube.com/watch?v=7avMd7v0mL4&t=8s.

Grant, Mark. *The Rise and Fall of the Broadway Musical*. Lebanon, NH: University Press of New England, 2005.

Green, Jesse. "Review: In 'The Cher Show,' I Got You, Babe. And You. And You." Review of The Cher Show, New York. *New York Times* (New York), December 4, 2018, sec. C, 1. Accessed February 8, 2021. www. nytimes.com/2018/12/03/theater/the-cher-show-review.html.

Gordon, David. "Shuffle Along to Close Abruptly on Broadway." Theatremania. Accessed June 20, 2022. www.theatermania.com/broadway/ news/shuffle-along-closing-date_76939.html.

Haagensen, Erik. "'Motown: The Musical' Bathes Us in Nostalgia." Review of Motown: The Musical, New York. *Backstage*. Accessed December 28, 2022. www.backstage.com/magazine/article/motown-musical-bathes-us-nostalgia -15186/.

Hanson, Kristan M. "Amar Ramasar." In *Encyclopaedia Britannica*. Accessed July 26, 2022. www.britannica.com/biography/Amar-Ramasar.

Healy, Patrick. "ArtsBeat: 'Fela!' Will Return to Broadway for a Summer Run." Artsbeat. Last modified June 11, 2012. Accessed July 26, 2022. http s://archive.nytimes.com/artsbeat.blogs.nytimes.com/2012/06/11/fela-will-r eturn-to-broadway-for-summer-run/.

Healy, Patrick. "Finding the Musical Hidden in a Punk Album." *New York Times* (New York), April 1, 2010, sec. C, 1. Accessed April 1, 2010. www. nytimes.com/2010/04/02/theater/02greenday.html.

Healy, Patrick. "'Scottsboro Boys' to Close on Dec. 12." ArtsBeat. Last modified November 30, 2010. Accessed September 23, 2022. https://archive. nytimes.com/artsbeat.blogs.nytimes.com/2010/11/30/scottsboro-boys-to-cl ose-on-december-12/.

Hershberg, Marc. "Audra McDonald Stars in New Lawsuit." Forbes.com. Last modified November 14, 2016. Accessed June 20, 2022. www.forbes.com/ sites/marchershberg/2016/11/14/audra-mcdonald-stars-in-new-lawsuit/?sh =1fb430f754c2.

Hoffman, Warren. *The Great White Way: Race and the Broadway Musical*. 2nd ed. New Brunswick, NJ: Rutgers University Press, 2020.

Holdren, Sara. "Theater Review: Can Carousel Be Brought Around?" Review of Carousel, New York. Vulture.com. Last modified April 12, 2018. Accessed December 27, 2022. www.vulture.com/2018/04/theater-re view-can-carousel-be-brought-around.html.

Howard University School of Law. "Black Lives Matter Movement." Law Library. Last modified 2018. Accessed October 21, 2022. https://library.law. howard.edu/civilrightshistory/BLM.

Bibliography 207

"How SpongeBob BROKE Broadway." Video. YouTube. Posted by Wait in the Wings, September 16, 2019. Accessed May 19, 2022. www.youtube.com/watch?v=IuzcyO9xewQ.

Hughes, Langston. *The Big Sea*. New York: Alfred A. Knopf, 1940.

Isherwood, Charles. "Stomping Onto Broadway With a Punk Temper Tantrum." Review of American Idiot, New York. New York Times (New York), April 21, 2010, sec. C, 1. Accessed January 16, 2021. www.nytimes.com/2010/04/21/theater/reviews/21idiot.html.

Jahdwani, Lavinia, and Victor Vazquez. "Identity Conscious Casting: Moving Beyond Color-Blind and Color-Conscious Casting." Howlround Theatre Commons. Last modified February 2, 2021. Accessed July 26, 2022. https://howlround.com/identity-conscious-casting.

Jarrow, Kyle. *The SpongeBob Musical*. N.p.: Concord Theatricals, n.d.

"Jersey Boys." *Jersey Boys*. Accessed January 9, 2021. www.jerseyboysinfo.com/.

Jones, Kenneth. "Protestors Take Aim at Scottsboro Boys Musical." Playbill.com. Last modified November 8, 2010. Accessed September 23, 2022. https://playbill.com/article/protestors-take-aim-at-scottsboro-boys-musical-com-173373.

Jones, Morgan. "How the LDS Church's Response to 'The Book of Mormon' Musical Is Actually Working." Deseret News. Last modified November 16, 2016. Accessed June 9, 2022. www.deseret.com/2016/11/16/20600593/how-the-lds-church-s-response-to-the-book-of-mormon-musical-is-actually-working.

Kenrick, John. *Musical Theatre: A History*. 2nd ed. London: Bloomsbury Methuen Drama, 2018.

Kerr, Alexandra. "A Historical Timeline of COVID-19 in New York City." Investopedia. Last modified April 5, 2021. Accessed October 14, 2022. www.investopedia.com/historical-timeline-of-covid-19-in-new-york-city-5071986.

Kessler, Kelly. *Broadway in the Box: Television's Lasting Love Affair with the Musical*. New York: Oxford University Press, 2020.

Kinshasa, Kwando M. "Editorial. On Committing a Cultural Felony: 'The Scottsboro Boys' Minstrel Show (New York), April 12, 2011." https://amsterdamnews.com/news/2011/04/12/on-committing-a-cultural-felony-the-scottsboro/.

Kircher, Madison Malone. "Jagged Little Pill's Lauren Patten Will Not Admit That She Steals the Show." Vulture.com. Last modified June 13, 2020. Accessed September 30, 2022. www.vulture.com/2020/06/jagged-little-pills-lauren-patten-steals-the-show.html.

Knapp, Raymond. *The American Musical and the Formation of National Identity*. 2nd ed. Princeton, NJ: Princeton Univ. Press, 2005.

Koltnow, Barry. "Berry Gordy, the Father of Motown, Sets Record Straight." *Orlando Sentinel* (Orlando, FL), December 19, 1994. Accessed December 28,

2022. www.orlandosentinel.com/news/os-xpm-1994-12-20-9412170897-st ory.html.

Kourlas, Gia. "A Dark 'Oklahoma!' Brings Barefoot Modern Dance to Broadway." *The New York Times* (New York), April 21, 2019, sec. AR, 16. Accessed July 26, 2022. www.nytimes.com/2019/04/16/arts/dance/okla homa-dream-ballet.html#:~:text=For%20the%20show's%20choreographer% 2C%20John,take%20this%20time%20to%20dream.%E2%80%9D.

Landau, Tina. "How Director Tina Landau Found the Broadway Musical in SpongeBob SquarePants." Interview by Ryan McPhee. *Playbill.com*. Last modified November 5, 2017. Accessed May 20, 2022. www.playbill.com/a rticle/how-director-tina-landau-found-the-broadway-musical-in-spongebob -squarepants.

Landau, Tina. "An Interview with Tina Landau." By Victoria Myers. *The Interval*. Last modified January 30, 2018. Accessed May 20, 2022. www. theintervalny.com/interviews/2018/01/an-interview-with-tina-landau/.

Landau, Tina. "Stage Directions: Tina Landau Gets Real about Being a Director Who Plays and Explores." Interview by Mervyn Rothstein. *Playbill.com*. Last modified July 5, 2018. Accessed May 20, 2022. https://playbill. com/article/stage-directions-tina-landau-gets-real-about-being-a-director-w ho-plays-and-explores.

Lardieri, Alexa. "New York Bans Large Gatherings, Closes Broadway as Coronavirus Spreads." *US News & World Report*. Last modified March 12, 2020. Accessed October 14, 2022. www.usnews.com/news/health-news/articles/ 2020-03-12/new-york-bans-large-gatherings-closes-broadway-as-coronavir us-spreads.

"LEDs and OLEDs." History of Lighting. Accessed September 2, 2022. http s://edisontechcenter.org/LED.html.

Lee, Ashley. "'Jagged Little Pill' Fumbled a Character's Gender Identity. The Tour Vows to do Better." *LA Times*, September 16, 2022. Accessed September 30, 2022. www.latimes.com/entertainment-arts/story/2022-09-16/ jagged-little-pill-jo-gender-identity-revisions?fbclid=IwAR1E7TmktBZAop UxRegNWzy0eXLUpDt0cI3AqCFkDZ1oQrQW5eORKyJVBvo.

Lenker, Maureen Lee. "How Moulin Rouge! The Musical Turned a Smash Soundtrack into a Broadway Show." *Entertainment Weekly*, July 23, 2019. Accessed May 12, 2022. https://ew.com/theater/2019/07/23/moulin-rou ge-the-musical-behind-the-music/.

Lewis, Christian. "One Step Forward, Two Steps Back: Broadway's Jagged Little Journey Toward Nonbinary Inclusion." *The Brooklyn Rail*, April2021. Accessed September 30, 2022. https://brooklynrail.org/2021/04/theater/One-Step -Forward-Two-Steps-Back-Broadways-Jagged-Little-Journey-Toward-Nonbin ay-Inclusion.

Bibliography **209**

"Longest-Running Shows on Broadway." Playbill.com. Last modified March 9, 2020. Accessed June 9, 2021. www.playbill.com/article/long-runs-on-broadway-com-109864.

Marks, Peter. "As Rock-Star Portrayals Go, It Doesn't Get Any Better than Adrienne Warren as Tina Turner." Review of Tina, New York. Washington Post (Washington, DC), November 7, 2019. Accessed February 8, 2021. www.washingtonpost.com/entertainment/theater_dance/as-rock-star-portrayals-go-it-doesnt-get-any-better-than-adrienne-warren-as-tina-turner/2019/11/07/79ee6c4c-0179-11ea-8bab-0fc209e065a8_story.html.

Marks, Peter. "'West Side Story' at the National Theatre." *Washington Post* (Washington, DC), January 9, 2009. Accessed July 6, 2022. www.washingtonpost.com/wp-dyn/content/article/2009/01/08/AR2009010803931.html.

McMaster, James. "Why 'Hamilton' Is Not the Revolution You Think It Is." Howlround Theatre Commons. Last modified February 23, 2016. Accessed July 31, 2022. https://howlround.com/why-hamilton-not-revolution-you-think-it.

McKinley, Jesse. "Read, Aim, Sing: 'Assassins' Hits Broadway." *New York Times* (New York), April 22, 2004, sec. E, 1. www.nytimes.com/2004/04/22/theater/ready-aim-sing-assassins-hits-broadway.html.

Mele, Christopher, and Patrick Healy. "'Hamilton' Had Some Unscripted Lines for Pence. Trump Wasn't Happy." *New York Times* (New York), November 19, 2016, sec. A, 10. Accessed July 31, 2022. www.nytimes.com/2016/11/19/us/mike-pence-hamilton.html.

Meyer, Dan. "Actors' Equity and SAG-AFTRA Reach Agreement on Streamed Theatre." *Playbill.com*. Last modified November 20, 2020. Accessed October 28, 2022. https://playbill.com/article/actors-equity-and-sag-aftra-reach-agreement-on-streamed-theatre.

Mink, Casey. "How a TV Ad Enticed Broadway Crowds Right after 9/11." *New York Times* (New York), September 12, 2021, sec. AR, 4. Accessed July 30, 2022. www.nytimes.com/2021/09/09/theater/9-11-broadway-new-york-commercial.html#:~:text=Following%20the%20Sept.,near%2Dempty%20houses%20for%20weeks.

"A Monetary Autopsy of Spider-Man: Turn Off the Dark." Vulture.com. Last modified November 24, 2013. Accessed June 14, 2021. www.vulture.com/2013/11/spider-man-leaves-behind-broadways-biggest-bill.html.

Mordden, Ethan. *Anything Goes: A History of American Musical Theatre.* Oxford: Oxford University Press, 2015.

Morning Edition. "'King Kong' on Broadway Is the 2,400-Pound Gorilla in the Room." Hosted by Jeff Lunden. Aired November 7, 2018, on NPR.

"'Moulin Rouge!' Director Baz Luhrmann on Turning the Film into the Tony-Nominated Broadway Musical." Video, 59:45. YouTube. Accessed May 12, 2022. www.youtube.com/watch?v=pGE9efj6b2I.

210 Bibliography

Mutie, Hope. "What's with the Trend of Turning Old Tweets into NFTs?" CryptoVantage. Last modified March 3, 2021. Accessed June 16, 2021. www.cryptovantage.com/news/whats-with-the-trend-of-turning-old-tweets-into-nfts/.

"Newsies (1992)." Internet Movie Database. Accessed August 1, 2022. www.imdb.com/title/tt0104990/?ref_=fn_al_tt_1.

The New York Times. "'Little Whopper' Welcome; New Play at the Casino a Good Farce, with Tuneful Music." Unsigned review of The Little Whopper, New York. October 16, 1919. Accessed June 8, 2021. www.nytimes.com/1919/10/16/archives/little-whopper-welcome-new-play-at-the-casino-a-good-farce-with.html.

Osatinski, Amy Sara. *Disney Theatrical Productions: Producing Broadway Musicals the Disney Way.* New York: Routledge, 2019.

Osatinski, Amy Sara. "Ghosts in the Machine: Digital Technology and Screen to Stage Musicals." In *IBroadway: Musical Theatre in the Digital Age*, edited by Jessica Hillman-McCord. Basingstoke: Palgrave Macmillan, 2018.

Paulson, Michael. "As Broadway Returns, Shows Rethink and Restage Depictions of Race." *New York Times* (New York), October 24, 2021, sec. A, 1. Accessed June 9, 2022. www.nytimes.com/2021/10/23/theater/broadway-race-depictions.html.

Paulson, Michael. "The Battle of 'Miss Saigon.'" *New York Times* (New York), March 19, 2017, sec. AR, 1.

Paulson, Michael. "Broadway, Baby? Curtains Go up in September, and the Box Offices Open Soon." *New York Times* (New York), May 6, 2021, sec. A, 1. Accessed October 21, 2022. www.nytimes.com/2021/05/05/theater/broadway-reopening-new-york.html?searchResultPosition=8.

Paulson, Michael. "Decision to Close 'Shuffle Along' Is Debated Along Broadway." *New York Times* (New York), June 25, 2016, sec. C, 3. Accessed June 20, 2022. www.nytimes.com/2016/06/25/theater/decision-to-close-shuffle-along-is-debated-along-broadway.html.

Paulson, Michael. "Despite Turnaround, 'Beetlejuice' Being Forced out of Theater." *The New York Times* (New York), December 11, 2019, sec. C, 1. Accessed August 1, 2022. www.nytimes.com/2019/12/09/theater/beetlejuice-broadway-evicted.html.

Paulson, Michael. "'Fun Home' Recoups on Broadway." *New York Times* (New York), December 13, 2015, sec. C, 3. Accessed June 6, 2022. www.nytimes.com/2015/12/14/theater/fun-home-recoups-on-broadway.html#:~:text=First%2C%20the%20producers%20kept%20costs,cost%20more%20than%20%2415%20million.

Paulson, Michael. "'Motown: The Musical' to Close for Second Time on Broadway." *The New York Times* (New York), July 23, 2016, sec. C, 3. Accessed December 28, 2022. www.nytimes.com/2016/07/23/theater/motown-the-musical-to-close-for-second-time-on-broadway.html.

Bibliography **211**

Paulson, Michael. "Phantom of the Opera,' Broadway's Longest-Running Show, to Close." *New York Times* (New York), September 16, 2022. Accessed October 21, 2022. www.nytimes.com/2022/09/16/theater/phantom-of-the-opera-broadway-closing.html.

Paulson, Michael. "Pregnancy Prompted Closing of 'Shuffle Along.' Should Insurance Pay?" *New York Times* (New York), November 16, 2016, sec. C, 3. Accessed June 20, 2022. www.nytimes.com/2016/11/16/theater/pregnancy-prompted-closing-of-shuffle-along-should-insurance-pay.html.

Paulson, Michael. "The Problem with Broadway Revivals: They Revive Gender Stereotypes, Too." *The New York Times* (New York), February 25, 2018, sec. AR, 18. Accessed July 26, 2022. www.nytimes.com/2018/02/22/theater/gender-stereotypes-carousel-my-fair-lady-pretty-woman.html.

Paulson, Michael. "Showtime on Broadway, Suspended." *New York Times* (New York), April 21, 2020, sec. C, 1. Accessed October 14, 2022. www.nytimes.com/2020/04/20/theater/broadway-closed-coronavirus.html.

Paulson, Michael. "'Shuffle Along' and Insurer Drop Pregnancy-Prompted Lawsuit." *New York Times* (New York), October 27, 2020, sec. C, 4. Accessed June 20, 2022. www.nytimes.com/2020/10/21/theater/shuffle-along-audra-mcdonald-insurer-pregnancy-lawsuit.html#:~:text=Scott%20Rudin%2C%20the%20lead%20producer,when%20its%20star%20became%20pregnant.&text=As%20a%20subscriber%2C%20you%20have,articles%20to%20give%20each%20month.

Paulson, Michael. "Two More Broadway Shows Close as Omicron Takes a Toll on Theater." *New York Times* (New York), December 23, 2021. Accessed October 21, 2022. www.nytimes.com/2021/12/23/theater/broadway-shows-close-omicron-waitress-thoughts.html.

The Playbill Staff. "Broadway's New West Side Story Releases Statement Regarding Casting Controversy." Playbill.com. Last modified February 13, 2020. Accessed September 30, 2022. https://playbill.com/article/broadways-new-west-side-story-releases-statement-regarding-casting-controversy.

Purdy, Stephen. *Flop Musicals of the Twenty First Century: How They Happened, When They Happened (and What We've Learned).* London: Routledge, 2020.

Riedel, Michael. "Spinning A $30M Show." *New York Post* (New York), May 2, 2007. Accessed July 1, 2022. https://nypost.com/2007/05/02/spinning-a-30m-show/.

Resnikoff, Paul. "'Motown: The Musical' Forced to Close after Two Weeks…." *Digital Music News*. Last modified July 24, 2016. Accessed July 26, 2022. www.digitalmusicnews.com/2016/07/24/motown-musical-closes-two-weeks/.

Reuters. "First Broadway Play Opens in NY since Lengthy Pandemic Shutdown." Reuters. Last modified August 5, 2021. Accessed July 30, 2022. www.reuters.com/world/us/first-broadway-play-opens-ny-since-lengthy-pandemic-shutdown-2021-08-05/.

212 Bibliography

Robertson, Campbell. "Fleeting Stage Glory, Savored and Survived." *The New York Times* (New York), May 19, 2008. Accessed June 9, 2022. www.nytim es.com/2008/05/19/theater/19glory.html#:~:text=But%20after%2017%20p reviews%2C%20a,its%20entire%20%242.5%20million%20investment.

Rooney, David. "A Gentleman's Gide to Love & Murder: Theater Review." Review of A Gentleman's Guide to Love & Murder, New York. *Hollywood Reporter*. Last modified November 17, 2013. Accessed June 7, 2022. www. hollywoodreporter.com/news/general-news/a-gentlemans-guide-love-mur der-656830/.

Rooney, David. "Shrek the Musical." Review of Shrek the Musical, New York. *Variety.com*. Accessed January 7, 2021. https://variety.com/2008/ film/awards/shrek-the-musical-4-1200472752/.

Rosky, Nicole. "Broadway By Design: Scott Pask, Finn Ross, Adam Young and Gregg Barnes Bring MEAN GIRLS from Page to Stage." Broadwayworld. com. Last modified June 2, 2018. Accessed June 18, 2021. www.broadwa yworld.com/article/Broadway-By-Design-Scott-Pask-Finn-Ross-Adam-Young -Gregg-Barnes-Bring-MEAN-GIRLS-from-Page-to-Stage-20180602.

Rothstein, Mervyn. "Stage Directions: Why a Decades-Long Connection to Carousel Led Jack O'Brien to Direct the 2018 Broadway Revival." Playbill. com. Last modified May 29, 2018. Accessed December 27, 2022. www.pla ybill.com/article/stage-directions-why-a-decades-long-connection-to-carou sel-led-jack-obrien-to-direct-the-2018-broadway-revival.

Rubin, Rebecca, and Brent Lang. "'West Side Story' Broadway Opening Night Sparks Protests." *Variety*, February 21, 2020. Accessed September 30, 2022. https://variety.com/2020/legit/news/west-side-story-broadway-op ening-night-protests-1203509630/.

Russell, Curtis. "Screen-To-Stage Musicals Database." Last modified 2020. Accessed June 8, 2021. www.documentabarbarism.com/academia-new.

Ryan, Patrick. "They Closed on Opening Night Due to COVID; Here's How 'Six' Bounced Back to Rule Broadway." *USA Today*. www.usatoday.com/ story/entertainment/music/2021/10/10/six-musical-broadway-interview-c ovid-pandemic-shutdown-reopening/5921224001/.

Savran, David. *A Queer Sort of Materialism: Recontextualizing American Theater.* Ann Arbor, MI: University of Michigan Press, 2003.

Scheck, Frank. "Green Day's American Idiot a Tough Sell on Broadway." *Hollywood Reporter*, April 10, 2010. Accessed January 16, 2021. www.reuters. com/article/us-stage-idiot/green-days-american-idiot-a-tough-sell-on-broa dway-idUSTRE63J6IO20100420.

Schumacher, Thomas. "THE GRAHAM SHOW Episode 4: Thomas Schu-macher, 'The Lion King, Newsies and Paying It Forward.'" Interview by Graham Douglass. Video. YouTube.com. Posted November 23, 2012. Accessed August 1, 2022. www.youtube.com/watch?v=7avMd7v0mL4.

Bibliography **213**

Shapiro, Lila. "'We Stand With Alexandra Waterbury': Inside a Protest of West Side Story on Broadway." Vulture.com. Last modified February 1, 2020. www.vulture.com/2020/02/west-side-story-broadway-protest-alexandra-waterbury-amar-ramasar.html.

Sheffield, Rob. "American Idiot." Review of American Idiot. *Rolling Stone*, September 30, 2004, 186. ProQuest 5000.

Soloski, Alexis. "'Hamilton' Was Just the Beginning. Hollywood Loves Broadway, Again." *New York Times* (New York), November 4, 2020. Accessed June 15, 2022. www.nytimes.com/2020/11/04/movies/broadway-movie-adaptations-prom.html?searchResultPosition=1.

"Spider-Man, The Lion King, and Life on the Creative Edge." Video, 18:16. Ted.com. Posted March2011. Accessed June 30, 2022. www.ted.com/talks/julie_taymor_spider_man_the_lion_king_and_life_on_the_creative_edge/transcript?language=en.

Stasio, Marilyn. "Legit Review: 'Motown.'" Review of Motown: The Musical, New York. Variety. Accessed December 28, 2022. https://variety.com/2013/legit/reviews/legit-review-motown-1200364348/.

Stempel, Larry. *Showtime: A History of the Broadway Musical Theater.* New York: W.W. Norton, 2011.

Stiehl, Pamyla, and Bud Coleman. *Backstage Pass: A Survey of American Musical Theatre.* Dubuque, IA: Kendall Hunt, 2013.

Stiehl, Pamyla. "Because She Said So: How Twyla Tharp and Movin' Out Legitimized the 'Dansical' as a Choreographic Domain/Diversion on Broadway." *Journal of American Drama and Theatre* 22, no. 2 (Spring 2010): 85–107.

Taylor, Millie. "I've Heard That Song Before: The Jukebox Musical and Entertainment." In *Musical Theatre, Realism and Entertainment*, 149–166. Farnham: Ashgate, 2012.

Thomas, Leah Marilla. "How Anaïs Mitchell's Musical 'Hadestown' Is Making Broadway History For Women." Bustle. Last modified May 6, 2019. Accessed June 9, 2022. www.bustle.com/p/anais-mitchells-hadestown-is-making-broadway-history-for-women-but-she-wants-it-to-be-normal-for-the-next-generation-17130069.

Tony Awards. Accessed July 5, 2022. www.tonyawards.com/.

Tran, Diep. "I Am Miss Saigon, and I Hate It." Editorial. *American Theatre*, April 13, 2017. Accessed July 8, 2022. www.americantheatre.org/2017/04/13/i-am-miss-saigon-and-i-hate-it/.

Tran, Diep. "SAG-AFTRA and Actors' Equity Feud over Streaming Rights for Theater Productions." Backstage.com. Last modified October 19, 2020. Accessed October 28, 2022. www.backstage.com/magazine/article/sag-aftra-actors-equity-theater-streaming-rights-jurisdiction-71925/.

Tran, Diep. "S.F. Theatre Director Bartlett Sher Shifts 'My Fair Lady' from Frothy Romance to Social Critique." Datebook. Last modified November 1, 2021.

Accessed July 6, 2022. https://datebook.sfchronicle.com/theater/s-f-theater-dir ector-bartlett-sher-shifts-my-fair-lady-from-frothy-romance-to-social-critique.

Vandevender, Bryan M. "'Kiss Today Goodbye, and Point Me Toward Tomorrow'. Reviving the Time-Bound Musical, 1968–1975." PhD diss., University of Missouri, 2014.

Vincentelli, Elizabeth. "Spidey's Back." Review of Spiderman: Turn Off The Dark, New York. *New York Post*. Last modified June 15, 2011. Accessed June 30, 2022. https://nypost.com/2011/06/15/spideys-back/.

The Visibility Report: Racial Representation on NYC Stages. N.p.: AAPAC, 2021.

Weissman Center for International Business at Baruch College. "NYCData." NYCData. Accessed June 14, 2021. www.baruch.cuny.edu/nycdata/.

Wetmore, Brendan. "'Beetlejuice' on Broadway is Breaking TikTok." *Paper*, October 3, 2019. Accessed August 1, 2022. www.papermag.com/beetlejui ce-broadway-tiktok-trend-1-2640689936.html?rebelltitem=1#rebelltitem1.

"What is an LED?" *LEDs Magazine*. Last modified September 1, 2004. Accessed September 2, 2022. www.ledsmagazine.com/leds-ssl-design/ma terials/article/16701292/what-is-an-led.

Whitfield, Sarah. "Framing and Reframing: Existing Ways of Looking." Introduction to *Reframing the Musical: Race, Culture and Identity*, xi–xxxii. London: Methuen Drama, 2021.

"Who's Going to the Theatre: Stats and Facts from Broadway." Theatreseatstore. com. Accessed June 14, 2021. www.theaterseatstore.com/blog/broadway-data.

"Wicked Broadway Reviews." Broadwayworld.com. Accessed June 7, 2022. www.broadwayworld.com/reviews/Wicked.

Wild, Stephi. "THE BOOK OF MORMON Creatives Will Convene to Address Concerns From Black Cast Members." Broadwayworld.com. Last modified March 12, 2021. Accessed June 9, 2022. www.broadwayworld. com/article/THE-BOOK-OF-MORMON-Creatives-Will-Convene-to-A ddress-Concerns-From-Black-Cast-Members-20210312.

Wolcott, James. "Pop Goes the Great White Way." *Vanity Fair*, July 1, 2011. Accessed September 2, 2022. www.vanityfair.com/culture/2011/07/musica ls-201107.

Wolfe, Jonathan, and Nick Corasaniti. "New York Today: Terrorism and Tourism." *New York Times*, November 3, 2017. www.nytimes.com/2017/ 11/03/nyregion/new-york-today-terrorism-and-tourism.html.

Woll, Allen. *Black Musical Theatre: From Coontown to Dreamgirls*. New York: Da Capo, 1989.

Wollman, Elizabeth L. *A Critical Companion to the American Stage Musical*. London: Bloomsbury Methuen Drama, 2020.

Young, Catherine M. "Sympathy for the Incel? On 'Oklahoma!' and Jud Fry in the #MeToo Era." Howlround.com. Last modified June 26, 2019. Accessed July 19, 2022. https://howlround.com/sympathy-incel.

INDEX

Page numbers in italics refer to figures. Page numbers in bold refer to tables.
Page numbers followed by 'n' refer to notes.

9 to 5 **189**, **196**
13 **116**, **188**, **197**
25th Annual Putnum County Spelling Bee **115**, **187**, **194**
42nd Street 52, **145**, **186**, **193**
110 In the Shade **146**, **188**, **197**

AAPAC *see* Asian American Performers Action Coalition (AAPAC)
ABBA xii, 60
Actor's Fund 176
Actors' Equity 15, 47n57, 157, 177, 184n15
Adams, Warren 80
Addams Family, The **116**, 122–123, **189**, **194**
Adventures of Tom Sawyer, The **114**, **186**, **199**
Adventures of Tom Sawyer, The (Twain) 121

After Midnight **57**, 59, **190**, **196**
Agreeable Surprise, The 148
Aguirre-Sacasa, Roberto 135
Ain't Misbehavin' 59
Ain't Too Proud **56**, 61, 62, 71, **192**, **195**
Aladdin **56**, **190**, **193**
Alice in Wonderland (Caroll) 121
All About Me **116**, 128, **189**, **199**
Allee, David S. 175
Allegiance xv, **117**, 126, 142n18, **191**, **197**
Alley, Tin Pan 58, 72
All Shook Up **54**, 61, **187**, **196**
Always Patsy Cline 59
Amazing Grace **117**, **191**, **197**
Amazing Spiderman, The (Lee) 123
Amelie, A NewMusical **191**, **198**
American Federation of Musicians 15

216 Index

American Idiot 76, **189**, **195**; case study of 71–75; significance of 18, **55**, 61

American in Paris, An **56**, 88, **190**, **194**

American Musical and the Formation of National Identity, The (Knapp) 1

American Psycho 88, **191**, **198**

American Theatre 158

Amour **114**, 121, **186**, **199**

Anastasia **56**, 88, 96–97, **191**, **194**

ancestral memory, idea of 160, 161

animated/family film musicals 88, 96

Annie **146**, **190**, **195**

Anything Goes 58, **146**, **189**, **194**

Anything Goes: A History of American Musical Theatre (Mordden) 148

Apple Tree, The **146**, **188**, **197**

Arad, Avi 134

Arlen, Harold 59

Armstrong, Billie Joe 71, 72–74

Arnold, Samuel 148

Asian American Performers Action Coalition (AAPAC) 11, 12, 159, 179–180

Assassins 4, **114**, 126, 142n19, **187**, **197**

"Audra McDonald Stars in New Lawsuit" (Hershberg) 139

autobiographical jukebox musical 61, 66–71

Avenue Q 18, **114**, 129, **187**, **193**

Aymé, Marce 121

Babbitt, Natalie 121

Baby It's You **55**, 61, **189**, **196**

Backstage 79, 177

Band's Visit, The xiii, 88, 90, 96, **188**, **191**, **194**

Bandstand **117**, **191**, **196**

Baum, L. Frank 120

Beach, Gary x

Beautiful: The Carole King Musical **56**, 61, 70, **190**, **193**

Beauty and the Beast 88, 96

Beauty and the Beast (film) xii

"Because She Said So…" (Stihl) 49

Bechdel, Alison 123

Beeple 92

Beetlejuice (film) 30

Beetlejuice the Musical 30–33, **192**, **195**

Beggar's Opera, The 57–58

Bells are Ringing 98, **145**, **186**, **198**

Be More Chill 30, 121, **118**, **192**, **196**

Be More Chill (Vizzini) 30, 121

Berger, Glen 27, 131, 132, 134, 135–136, 143n34

Berkley, Busby 149

Bialystock, Max xi

Big Fish **190**, **197**

Big River **145**, **187**, **198**

Big Sea, The (Hughes) 136

Bikini Bottom, idea of 99–100, 110n34

Billington, Michael 78

Billy Elliot 96, **188**, **193**

biographical jukebox musical: case study of 78–80; multiple artist 61–62, 78–80

BIPOC *see* Black, Indigenous, and People of Color (BIPOC)

Black, Indigenous, and People of Color (BIPOC) xv, 7, 8, 12

Black Crook, The 119–120, 148

Blackface minstrelsy 35–36, 38

Black Lives Matter Movement 21, 130, 178–179

Blaemire, Nick 128

Block, Stephanie J. 66

blockbuster film musicals 88, 95, 96

Bloody Andrew Jackson **116**, **189**, **197**

Bloom, Leo xi

Boheme, La 48, **187**, **196**

Bombay Dreams xv, **115**, **187**, **196**

Bonnie and Clyde **116**, **189**, **198**

book, original musicals based on 120–122

Book of Mormon, The xiii, xiv, **116**, 129–131, 180, **189**, **193**

"Boulevard of Broken Dreams" (song) 71

Boy From Oz, The **54**, **187**, **195**

Boys from Syracuse, The **145**, **186**, **198**

Index **217**

Brantley, Ben 57, 68–69, 77, 89, 121, 129–130

Breslin, Michael 176

Brickman, Marshall 66, 67

Bridges of Madison County, The **190**, **197**

Brigadoon 149

Bright Star **117**, **191**, **197**

Bring It On! **190**, **196**

Broadway Advocacy Coalition 179, 180

Broadway for Black Lives Matter 179

Broadway Idiot (documentary) 71–72, 73–74

Broadway in the Box (Kessler) 108

Broadway League 81n8, 90, 136, 143n34, 148, 173

Broadway productions, cost of 89–91

Broadway reopening 181–182

Broadwayworld.com 34, 93, 130

Broderick, Matthew x

Bronx Tale the Musical, A **191**, **194**

Brooklyn **115**, **187**, **196**

Brooklyn Rail, The 42

Brooks, Mel x

Brooks, Said xi

Brown, Michael 179

Buddy: The Buddy Holly Story 59

Buffone, Trevor 32

Bullets Over Broadway **190**, **196**

bumpers 30

Bundy Laura Bell 107

Burke, Turana 171n44

Burstein, Danny 174–175

Bush, George W. 18

Bye Bye Birdie **146**, **189**, **197**

By Jeeves **114**, **186**, **198**

Byrne, Kevin 64

Cabaret xiv, 35, 120, **147**, **190**, **195**

Cage Aux Folles, La **145**, **146**, **187**, **189**, **195**, **196**

Calloway, Cab 59

cancel culture 40

Caroline, or Change **115**, **187**, **196**

Caroll, Lewis 121

Carousel: importance of **147**, 149, 152, 156, **192**, **196**; revisionist revival, as case study 165–168

Carter, Tim 160

Cash, Johnny 62

Catch Me If You Can **189**, **196**

Catered Affair, A **188**, **197**

Cats **147**, **188**, **191**, **194**

Cats (film) 106

Cerniglia, Kenneth 103

chamber musical 171n37

Chapin, Harry 59

Chaplin **116**, **190**, **196**

Charlie and the Chocolate Factory **56**, **191**, **195**

Chauvin, Derek 178

Chavkin, Rachel 125

Cher Show, The **56**, 66, **192**, **195**

Chicago 35, 90

Chicago (film) 106

Chicago Tribune 74

Chita Rivera **57**, **187**, **198**

Chitty Chitty Bang Bang **54**, **86**, **196**

Chorus Line, A **146**, 151, 152, **188**, **194**

Christmas Story, A **190**, **198**

Circle Jerk 176

Class Act, A **54**, **186**, **197**

classic film musicals 88

Coleman, Bud 170n14

colorblind casting 165, 167

color-conscious casting 167–168

Color Purple, The **86**, **147**, **187**, **191**, **194**, **195**

Come Fly Away 49, **55**, **189**, **196**

Come from Away 107, **117**, 126, 176, **191**, **193**

comic book/strip, original musicals based on 122–124

Company **146**, **188**, **196**

controversies, 20 seasons of 35–43

Corbello, Donna 69

costume designers 9

COVID-19 shutdown 174–181

Cox, Gordon 74

Crazy for You 60

218 Index

Crumm, Max 107
Cry-Baby 88, **188**, **198**
Cullors, Patrisse 178
cult classic film musicals 88, 96
cultural movements, 20 seasons of 20–22
Cuomo, Andrew 173
Curtains **115**, **188**, **194**

Dahl, Roald 120
Dames at Sea **117**, **191**, **197**
Dance of the Vampires **85**, **187**, **198**
DanceOn 103
dansicals: importance of 5, 6; meaning and significance of 49, *51*
"Day of Accountability, A" forum 179
"Day of Healing, A" forum 179
"Day of Listening, A" forum 179
Deadline 182–183
Dear Evan Hansen 28–29, 34, **117**, **191**, **193**
Deaville, James 33
de Blasio, Bill 181
de Keersmaeker, Anna Teresa 39
de Mille, Agnes 162, 165
designers 9
DeVito, Tommy 69
Diana 107, 176
Dickens, Charles 121
digital media, impact on production marketing 29–30
digital scenography 93
directors and choreographers 8
Dirty Rotten Scoundrels **86**, **187**, **194**
Disaster! **56**, 62, **191**, **198**
Disney's Beauty and the Beast 63
Disney Company xii, xiii
Disney Theatrical Productions xii, 21, 29, 96, 102, 104, 105 111n60
Disney Theatrical Productions (Osatinski) 29–30
Disney Theatricals *see Disney Theatrical Productions*
diversity, in Broadway xiv–xvi
Dixon, Brandon Victor 20, 138

Doctor Zhivago **191**, **198**
Dodger Theatricals 67
Domingo, Coleman 38
Donahue, Tim 90
Dorsey, Jack 92
Downs, Olin 160
Dr. Seuss' How the Grinch Stole Christmas **115**, **147**, 168, **188**, **197**
Dr. Seuss's How the Grinch Stole Christmas (Seuss) 121
Dracula, The Musical **115**, **187**, **196**
Dreamgirls (film) 106
DreamWorks 133
Drowsy Chaperone, The **115**, **188**, **194**
Dudley, Bide 86
Dylan, Bob 49, 61

Ebb, Fred 35
Eisenhauer, Peggy 9
"Elephant Love Medley" (song) 76
Elf **147**, 168, **189**, **190**, **198**
Elice, Rick 66, 67
Ellington, Duke 59
Elvis: The Legend Lives 81n8
Entertainment Weekly 76
Erivo, Cynthia 122
Escape to Margaritaville **56**, **192**, **197**
Estefan, Gloria 71
Everage, Dame Edna 128
Everyday Rapture **55**, 62, **189**, **197**
Everydays (digital art work) 92
"Everything All at Once" (Ted Talk) 100–101
Evita **146**, **189**, **195**
Expressionist Explosion 162
extratextual narrative 167–168

Fake Friends 176
Falsettos **147**, **191**, **197**
Faust 120
Fela! **55**, 62, 80, **147**, 168, 169, **189**, **190**, **195**, **198**
Fiddler on the Roof **145**, **147**, **187**, **191**, **194**, **195**
Fierberg, Ruthie 140

Index **219**

Finding Neverland 89, 91, **188**, **190**, **194**
Finian's Rainbow **146**, **189**, **197**
Finley, Chase 39
First Date **117**, **190**, **196**
Fish, Daniel xiv, 161, 163
Fitzpatrick, Felicia 36
Flop Musicals of the 21st Century (Purdy) 128
Flower Drum Song **145**, 153, **186**, **196**
Floyd, George 21, 178
Flying By Foy 27
flying technology 27
Foley, Patrick 176
Follies **145**, **146**, **186**, **189**, **196**, **197**
Footloose 60
Forbes.com 139
"For Now" (song) 18
Foster, Sutton 31, 178
Foxwoods Theatre xiii
Franklin, Marc J. 182–183
Freedom Party 36
Freischütz, Der 120
Friedman, Sonia 130
Friml, Rudolf 86
Frith, Simon 64
Frogs, The **115**, 141n15, **187**, **197**
Frozen **56**, 178, **192**, **194**
Fuchs, Emily 64
Full Monty, The **85**, 88, **186**, **194**
Fun Home xv, **117**, 120, 122, 123–124, 125, **188**, **191**, **194**
Fun Home (Bechdel) 123
Funny Thing Happened on the Way to the Forum, A 149

Galella, Donatella 19, 155
Gardener, Elysa 121, 122
Gardiner, James 128
Garefino, Anne 130
Garfinkle, David 132
Garner, Eric 179
Garza, Alicia 178
Gaudio, Bob 67
Gay, John 57
Gelles, Barrie 100

Gentleman's Guide to Love and Murder, A **116**, 120, **190**, **194**
Gere, Richard 106
Gershwin's Porgy and Bess, The **146**, **189**, **195**
Getting the Band Back Together **118**, 128, **192**, **198**
Ghost: The Musical 26–27, 88, 93, **190**, **196**
Gigi **147**, 156–157, **190**, **197**
Girl From the North Country **57**, 61, **192**, **197**
Glory Days **115**, 120, 127–128, 129, **188**, **199**
Glover, Savion 138
Godspell **146**, **189**, **196**
Goodbye Entertainment 133
Good Vibrations **54**, **187**, **197**
Gordy, Barry 61, 78, 80
Graham Show, The (television) 103–104
Grammer, Kelsey 89
Grande, Ariana 122
Grant, Mark N. 23
Grease **146**, 150, **188**, **194**
Grease (television) 107
"Great American Musicals in Concert" (New York City Center) 150
Great Performances (television) 107
Great White Way (Hoffman) 2, 36
Green, Jesse 66
Greenberg, Florence 62
Green Day 61, 71, 73
Green Grow the Lilacs 124
Greenwich, Ellie 59
Grey Gardens **86**, **188**, **195**
Groundhog Day **191**, **196**
Guardian, The 78
Guys and Dolls **146**, 150, **188**, **197**
Gypsy **145**, **146**, **187**, **188**, **195**, **195**

Haagensen, Erik 79
Hadestown xi, xiv, xv, 17, **118**, 125–126, **192**, **194**

220 Index

Hair **146**, **147**, 168, 169, **188**, **189**, **194**, **198**
Hairspray **85**, 96, 106, **186**, **193**
Hall, Katori 63
Hamilton xi, xiii, xv, 19–20, 107, 108, **117**, 126, 138, 154, 176, 181, **191**, **193**
Hamilton, Alexander 19
Hammerstein, Oscar 86, 149, 153, 160, 165
handheld microphones, for performance 163–164
Hands on a Hardbody **190**, **198**
Hanks, Bailey 107
Hansen, Rhiannon 107
Hanson, Ashley 10
Harbach, Otto 86
Harlem Renaissance 137
Head Over Heels 43, **56**, **192**, **196**
Hedwig and the Angry Inch **117**, **190**, **194**
Hello Dolly 124, **147**, **191**, **194**
Hello Entertainment 133
Henry, Joshua 138, 167
Hereda, Kai 10
"Heroes" (song) 76
Herold, Patrick 99
Hershberg, Marc 139
Heywood, Christopher 4
Higgenbotham, John 162
high art 91
High Fidelity **86**, **188**, **199**
Hilferty, Susan 122
Hillenburg, Stephen 97, 98, 99
Hilton Theatre 132
historical event and person, original musicals based on 126–127
history, 20 seasons of 14–18
Hoche, John 95
Hoffman, Warren 2, 36–37
Holdren, Sara 166
Holiday Inn, The New Irving Berlin Musical **56**, **191**, **197**
Holler If Ya Hear Me **56**, 62, **190**, **198**

Hollywood Reporter 74, 175
Honeymoon in Vegas **190**, **197**
Horniman, Roy 120
Horton Hears a Who (Seuss) 121
Hot Feet **54**, 62, **188**, **197**
How Do You Solve a Problem Like Maria? (television) 107
Howlround Theatre Commons, The 168
How to Succeed in Business Without Really Trying **146**, **189**, **195**
Hughes, Langston 59, 137
Humphries, Barry 129
Hurlburt, Autumn 107
Hwang, David Henry 153

"I'm Not A Loser" (song) 101
"I Cain't Say No" (song) xiv
Iconis, Joe 30
identity conscious casting 168
"Identity Conscious Casting" (Jadhwani and Vazquez) 168
"I Enjoy Being a Girl" (song) 153
If/Then **117**, **190**, **195**
"I Get a Kick Out of You" (song) 58
Imbruglia, Natalie 76
independent/foreign film category 88, 96
In My Life **115**, **187**, **198**
intellectual property (IP) *see* IP musicals
Internet Broadway Database, The 148
Interval, The 99
In the Heights xv, 17, **115**, 154, **188**, **193**
Into the Woods **145**, **186**, **196**
Into the Woods (film) 106
In Transit **118**, **191**, **196**
iPhone 17
IP musicals: as king xiii–xiv; rise of xi–xiii
Irving Berlin's White Christmas **55**, **147**, 168, **188**, **189**, **198**
Isherwood, Charles 74, 122
Israel Rank (Horniman) 120
It Shoulda Been You **117**, **190**, **196**
"I Will Always Love You" (song) 76

Index **221**

Jackman, Hugh 31, 178
Jackson, Michael 78
Jackson, Michael R. 179
Jadhwani, Lavinia 168
Jagged Little Pill 41–43, **57**, **192**, **196**
Jane Eyre **114**, **186**, **196**
Jarrow, Kyle 97
Jazz Singer, The (film) 109n1
Jekyll and Hyde **146**, **190**, **198**
Jelly's Last Jam 60
Jersey Boys: case study of 66–71; significance of **55**, 61, 82n32, **187**, **193**
Jesus Christ Superstar **146**, **189**, **197**
Joel, Billy 49, 50
Jones, Chris 74
Jones, Christine 74–75, 83n56
Jones, Kevin 74
Jones, Rebecca, Naomi xiv
Jordan, Julie 166
Josken, Greg V. 29
Jukebox Musical, The (Byrne and Fuchs) 64
jukebox musicals xi–xii, 5, 13n11, 23, 119, 136; in 20 seasons **54–57**; appeal of 63–66; case studies of 66–80; history and development of 57–58; meaning and significance of 49, *50*, 51–52, *51*; representation and 62–63; and revue compared 58–60; types of 60–62

Kander, John 35
Katz, Natasha 9
Kern, Jerome 58, 149
Kessler, Kelly 108
Kieve, Paul 26
King, Carole xii
King and I, The xiv, **147**, **190**, **195**
King Kong 94–95, **192**, **195**
Kinky Boots 88, 96, **190**, **193**
Kinshasa, Kwando M. 37
Kircher, Madison Malone 42
Kiss Me Kate **147**, **192**, **197**
Kitt, Tom 72, 74
Knapp, Raymond 1

Kourlas, Gia 162
Kron, Lisa xv, 124, 125

Lady Day at Emerson's Bar & Grill 138
Lahr, John 96
Landau, Tina 97, 98–102
Lane, Nathan x, 123
Lapine, James 121
"Last Night on Earth" (song) 72
Last Ship, The **117**, **190**, **197**
Laurents, Arthur 153–154
Leader of the Pack 59
Leap of Faith **190**, **199**
LED *see* light-emitting diode (LED)
Lee, Baayork 151–152
Lee, Eugene 122
Lee, Jeff 27
Legally Blonde: The Search for Elle Woods (television) 107
Legally Blonde the Musical (television) 107, **188**, **194**
Leiber, Jerry 59
Lenker, Maureen Lee 76
Lennon 55, **187**, **198**
Lestat **115**, **187**, **198**
Letts, Tracy 98
Levine, Justine 76
Lewis, Christian 42
Lewis, Jerry Lee 62
light-emitting diode (LED) 24–25, 26, 93
Lighting & Sound America 25
lighting design 9
Light In the Piazza, The **115**, **187**, **194**
Lightning Thief, The **118**, 141n15, **192**, **197**
Lincoln's Inn Fields Theatre (London) 57
Lion King, The: film xii, xiii–xiv; significance of 88, 90, 96, 102, 105, 133, 181; and *Spider-Man* processes compared 133–134
Little Mermaid, The **55**, **188**, **194**
Little Night Music, A xiv, **146**, **189**, **195**

222 Index

Little Shop of Horrors **145**, **187**, **195**
Little Whopper, The 86–87
Little Women **115**, **187**, **196**
Live from Lincoln Center (television) 107
Look of Love, The **57**, **187**, **198**
Lopez, Robert 129
Lovemusik **55**, **188**, **198**
low art 91, 92
Luhrmann, Baz 75
Lunden, Jeff 95
LuPone, Patti xvi
Lysistrata Jones **116**, **189**, **198**

Mackintosh, Cameron 157
Maguire, Gregory 120
Mamma Mia **54**, 60, 67, 82n32, **186**, **193**
Mamma Mia and Beautiful xiii
Man of La Mancha **145**, **187**, **195**
Marks, Peter 65, 154
Marlow, Toby 173, 174
Marquis Theatre 33
Martin, Trayvon 179
Martin Short **115**, **188**, **196**
Marvel Entertainment 132, 134, 135, 143n41
Mary Poppins **55**, **188**, **193**
Matchmaker, The 124
Matilda the Musical **116**, 120, **190**, **193**
Maxwell, Alexa 39
Mayer, Michael 71–72, 74
McCallum, Kevin 173–174
McDonald, Audra 138–140
McKinley, Phil 135
McMaster, James 19
McPhee, Ryan 99
Mean Girls 25–26, 27, 88, 93, 178, **192**, **194**
Mean Girls (film) 25
Memphis **116**, 127, **189**, **194**
Menken, Alan 103
Menzel, Idina 122
#MeToo movement 166, 171n44
middlebrow, concept of 91–92

Million Dollar Quartet **55**, 62, **189**, **195**
mini-concert 70
Miranda, Lin-Manuel xv, 154
"Miseducation, The" forum 179
Misérables, Les 52, 120, **146**, 157, **188**, **190**, **194**, **195**
Misérables, Les (film) 106
Miss George Washington (silent film) 86
Miss Saigon **147**, 157–159, **191**, **195**
Mitchell, Anïas 125
Mitchell, Brian Stokes 138
MJ the Musical 176, 178, 179
Mordden, Ethan 148
Morissette, Alanis 41
Morrison, Matthew 89
Moss, Lucy 173
Motown: The Musical: case study of 78–80; importance of **56**, 61, 62, 63, **147**, 169, **190**, **191**, **194**, **198**
Motown Record Corporation 78
Moulin Rouge: case study of 75–78; importance of **57**, 96, 174, **192**, **195**
Movin' Out 49, 50, **54**, **187**, **193**
Mrs. Doubtfire 43
Muller, Jessie 167
multiple artists: biographical jukebox musical 61–62, 78–80; new story jukebox musical 62, 75–78
Musical Theatre, Realism, and Entertainment (Taylor) 64
Music Box Theatre 137
Music Man, The 31, 178
Myers, Victoria 99
My Fair Lady **147**, 152, 156, 166, **192**, **194**
Mystery of Edwin Drood, The **146**, **190**, **196**
myth, original musicals based on 125–126

Natasha, Pierre, and the Great Comet of 1812 **118**, **191**, **195**
Nayfack, Shakina 43

Index **223**

Nederlander, The 104
Neuwirth, Bebe 123
Never Gonna Dance 54, 85, **187**, **197**
Newsies: case study of 102–106;
    importance of 21, 29, **55**, 107,
    189, **194**
Newsies: Stories of the Unlikely Hit
    (Cerniglia) 103
Newsies (film) 29, 103
Newsies Live 112n75
new story jukebox musical: multiple
    artist 62, 75–78; single artist 61,
    71–75
New York City Center 149, 150
New Yorker, The 122
"New York, New York" (song) 15
New York Post 132, 136
New York Times 74, 86, 89, 121, 129,
    130, 139, 153, 160, 162, 165, 175,
    181
Next To Normal 72, **116**, **189**, **194**
NFT *see* nonfungible tokens (NFT)
Nice Work If You Can Get It **55**, **190**,
    195
Nickelodeon cartoon 97, 98, 102
Night That Made America Famous, The
    59
Night with Janis Joplin, A **56**, **190**,
    196
Nine **145**, **187**, **196**
No, No, Nanette 149–150
nonbinary characters, representation
    and denial of 41–43
nonfungible tokens (NFT) 92
nostalgia: in jukebox musicals 64, 79;
    significance of xii–xv; *see* IP
    musicals
Nottage, Lynn 179
Nunn, Trevor xiv
Nwandu, Antoinette Chinonye 16
NY1 122

Obama, Barack 18–19
O'Brien, Jack 166, 167
Occupy Wallstreet Movement 21
O'Keefe, John 148

Oklahoma!; revisal, as case study
    160–164; significance of xiv, xv,
    124, **145**, **147**, 149, 154–155, **186**,
    192, **195**
*Oklahoma! The Making of an American
    Musical* (Carter) 160
On A Clear Day You Can See Forever
    146, 153, **188**, **198**
Once **56**, 88, 96, **189**, **194**
Once on This Island **147**, **152**, **191**,
    195
One Mo' Time **57**, **186**, **199**
On the 20th Century **147**, **190**, **196**
On the Town **147**, 152, **190**, **195**
On Your Feet **56**, 61, 62, 63, 70–71,
    191, **194**
opera/etta musicals 5
"Oral History of *The Scottsboro Boys*,
    The" (Fitzpatrick) 36
original musicals 5–6, **114–118**; based
    on book 120–122; based on comic
    book/strip 122–124; based on
    historical event and person
    126–127; based on myth 125–126;
    based on play 124–125; case
    studies of 131–140; meaning and
    significance of 49, *50*, *51*, 52;
    musical inventions and 127–131;
    percentage of musical in *119;*
    source material of 118–120
Osnes, Laura 107
Ost, Tobin 104
Oswald, Lee Harvey 126

Pacific Overtures **145**, **187**, **198**
Pajama Game, The **146**, **187**, **196**
Pal Joey **146**, 149, **188**, **197**
Paper 31
Papermill Playhouse 104
Paradise Square 179
Parker, Trey 129
Pasich, Kirk A. 139
Pask, Scott 25, 93
Passe-Muraille, Le (Aymé) 121
Passing Strange xv, **116**, **188**, **196**
Pass Over 16

224 Index

Patriot Act 18
patriotic tourism 4
Patten, Lauren 42, 43
Patterson, Jim 90
Paulson, Michael 130, 139, 165, 175, 176, 181, 182
Peck, Justin 165
Pence, Mike 20
People in the Picture, The **116**, 126, **189**, **198**
Percy Jackson Musical, The **118**
Performing Rites (Frith) 64
Perkins, Carl 62
Phantom of the Opera, The (film) 106
Phantom of the Opera, The 90, 120, 182
Phillips, Dewey 127
pilot production 104
Pippin **146**, **190**, **194**
Pirate Queen, The **115**, **188**, **197**
Platt, Ben 34
play, original musicals based on 124–125
Playbill 99, 100
Playbill.com 34, 36, 140, 166
Polk, Flora 37
Pop Goes the Great White Way (Wolcott) 23, 87
Porgy and Bess 149, 150
Porter, Billy 138
Porter, Cole 58
post-show concert 70
Presley, Elvis 62
Pretty Woman (film) xii
Pretty Woman: The Musical 88–89, **192**, **195**
Prince of Broadway **57**, **191**, **197**
Princess Musicals 58, 81n4
Princess Theatre 81n4
Priscilla Queen of the Desert **55**, **189**, **194**
"Problem with Broadway Revivals, The" (Paulson) 165
Producers, The x–xi, **85**, 96, 106, **186**, **193**

projection/video design 10, 13n13, 27, 93
Prom, The **118**, **192**, **195**
Promises, Promises **146**, **189**, **195**
Pryce, Jonathan 157
Purdy, Stephen 128
Pygmalion (Shaw) 152

Quart, Ann 104
Queer Sort of Materialism, A (Savran) 91

racism: in America 19–20; controversies and 36–39
Ragtime **146**, **189**, **198**
Ramasar, Amar 39–41, 167, 171n47
Randolph-Wright, Charles 80
Ratatouille: The TikTok Musical 176
recycling of musical material, as trend 23–24
Reframing the Musical (Whitefield) 2
remounts: in 20 seasons **147**; importance of 48, 79, 80, 168–169
revisals: case study of 160–164; importance of 153, 154
revisionist revivals: case study of 165–168; importance of 152
revivals 24, 48; in 20 seasons **145–147**; case studies of 160–168; history of 148–151; original musicals and 52; possibility of 155–159; types of 151–154
revue musicals 5; in 20 seasons **57**; and jukebox musical compared 58–60; meaning and significance of 49, *50*, *51*
Riedel, Michael 132
Riggs, Lynn 124
Ring of Fire **55**, **187**, **198**
Rise and Fall of Broadway Musicals, The (Grant) 23
Rock of Ages 17, **55**, 62, **188**, **193**
Rocky 88, 93–94, **190**, **196**
Rocky Horror Show, The **85**, **186**, **195**
Rodgers, Mary 157
Rodgers, Richard 86, 160, 165

Index 225

Rodgers and Hammerstein's Cinderella 3, 48, **56**, **190**, **194**
Rogers, Scott 27–28
Ross, Diana 78
Rothman, Carol 166–167
Rothstein, Mervyn 100, 166
"Roxanne" (song) 76
Rudin, Scott 31, 41, 130, 140, 165, 166
Ryan, Patrick 173

SAG-AFTRA 177, 184n15
Sans, Jeremy 121
Sater, Stephen 125
Saturday Night Fever 60
Savran, David 91–92
scenic design 9
Sceptor Records 61–62
Schaeffer, Eric 128
Scheck, Frank 74
Schell, Nora 47n57
School of Rock **191**, **193**
Schrader, David 105
Schumacher, Thomas 103–104
Scott, Sherie Rene 62
Scottsboro Boys, The 35–39, **116**, 127, **189**, **198**
screen-to-stage musicals xii, 5, 23, 119, 151; in 20 seasons **85–86**; bias against 88–89; case studies of 97–106; high, low, and middlebrow art in 91–92; history and development of 86–87; LED technology in 93; meaning and significance of 49, *50*, 51–52, *51*; scenic innovations in 93–94; as technologically driven 28; types of 87–97
Second Stage 167
Seussical **114**, 121, **186**, **196**
Shaw, George Bernard 152
She Loves Me **147**, **191**, **196**
Sher, Bartlett 152
Shevlove, Burt 149
Shiek, Duncan 124
Show Boat 149, 150

Showtime (Stempel) 150
"Showtime on Broadway, Suspended" (Paulson and Allee) 175, 176
Shrek (films) 88, 96, 133
Shrek the Musical 63, 88, 96, 107, **188**, **195**
Shubert Organization 31
Shuffle Along: case study of 136–140; significance of **117**, 143n41, **191**, **197**
Sideshow **147**, **190**, **198**
Signature Theatre 128
"Silly Love Songs" (song) 76
Sinatra, Frank 49
single artist: autobiographical jukebox musical 61, 66–71; new story jukebox musical 61, 71–75
Sister Act **189**, **194**
Six xvi, 4, 16, 173–174, 176
Smokey Joe's Café 59
social media, impact on Broadway 17, 28–33
Something Rotten **117**, **191**, **194**
Sondheim, Stephen 4, 59, 149, 154
Sondheim on Sondheim **57**, 59, **189**, **197**
Song of Spider-Man (Berger) 27, 132, 134, 143n41
Soul Doctor **56**, **190**, **198**
sound design 10
Sound of Music, The 107
South Pacific **146**, **188**, **194**
South Park (television show) 129
Spamalot **86**, 96, **187**, **193**
Spider-Man, The Lion King, and Life on the Creative Edge (TED Talk) 135
Spider-Man: Turn Off the Dark xiii, 27, 63, 90, 110n15, **116**, 120, 122, 123, **189**, **194**; case study of 131–136; failure of 132; and *The Lion King* processes compared 133–134
Spiegel, Steve 123

226 Index

SpongeBob SquarePants: case study of 97–102; significance of 88, 91, 97, 107, **191**, **195**
Spotify 30
Spring Awakening xi, xv, **115**, 124–125, **147**, **188**, **191**, **194**, **196**
Springsteen, Bruce 16, 181
Springsteen on Broadway 16
St. James Theatre x, 16
Stage Money (Donahue and Patterson) 90
stage representations 11–12
stage-to-screen musicals 106–108
Star Dust 58
Stempel, Larry 150
Steppenwolf Theatre 98
Stew xv
Stiehl, Pamyla 49, 170n14
Stoller, Mike 59
Stone, Matt 129
Story of My Life, The **116**, 128, **188**, **199**
Strange Loop, A xvi, 179, 182–183
streaming platform, on internet 176–177
Stroker, Ali xiv
Stroman, Susan 35
Summer: The Donna Summer Musical **56**, 62, **192**, **195**
Sunday in the Park with George **146**, **147**, **188**, **191**, **196**, **198**
Sunset Boulevard **147**, **191**, **196**
superfans and stagedooring 33–34
Superior Donuts 98
Sweeney Todd **146**, **187**, **195**
Sweeney Todd (film) 106
Sweet Charity **145**, **187**, **196**
Sweet Smell of Success **85**, **186**, **197**
Swinging on a Star 57
"Sympathy for the Incel?" (Young) 164

Taboo **54**, **187**, **197**
"Take on Me" (song) 76
Tale of Two Cities, A **116**, **188**, **198**

Tale of Two Cities, A (Dickens) 121
Tariya, Khadija 95
Tarzan: The Musical 27, 28, **55**, 60, **86**, **188**, **195**
Taylor, Mille 64
Taymor, Julie 90, 96, 102, 132, 133–135
technologically advanced scenography and staging 24–28
Temptations xii
Tesori, Jeanine xv, 124, 125
Tharp, Twyla 49
Theatrical Rights Worldwide 123
Thompson, David 35
Thoroughly Modern Millie **85**, 96, **186**, **194**
Thou Shalt Not **114**, **186**, **197**
Threepenny Opera, The 48, **146**, **187**, **197**
TikTok 31–32, 33
TikTok Broadway (Buffone) 32
Timbers, Alex 75
Time Out New York 121
Times They Are a-Changin', The 49, **55**, **188**, **198**
Tina: The Tina Turner Musical **57**, 62–63, 65, 71, **192**, **195**
To Be Loved (Gordy) 78, 79
Tolstoy, Leo 120
Tometi, Opal 178
Tony Awards x, xiv–xvi, 16, 180, 182–183; jukebox musicals and revues and 71, 74, 83n56; original musicals and 122, 124, 125, 129, 130, 136, 138, 139; revivals and remounts and 150–151, 165, 167; screen-to-stage musicals and 90, 96, 97, 102
Tootsie 43, **192**, **195**
"Torn" (song) 76
Torre, Roma 121
Tracz, Joe 30
traditional revivals 151–152
Tran, Diep 158, 159, 177
trends, 20 seasons of 22–34

Index   227

Trump, Donald 18, 174
Tuck Everlasting **117**, **191**, **198**
Tuck Everlasting (Babbitt) 121
Turner, Tina xii, 62
Twain, Mark 121
Two Rivers Theatre 30

Urban Cowboy **85**, **187**, **198**
Urinetown **114**, **186**, **194**
USA Today 121, 173
U.S. politics, 20 seasons of 18–20

Valli, Frankie 66, 67, 69, 70
Vandevender, Bryan 149, 150, 151
Van Hove, Ivo 39
Vanity Fair 23, 87
Variety 75, 122
Vazquez, Victor 168
Viewpoints 98–99
Vincintelli, Elizabeth 136
Violet **117**, **190**, **197**
Visit, The **117**, **191**, **198**
Vizzini, Ned 30, 121
Vulture 42, 166
Vulture.com 90

Waitress xiii, 17, **191**, **193**
"Wake Me Up When September Ends" (song) 71, 73
Waller, Fats 59
Walt Disney Corporation 21, 133
War and Peace (Tolstoy) 120
War Paint **118**, **191**, **196**
Warren, Adrienne 65, 66, 71
Washington Post 154
Watanabe, Ken xiv
Waterbury, Alexandra 39
Webb, Jason Michael 179
Webber, Andrew Lloyd 107, 120
Wedding Singer, The **86**, **187**, **196**
Wedekind, Frank 124
Weidman, John 4
Weinstein, Harvey 166
"We See You White American Theatre" 21–22, 179

West Side Story xv, 39–41, **146**, 149, 153–154, 171n47, **188**, **192**, **194**, **198**
Wetmore, Brendan 31
White, Noni 103
White Christmas 88
Whitfield, Sarah 2
whiteness 2, 20
Who's Tommy, The 59, 60
"Why *Hamilton* Is Not the Revolution You Think It Is" (McMaster) 19
Wicked xiii, xiv, **115**, 120, 121–122, 181, **187**, **193**
Wicked (film) 106
Wicked (Maguire) 120
Wild, Stephi 130
Wilder, Thornton 124
Williams, Jacob 95
Williams, Michelle xiv
Wilson, Patrick xiv
Windman, Matt 156–157
Winter Garden Theatre 31, 32
Wolcott, James 23, 87
Wolfe, George C. 137
Woman in White, The **115**, **187**, **197**
Women on the Verge of a Nervous Breakdown **189**, **198**
Wonder, Stevie 78
Wonderful Town **145**, **187**, **195**
Wonderful Wizard of Oz, The (Baum) 120
Wonderland **116**, **189**, **198**
Woods, Elle 107
Woodward, Rex 69
writing team 8

Xanadu 17, **55**, 60, 88, 141n15, **188**, **194**

Year with Frog and Toad, A **114**, **187**, **198**
yellowface casting 157, 170n27
Young, Adam 25
Young, Catherine M. 164
Young, John Lloyd 68–69

228 Index

Young Frankenstein **188**, **195**
YouTube 17

Zakrin, Lauren 107
Zank, Ronald 87

Zapruder, Abraham 126
Zellweger, Renee 106
Zeta-Jones, Catherine xiv
Zinn, David 100, 101
Zoom conferences 176

Printed in the United States
by Baker & Taylor Publisher Services